The Mirage And The Mirror

Thoughts On The Nature Of Anomalies In Consciousness

The Mirage
and the Mirror

Thoughts on the Nature
of Anomalies in Consciousness

Richard Chambers Prescott
Richard Prescott, 1998

Originally Published By
GRASCOTT PUBLISHING

"Your own Atma
is the Divine Mother."

Swami Aseshananda
1899 - 1996

"You are Immortal. Nothing can effect you."

Swami Bhashyananda
1917 - 1996

"The body is Sakti. Its needs are Sakti's needs; when man enjoys, it is Sakti who enjoys through him. In all he sees and does it is the Mother who looks and acts. His eyes and hands are Hers. The whole body and all its functions are Her manifestation. To fully realize Her, as such, is to perfect this particular manifestation of Hers which is himself. When the Mother is seen *in* all things, She is at length realized as She is when *beyond* them all."

Sir John Woodroffe

COLLECTED TITLES

The Sage
Moonstar
Neuf Songes
The Carouse of Soma
Lions and Kings
Allah Wake Up
Night Reaper
Dragon Tales
Dragon Dreams
Dragon Prayers
Dragon Songs
Dragon Maker
Dragon Thoughts
Dragon Sight
Kings and Sages
Three Waves
The Imperishable
The Dark Deitess
Years of Wonder
Dream Appearances
Remembrance Recognition and Return
Spare Advice
Tales of Recognition
Racopa and the Rooms of Light
Hanging Baskets
Writer's Block and Other Gray Matters
The Resurrection of Quantum Joe
The Horse and The Carriage
Disturbing Delights: Waves of The Great Goddess
Kalee Bhava: The Goddess and Her Moods
Because of Atma
The Skills of Kalee
Measuring Sky Without Ground
Kalee: The Allayer of Sorrows
The Goddess and the God Man
Living Sakti
The Mirage and the Mirror
Inherent Solutions To Spiritual Obscurations

I must thank a few friends for their kind letters, which have daily encouraged me to continue and complete this text:

Barbara G. Walker Author of *The Women's Encyclopedia of Myths and Secrets*: "Naturally, I am pleased by any profession of reverence for the Goddess."

Rufus C. Camphausen Author of *The Divine Library*: "You have so specialized a knowledge that I wonder what country (I mean culture) you've been born and raised in."

Swami Chetanananda: "Never give up writing --it is a good habit that clears understanding and keeps the mind in a higher plane, and it may also help others."

Swami Tyagananda: "We appreciate your efforts in trying to express different aspects of Vedanta philosophy."

Tenzin Wangyal Rinpoche, Author of *Wonders of the Natural Mind* and *The Tibetan Yogas of Dream and Sleep:* "And thank you for your books for our Ligmincha library. They will greatly benefit other people."

Dr. Raymond Moody Author of *Life After Life*: "I truly appreciate your thoughtfulness."

William Bond Author of *Gospel of the Goddess*: "Looking through your poems in *Dragon Thoughts* they seem to me to feel the same as the Tao Te Ching which has been a "Bible" for me over the years." "Thank you for *Measuring Sky Without Ground.* Looking through your book I do agree with most of what you say. Although I do have a different idea about getting rid of the ego. I feel man needs to develop his ego to learn how to love himself and how to become an individual. Until he reaches a state where he is so secure in his love of himself, that he no longer needs to search for "ego gratification." In this secure state he is able to now be humble and surrender to the Great Mother knowing he will not be swallowed up by Her and start to learn how to love others." And, "Thank you for your two books, it does amaze me how many books you are able to write on Kali."

Dr. Alfred Collins Author of *Fatherson* and *From Brahma to a Blade of Grass:*"I see again that you are a talented writer; some of the poems are very expressive and moving. I suppose your style is something like Walt Whitman's, among American writers." "Thanks for *Measuring Sky*... very interesting, very sincere."

Swami Bhashyananda: "I have gone through the manuscripts with great interest. You have genuine writing ability and the talent for using your imagination to express some of your spiritual intuitions. I was impressed to read what you have written. The thoughts are very valuable and elevating."

Swami Chidbhasananda on, *The Lamp of the Turiya,* from *Because of Atma.* "It is really a masterpiece coming from the bottom of your experience, and there is no artificial make-up in your composition. Our additional thanks and gratitude to your Kindself."

Amy Richards, assistant to Gloria Steneim: "So thank you for writing and also for sharing your humanity."

Anonymous by request of Author: "You are so kind, so wildly generous. We send our blessings on your work and writing hand."

Helen Fedro - Publisher: "The pieces I examined were very intriguing."

Swami Swahananda, Vedanta Society of Southern California, on *The Lamp of the Turiya*, from *Because of Atma* : "A very scholarly presentation."

Jo Kyle - Publisher: "We found your work most interesting and inspiring."

Artemis - Publisher: "I think you are trying to compete with Tolstoy or producing the equivalent of the Holy Koran. The pieces are superb."

Swami Atmavratananda: "I love your various books."

Sushri Braja Parikari Didiji: "I read your article, it was really very good."

Swami Vamanananda, Ramakrishna Mission Ashrama, West Bengal: "We would appeal to your goodself to contribute an article from your powerful pen and certainly it will add worth and prestige to our volume."

Swami Varadananda: "I wanted to thank you for the article on "The Indian Idea of Death," which you sent me. You are doing good work in spreading Sri Ramakrishna's message. As people become exposed to the teachings of Vedanta from various sources, it will gradually make an impression. By publishing your article in a non - Vedanta magazine, you have reached a whole new audience, which had perhaps never heard about these ideas."

Jerry Zientara - Librarian: "I shall also gladly point the books out to students and researchers interested in Tantra, Goddess Worship, and Spirituality outside the Western traditions."

Carola F. Sautter - Publisher: "This project seems to us to be an important one."

Arthur P. Young, Director, Northern Illinois University Libraries: "I am very pleased to acknowledge your recent contribution of materials. These are most welcome since they assist us in instructional and research programs of the university. It was good of you to remember us."

Swami Tathagatananda, Vedanta Society of New York: "I sincerely congratulate you for writing about Ramakrishna. Although we are working here for one hundred years, still, I am sorry to mention, very few intellectual Americans are showing their genuine interest in making a successful attempt to project the universal idealism of Ramakrishna. In the twenty-first century, we are reaching the Global Village which requires our cosmopolitan outlook to be fit for this Global Village. But the old ideas, thoughts and prejudices are still very prominently molding our lifestyle. This is quite natural. But still, you are doing your best through your creative writing to make people more liberal and universal. May God bless you with enthusiasm and right perspective."

Barry Scott, Ohio University Libraries: "Your contribution will enrich the Libraries' collections and help us to better serve the Ohio University Community. We appreciate your interest and hope you will continue your support of the Ohio University Libraries."

Swami Manishananda: "I am enjoying your book *Measuring Sky Without Ground* immensely. Your phrases are excellent. I especially like imagery such as "our souls kidnapped by crusty old belief systems."

Dr. Stanley Krippner, Saybrook Institute, Graduate School and Research Center: "We all appreciate your generosity. Thanks for the unique books. I am sure our students will find the books interesting, as is usual with your publications."

Swami Yatatmananda, Sri Ramakrishna Math, Mylapore, India: "We greatly appreciate your kind gesture. The books are an invaluable addition to our Library. The books have an attractive get up and bold prints which make reading them a pleasure. The topics chosen are also of immense interest and we are sure that a lot of our members will benefit from the addition of these books. Thanking you."

Dr. Miriam Robbins Dexter, author of *Whence The Goddess* and editor of *Varia on the Indo-European Past* and *The Kurgan Culture and The Indo-Europeanization of Europe* by Marija Gimbutas: "Thanks very much for the copies of your book. I will be giving a workshop in Greece in two days and I shall bring copies of your books with me to give to colleagues. My best." "Kalee... if you send a signal my circuit is open." In *Kalee Bhava* and *The Skills of Kalee*, both inspired books of meditations, Richard Prescott speaks with directness and deep feeling to the immanent Goddess Kali." "Your *Tales of Recognition* were charming. I particularly enjoyed *Racopa the Tibetan* and *The Spiritual Wars of the Planet Earth*. I appreciate the positive hopeful quality of your work. Your meditations give a beautifully personal and spiritual picture of you - that you rejoice in being a poet, and a writer of prose. I particularly enjoy the fact that the Goddess calls you Her "honey boy" - recalling Inanna calling Dumuzi Her "honey man."

Swami Prapannananda, Vedanta Society of Sacramento: "I appreciate your kind thoughts. The books will be kept in the reading room. I wish you continued success in your writing and publishing work. With our greetings and best wishes."

Northwestern University Library, Illinois: "Thank you very much."

Elizabeth Usha Harding, Kali Mandir, author of *Kali: The Black Goddess of Dakshineswar*: "Just wanted to thank you very much for the gift of the books. We really appreciate it and they will be in the library. Jai Ma."

Swami Shivarupananda, The Ramakrishna Vedanta Centre, England: "Thank you for the books which we received this morning. They will be a welcome addition to our library."

Dr. Allen R. Freedman, Vedanta Society of Western Washington: "On behalf of the Vedanta Society I would like to thank you very much for your kind and generous donation of your latest book *Living Sakti* to our society. Please accept my best wishes. Yours in Thakur, Ma and Swamiji."

Carolyn H. Aamot, University of Washington: Your generosity is very much appreciated. Thank you again."

Lakshmi Narayan, Krotona Library, "We appreciate your kind donation to Krotona Library. Thanking you again."

Ramakrishna Ashrama, Argentina: "Very interesting. Thank you very much."

Mangala Takacs, Vedanta Society of Southern California, San Diego: "Swami Atmarupananda asked me to write to you to thank you for copies of *Because of Atma* and *Living Sakti* that you sent for our Library. I find your statement of purpose quite interesting - the world needs more original manuscripts! Best wishes in your publishing work. Yours in Peace."

Swami Dayatmananda of the Ramakrishna Vedanta Centre in the U.K.: "Mother is working through you no doubt."

Ramakrishna Ashrama, Argentina: "Appreciating your analysis and thoughts on some interesting topics we placed your books in our public and personal libraries here."

Dr. Bruce Greyson, M.D. University of Connecticut: "Thank you for letting me see the enclosed selections of articles on existence, consciousness, and the mysteries of life and death. I enjoyed reading them, and as a clinical psychiatrist, I was particularly impressed by the wisdom and compassion in your article, *Depression: A Spiritual Dilemma.*"

Haragano, author and teacher: "Dearest Ricky, poet visionary, and dear companion to a wonderful lady, thank you for sharing your poetry and dreams with me and others of our kind."

Such dear inspirations as theirs have helped me to put my thoughts into the illustration of words that form this text.

Swami Chetanananda, The Vedanta Society of St. Louis: "Thank you for sending us copies of your book *The Goddess and the God Man.* I shall keep one copy for myself, and place the others in our library and book store. I wish you good luck in spreading the message of Vedanta through your Grascott Publishing Company."

The Bear Tribe: "Thank you for your gift. We will be glad to enjoy them and have them in our library."

Swami Yogeshananda: "I do look forward to absorbing the fascinating comments in *Dragon Sight* and also finishing *Measuring Sky Without Ground* which I have begun."

Aoumiel: "Thank you very much for the new volumes for my library! As always, I enjoy reading your perspective on the balance of light and dark in the Divine. Bright Blessings to you and your work. I hope your heartfelt writings get a wide distribution."

Swami Atmaramananda, Prabuddha Bharata, India: "We are glad to receive your gift of *Measuring Sky Without Ground* for our library and bookstore. The packet arrived last week."

The Ramakrishna Vedanta Centre, England: "Swami Dayatmananda would like to thank you for your kindness in sending to us your recent books which we received this morning. Very much appreciated!"

Effie Brown, Shenoa Retreat, California: "I am sure we will enjoy these unique and interesting books. It was very kind of you to remember us in this way."

Diane Kent, Salt Spring Centre, BC, Canada: "Thank you very much for your book donation. I dipped into the covered for a few moments and saw the work of a true Kali devotee. It will be a pleasure to read and I'm sure that many of our guests will enjoying reading them."

Swami Prabuddhananda, Vedanta Society of Northern California: "I was glad to receive your packet of books - *The Goddess and the God Man* and *Disturbing Delights*. Thank you for sending me these books."

Susana Andrews, Tantra Magazine: "I am delighted. Thank you for your generous gift of publications and also for your gift of service to the Goddess."

Swami Atmavratananda, Vivekananda Vihar, New York: "So fulfilled to see you are so filled with our Maha Kali. Yours in Love and Peace."

Swami Chidbhasananda, Vedanta Centrum R.V.V.N., The Netherlands: "We acknowledge with grateful thanks the receipt of *The Goddess and the God Man* and *Disturbing Delights*. Again, with our hearty thanks. May Sri Ramakrishna, Holy Mother and Swamiji shower their choicest Blessings on you and your family, is our earnest prayer at Their Feet!"

Cassia Berman, author of, *Divine Mother Within Me*: "everything I read, Ma authentically shines and plays through. I rejoice to find a kindred spirit and it means so much to me that you have been enjoying my work too. Those books are like a silver treasure chest, in every drawer of which Ma is sparkling. Thank you."

Lakshmi Narayan, Head Librarian, Krotona Library: "We acknowledge with deep gratitude your donation to the Krotona Library."

St. John, Secretary, The Lama Foundation: "Thank you so much for the books. People have already carted them off to read! Please keep us in your thoughts and prayers."

Karin J. Miles, Director, Cloud Mountain Retreat Center: "We do appreciate your recognition of our Dharma library, and your generous gift. It is certain that the books will be reviewed and read by at least some of the practitioners who pass through this Center. Thank you for your kindness."

Self Realization Fellowship, The Mother Center: "Our Encinitas Ashram Center informed us of your generous donation of a number of books for our library. It was kind of you to think of us. Please accept our gratitude for your thoughtfulness. May God bless you always. In divine friendship."

Swami Adiswarananda, The Ramakrishna Vivekananda Center, New York: "Please accept our thanks to you for your gift of *Measuring Sky Without Ground*. We appreciate your kind thoughts. I wish you continued success in your writing and publishing work. With our greetings and all best wishes."

Indralaya Library, Orcas Island: "Thank you for your donation... they are very much appropriate and appreciated. Always a treat to have new ideas offered."

Carolyn H. Aamot, University of Washington Libraries: "On behalf of the University of Washington Libraries, it is my privilege to express our gratitude. We welcome your interest in the University Libraries and value your support. Contributions of materials help enrich our collection for the many students, faculty and others who daily rely on its resources for study and research. Please be assured that your publications will be carefully reviewed for addition to our holdings."

Joni Cooke, Shoden, Mount Baldy Zen Center: "Thank you very much for this lovely silver book. We are not encouraged to read here at the monastery however, I just took a brief look through your collected titles and my sense is that it is wonderful that you are out there publishing exactly what pleases and interests you. I hope things go well in your publishing business, and I will put "The Mirage and the Mirror" in our library."

Self Realization Fellowship, Mother Center: "Thank you for your thoughtfulness and generosity. Our ashram in Encinitas received your donation also and asked us to convey their gratitude for your kindness. May the love of God be with you always, guiding you in all your worthwhile endeavors. In divine friendship."

Swami Murugananda, Satchidananda Ashram – Yogaville: "Thank you for your donation of spiritual books to our library. They are now all classified and cataloged and on our shelves for use by our community."

Ramakrishna Ashrama, Argentina" Swami Pareshanandaji and all of us here are very thankful for sending copies of your latest creation, "The Mirage and the Mirror." We wish you a new year of more and more deep and bright thoughts. With all affection."

The Ramakrishna Mission Institute of Culture, Gol Park, Calcutta: We acknowledge with thanks the receipt of the books noted below which you have sent for use is our library. We are sure our readers will find the books useful."

Swami Shivarupananda, Vedanta Centre, England: Thank you once again for the copies of *"The Mirage and the Mirror"*, received with gratitude and appreciation. Yours in the Eternal."

Subhabrata, Mothers Trust/Mothers Place: *The Mirage and the Mirror* will be a very valuable addition to our library. We are grateful for your continuing contributions to the ashram. We send our blessings and best wishes to you and hope to hear from you soon. Your in service of Mother."

Dr. Kenneth Ring, Author of *Life After Death* and *Heading Toward Omega* : "I very much respect the learning you so easily express concerning the nature of death and the state of consciousness it engenders. And I am glad you are continuing to be one of those authors of the modern book of the dead and thereby helping to bring the ancient wisdom to a new generation of beings." "I am happy to know that you continue to be a prolific writer and weaver of story-magic."

Linda Johnsen, author of *Daughters of the Goddess: The Women Saints of India:* "Reading over the expressions of your soul, I also felt an intense poignancy. In this culture who is there to be inspired by words such as yours, by visions such as Hers? We live in such a wasteland, Richard. And at the same time this spiritual desert is a heaven world Mother has created for us so that we can do sadhana (spiritual practice) well fed in heated homes. I accept Her blessing of contemporary American life with gratitude and despair. The Divine One will never let us go. May we never let go of Her! Bowing to the Goddess in you." & "I certainly wish I was as continuously inspired as you and could keep producing books at such a prodigious rate! And all for the glory of Mother." "Thanks so much for *Measuring Sky Without Ground*. What a wonderful title! I especially appreciated your point that, "Mother is not a lesser form that needs destroying." When Ramakrishna attacked the form of Kali with the sword of discrimination, it was Kali's own sword he was using, jnana sakti."

Penny Slinger, artist and author of numerous books, *The Path of the Mystic Lover* being but one of her titles: "No one can write as you do without it being forged in the bliss of Her divine fire, no one comes to Her knowledge without being prepared to offer themselves in the flames... only they know the passion of this surrender! Beautiful poet, I salute you, for you are doing the work, the great work of preparing the vessel so She may flow through.. oh how I too ardently long for there to be nothing left of me but the Goddess! I honor you for honoring Her." & "I appreciated *Dragon Sight* deeply... I have absorbed it and pay homage to you for not only attempting but actually executing such a work. Thank goodness, thank Goddess, for beings like you."

Swami Dayatmananda of the Ramakrishna Vedanta Centre in the U.K.: "Mother is working through you no doubt." & "Advaita is one philosophy which is the goal and the path. I think it harmonizes all other religious paths in love and understanding. You have caught the spirit of this marvelous philosophy aright. May the Lord now graciously grant you its right realization is my fervent prayer."

Swami Bhaskarananda, author of *The Essentials of Hinduism*, on *Measuring Sky Without Ground*: "People are victims of their conditioning. That is the reason why people of the East and people of the West sometimes think differently. Richard Chambers Prescott has grown up in the West. He has had Western conditioning. Yet his inquiring mind has taken him to the shores of Eastern knowledge - particularly the knowledge of Hindu philosophy and religion. He is one of the few Western friends I know who have tried to explore the wealth of Hindu wisdom with the mind of an ardent and admiring student, and not that of a chance traveler or a supercilious surface-taster. The articles contained in this book clearly reflect his open-mindedness, impartial self-examination, and mental enrichment attained through the exploration of both Eastern and Western wisdom. Rudyard Kipling once said, "Oh, East is East, and West is West, and ne're the twain shall meet." Mr. Prescott has proved him wrong. In him the wisdom of the East and the wisdom of the West seem to have blended together in perfect harmony." And, "Your writings are very precise and clear, and therefore, they will help readers to understand some of the Vedantic ideas more easily. Please keep up the good work!"

Swami Muktirupananda, Advaita Ashrama, the Himalayas: Editor for *Prabuddha Bharata:* "I have gone through all of your review articles, they are very good and reveal the depth of the writer. Please try to share your mature thoughts with the reader of this spiritual journal." "So many books have been coming out from your facile pen and rich brain. I will keep the copies of your books in our Advaita Library. You have rightly pointed out that Turiya is the state of pure beingness. It is eternal existence without any name and form. It is the ego with the sense of 'I am this' and 'I am that', that thinks it undergoes changes. This information we have gathered in our heads about ourselves gives us the idea that we are limited, powerless. But, these definitions that one is American, or Christian, or husband, or wife, rich or poor, are added to one's pure beingness. These are external descriptions gathered in the course of time. We believe we are these definitions and suffer. Behind all these external decorations there is One who existed prior to all these. To see thoughts appearing in the mind, there must be somebody to see. So he must be in existence before there was any thought. 'You' as pure being exist prior to all thoughts. This pure being cannot be defined, because of it, everything else arises. It is prior to all. Spiritual practice is to throw out all we have accumulated from the external world. When all that rubbish stuff is thrown out, when the mind is cleaned what remains is Reality, beyond all words."

Swami Smaranananda, General Secretary, Belur Math: "Glad to receive your letter dated nil together with three copies of books. Thank you. The books have been kept in our Math Library and Probationers' Training Centre Library. With best wishes and greetings."

CONTENTS

An Explorative Study of the Intimate Relationship
of the Goddess Kali
with Sri Ramakrishna of Dakshineswar

The Poem: Sakti Karma

The Lamp of the Turiya
The Light of Self Evident Consciousness

References

Author's Preface

Kalee Bhava: The Goddess and Her Moods, was born out of torment and love crashing together like lightning hitting the Earth to ignite life into existence. It is nothing but passion for the spiritual. This book was the work of Healing Sakti in my life. I began to heal what has seemed to be a never ending torrent of wounds, everything from the wounds of Jesus, to the wounds of inability to attain Advaita (non-dual transcendence) permanently. The distorted imprint of this world leaves us with many delusions, scars, and schisms: sexual, psychological, and religious. My healing began as I began to embrace the Image of Kali as my Ishta Sakti, the Chosen Ideal of Spiritual Power.

Because of Atma: Essays on Self and Empathy was the work of Vedanta Sakti coming back to me. It is my inquiry into the Pure Atma, true self as What is Behind and yet Within the Curtain of Enchantment. But I must confess my own non-originality. If Ashtavakra describes the Atma as "glory" and thousands of years later Swami Abhedananda describes Atma as "glory" and then perhaps a decade or two after that someone else uses the very same word, well, who is then original? No one person is the holder of Truth, it is Truth that is the Holder of every individual. *The Lamp of the Turiya* was translated into Dutch and republished in the journal *Vedanta*. *Spiritual Solutions to Psychological Equations* was republished in *The New Times*. *Bursting the Sharp Midpoint of the World Mind Cultus* was republished in *Prabuddha Bharata* and *The New Times*.

The Skills of Kalee came later as a process of autonomous self arrival. As it is with almost all writing and poetic efforts, some of it is a scholarly construct and some is spontaneous creativity. As it is, I think the feeling within each sentence speaks for itself. This manuscript was the work of Loving Sakti in my life. The text is an exercise in the practice and application of learning to love and to use my own mind as an instrument for loving the Goddess.

Measuring Sky Without Ground: Essays on the Goddess Kali, Sri Ramakrishna and Human Potential came out of thinking upon Turiya Sakti, that is Mother's Advaita returned from the waking, dreaming, and deep sleep states back into the fourth state (turiya), at least, in a cerebral perspective, but expressed with powerful feeling. For me it was like the dawn of spiritual life inside my heart. The title essay, *Measuring Sky Without Ground: A Pragmatic Psychology of Non-Duality* was republished in *The New Times*.

Kalee: The Allayer of Sorrows is a return address to some important historical and spiritual subjects which for me are a salute to Tantra Sakti and how She has expressed Herself in my life. From this text, *The Radical View of Kali: A Study in Religious Distortion* was republished in the journal *Matriarch's Way*. *The Guru Problem: Spiritual Trauma and Abuse in the Causal Dynamic of the Guru Dilemma* was republished in *The New Times*.

The Goddess and the God Man: An Explorative Study of the Intimate Relationship of the Goddess Kali with Sri Ramakrishna of Dakshineswar was my greatest pleasure and joyful labor, being in itself a work on pure Kali Sakti. It is a probing search, and an unworthy attempt to fathom the depth of his spiritual experience, written at the borderline where the absolute transcendent Goddess expressed Herself in the person of Sri Ramakrishna of Dakshineswar (1836-1886).

Living Sakti: Attempting Quick Knowing in Perpetual Perception and Continuous Becoming, I prayed, was to be my culmination, after thirty years of writing, perhaps that I now might live in Peace. To enjoy what has been discovered in Sakti and to live what has been uncovered by Sakti.

But Mother would not let me rest and just live in Her Sakti. She once again forced me to continue writing and so the eighth text was born from my mind womb wherein She could not resist impregnating me with more thoughts on Her. So *The Mirage and the Mirror* was born. It was written from the Perspective of the Witness Consciousness (The Mirror). All else is the Mirage. As to whether or not, in the Final Conclusion, the anomalies within the Mirage are considered to be real or unreal, is up to you, as both the Tantric and Vedantic views are given. Either view, is still only a consideration within that Consciousness, the Mirror. It is the work of Clear and Lucid Advaita Sakti.

These eight texts are what I see as eight parts/stages of one book which is the embodiment of my devotion to the Goddess. The overall title of these eight book/stages is *Advaita Sakti: A Poet's Journey To The Goddess.* Advaita, of course, is Non-Duality. Sakti is the Immeasurable Power or Energy of the Divine Mother as Pure Consciousness and Pure Love.

I am simply a poet who loves the Goddess. I am just one seeker of Truth who has written down his thoughts as so many of us have done. I am no one special and knowing that this is so, is one of the most healing emotions I have ever experienced. The emotions we entertain become the moods we live in and for me, the Sweet Current of Love is the mood in which I would wish to spend as much time as may be. While working on these texts, *Advaita Sakti*, the most excellent thing that I learned in the process, is that it is for the Sake of Her, not I. You may taste these thoughts, you may swallow these words, or, as you choose, you may spit them out. I lay no claim to these works. Ego is a massive cloud that consumes the body idea, the content of feelings, and the mind's addressing of one's life, so with that I try not to identify. May She protect and inspire the emerging of the Love that is within you.

Kalee and the Sacred Feminine
An Initial Blessing of Her Direct Reality

The Celts called Her Kele, the prehistoric Tantrikas called Her Kali, I cherish the name Kalee as a more universal invocation. For She was never confined to any one culture, place or people. The Sacred Divine Feminine is present everywhere, though the path has been suppressed by the hardness and fear of the dominator mind. But things are changing in an uphill battle of idealism at the level of spiritual education.

To separate the mind from the heart makes for a one sided person. To divide the masculine and the feminine does an even worse thing to the human spirit. It robs the soul of it's full inheritance. That is why the essential duality of the male and female must be brought together into One Unity, for this breaking of the two halves is the wound of the world.

The Sacred Feminine is the most cherishable in the world, the essential primal sentiment of all living beings. This is the first Great Emotion that we learn when we enter this world of life. That is why the restoration of the Great Sentiment is so important to becoming a spiritually alive and a real human being. The denial of the Profound Sentiment is the root cause of so much suffering, individually and universally.

Kalee is my Disturbing Delight. Disturbing because She puts asunder the agitations of our crowded concrete conceptions of what we perceive this relative life to be. She is Delight because She is greatly pleasant to know. She is Delight because She is the Fearless Loving Untrammeled Unconditioned Light which is such a Great Delight to welcome and invite into the Sense of the Great Self.

Sri Ramakrishna of 19th century Dakshineswar saw Her as a Living Being. She would stand on the balcony of the Temple and watch the night lights of Calcutta reflecting over the waters of the Ganges. He would commune with Her, talk with Her, become One with Her in Samadhi (an ecstatic spiritual state). He was moved, guided, taught, comforted, enlightened by the Divine Mother Kali. What are mere human relationships compared to this? A living relationship with the Transcendent Infinite Goddess. It was She who brought him into the theater of the world stage and She who withdrew him back to the Infinite when the play was done.

What can we say? The Goddess Principle of Sheer Identity in Consciousness is called by many names. These precious names are too many to number. So I will dwell on and within Kalee. She is Kha, the Pure Space of Ineffable Consciousness, the True Self_ and She is Li, from lila, the wondrous cosmic play that is spread out before you, the universal tragic comedy

iv

drama we see in front of our eyes.

She is the Breather (Infinite Formless Brahmanic God Consciousness) and She is the Breath expelled as the Finite manifesting as your four states of self consciousness, none other than the waking-dream-sleep-Self paradigm. Our entire self conception is within the parameter of this paradigm which is but an emanation of Her Universal Immensity. So what is this thing we call who, you, me?

S/he is Two-ness, S/he is Not Two-ness and S/he is the Resolution of Reality in the Threshold Between. S/he is Identity in the Sheer Force of Consciousness so much more than the feminine-masculine limitations of embodied awareness. S/he is union and unity, birth, death, rebirth, transcendence and cycle, celebration, tragedy, joy and freedom. Every word invokes Her. Every thought rises out of Her. Every feeling dark or light emerges out from Her Infinite Sentiment.

Her Jewelries are the catholicity of the Waking States. Her Garments are the universality of the Dream States. Her Fragrances are the empyrean cosmic canopy of the Depth of Dreamless Sleep States. Her Self is the Self Conclusive! Kalee is passion, mysticism, Deitess and Essence.

The Mood Tone of Facing Her in Every Direction and in the Directionless Free Transcendent Above the Highest Point of the Spiritual Horizon are words trapped by finiteness hopelessly speaking of the Unspeakable Goddess. She is the Moment of Rapture when all this is realized and She is the Coming Back to the realm of what we refer to as world, life, death, relativity. O Mother Goddess Kalee, remove from my mind this last barrier!

My flesh and blood is the Fluid of Your Mind O Best Kalee. My dreaming consciousness is the Fluid of Your Heart Sentiment. The original and final idea of what I call me is a wave thought on the Fluid of Your Sea of Dreamlessness. O Kalee, You are right in front of my eyes and The One who is seeing through my eyes and all the eyes of the mortal realm of generation, intensity, magnitude, the Spring Tide that sweeps the scope of Boundless Void and Ample Sphere from Indus to Pole, from China to Peru.

Introduction
Formulas of Consciousness

I have only seen two genuine miracles occur in this life. One is the spiritual humility to ask another human being for forgiveness. The other is the spiritual dignity to forgive the one who asks. In these two miracles, Love shines beautifully. One may spend years walking up and down the driveway of figuring. What will be accomplished? Will you change what is meant to be? Will all the figuring in the world ever change what will never happen? The mind is such a curious puzzle. Consciousness watches the mind as it goes from agitation to peace to agitation. Increasing the allotment of the mind's peaceful energy is the great work to be done. It is the tireless work of Love.

We are all born into this world and here we are told now and then what Love is and usually these definitions are wrong. Love is the incomprehensible true state of the Self. You see, if one lives and dies only within the experience of the Karmic "I" which says to itself, I have done this good thing therefore I shall be rewarded with pleasure or, I have done this wicked thing therefore I shall suffer, that condition of the experience of consciousness is extremely limited in its capacity to feel the Energy of Love. Love really knows nothing of that conscious condition of the Karmic "I", for Love does not think in relation to a karmic payback of either sort. But the Love within us as the true reality of Self (atma) may indeed suffer and may indeed feel joy, but this Love knows without a particle of doubt that the reason for this dualistic cause and effect experience is only that the Love within may Learn more of what Love is in Reality. Also the greatest realization in the world is to know that this Love may voluntarily accept suffering upon itself in order to remove that suffering from another soul, mind, or body, without it being ever thought of as karmic payback. When the mind realizes there is no Karmic "I" then thinking changes, there is a flow of Love within the stillness of the heart that comprehends just about everything without a great deal of figuring.

I have but one effort in this life which is to walk the Earth with Humility. I just have to humble myself to Everything for I realize I know nothing at all. I am no longer so arrogant to think in myself that my mind is not influenced by the environment or the people around me, so I humble and surrender myself to the surrounding energies of persons and environments and by this I can see and feel into their deeper reality. I heard my dear friend Swami Bhaskarananda tell a story. I shall retell it. A man was walking by a river. He came to a tall bridge where he saw another man preparing to jump in order to end his life. He cried out please do not jump. Let us talk. So he climbed up the bridge and they talked for four hours. At the end of their conversation, they both jumped off the bridge. So if you do not think you are influenced by environmental and psychic surroundings, well, you will learn humility eventually.

The problem of subtle psychological ego-based comparison is deadly business, spiritually speaking. Atma is not found by an ego comparison with another human being, not even with the finest examples of human spiritual life. It is your own experience to be tried and tested in your own way with your own energy. All connections, whether of attraction, longing, need, or repulsion, offense, defense, and dislike, are ultimately deceptions on the Pure Consciousness of your own Atma, which is beautifully independent of the comparison problem. As this experience is the stabilization of your own sakti (conscious power) in the Sakti (Shak-tee) of the Goddess.

This text is written from the posture that everything seen in the Mirror of Consciousness as the Witness Power is nothing but a mirage. We go back to a Primordial Experience of a First Consciousness. If one contemplates a religion, a teacher or a tradition following the ancient thought of who was before that teacher, and what was before that religion or tradition and with that keeps going back and back, one's mind finally arrives at the Primordial Origin. There one discovers the Great Principle which is literally the First Root, the First Take, the First Hold, which is the First and Original Truth. Once this is realized one comes to know that one is not a disciple of any person or any path. A disciple is one who is in the discipline of another person or some path or tradition. If one has reached the Original State or even just a glimpse of it, then how can that be that one would still be a disciple of someone or something? The practice of a traditional path or a teacher of some kind may or may not be with you at all times. One must be honest, who practices their path or sits in the presence of their teacher twenty four hours a day? But Life is always with you, so Life and even so Life in its Original State is always with you as the Reality of You (the Atma). That is my only discipline and Love is its Result!

I give no value to my worries. What I say or do not say can have no effect on the True Love in You. Nor can I cause the Cause of Love in you. It has always been so in regard to anyone's experience. That Love comes of its own as the Teacher called Life wears us down until we surrender to the Beautiful Original Experience of Love as what Is! And it seems to be true that an intellectual illumination is but a flash of momentary insight. Whereas the emotional illumination of Love stays with us. For you see, emotion imprints memory and brings changing power. We have thousands of sensory, mental and intellectual surveillances occurring every hour, but only those that are connected with an emotional imprint are remembered.

The central cognitive ideal of this text is under the spiritual protection and guidance of Mother Kali. It is by thinking of Her that the ideas written forth in the following pages came to my mind. I don't know why. But I humble myself to Her as She is! Ramakrishna (1836-1886) speaks of turning the mind within oneself so you can go to Kali as the Wish-Fulfilling Tree. This is the real cognitive spiritual power, not just the human mind wishing for this and that, petty things of the passing world, as Love (the Atma) is what will be manifest by this cognitive spiritual power. Paramahansa Yogananda, the author of the famous book, *Autobiography of a Yogi*, had this experience of manifesting the visible living Goddess when he visited the Dakshineswar Temple where Sri Ramakrishna had lived and worshiped the Goddess. When we think of these manifestations in consciousness it is important to realize that they come out of the conscious power of Chitrini (the Sakti of Consciousness). It should come as no surprise. Also, at one time Yogananda wanted M., the recorder of *The Gospel of Sri Ramakrishna*, to be his teacher, but M. knew there was another for the precious yogi. Nevertheless, they had a few extraordinary experiences in each other's company.

Most of the time people do not realize how powerful the cognitive conscious force of religious thought is and its effect on humanity. For generating Love or generating fear. To cherish or to destroy. You see, if one holds to a singular exclusive religious ideal in the shape of a person or a religion, one cannot but help to develop an unhealthy xenophobic alienation toward everything else that is not included in one's ideal. This is most destructive and creates such madness of warlike aggressivity. A case example is early Jewish destruction of every other religious community they could find and destroy out of the religious justification that their God said to do it. A very negative example of the power of dark cognition. This religious system and others of that type or sort are responsible for so much of the fearful apocaphobic millennial mentality that just delegates the world's future to God's vengeful devastation. In reality there is no problem on the Earth today that cannot be solved by the active desire and spiritual balance within the human spirit combined with intelligence in solving the problems of the Earth. Whereas Buddhism has never sought to destroy others, but demonstrates high compassion for all beings with the amazing ideal that any being, past, present or future may at one time be one's mother and that all beings tremble at the great fright of death. And so compassion should always be shown. I am speaking of pure Buddhist culture that only shows peace to others. But if you mix Buddhism with Samurai culture, the peaceful ideal will be there but the samurai part will go off on the route of killing and death.

There are really so many examples of the psychic influence of cultural phenomena. Religious beliefs can arise out of environmental conditions. It is believed that the ancient Harrapa valley of India was a matriarchal society. Men had a more passive and gentle role than they do today. Much of their time was used for the contemplation of spiritual questions and conditions. As the matriarchal dynamic directed most of life's activities and functions, the idea of the Purusha (Soul) as the Witness or Watcher of life may have arose. And so Prakriti (the Dynamic Power of Nature) was then thought to be more of the energetic power in the universe, the world, and society. This was the formation of early Samkhya, founded by Kapila. It is an interesting thought in itself which should be applied to the question of how our environment of today affects our thought development and affects our response to this environment itself, as we should be Poets of the Earth and give our Love to all life that is here, now. The solutions to the problems of the Earth are certainly present and innate and are being born forth as women who are naturally cherishing of life, rise in their active power directing more and more of our world's dynamics.

For one thing, the Tantra is most honest about the comparative horror and beauty which is just naturally here in the world. It deals directly with the dualism of our experience without a bunch of superstitious hoohah, for the most part. The truth is that Tantra addresses the contradictions and confusions of life. For it takes into consideration the path of erotic love and the path of no erotic love, as a love transmuted into spiritual romance and the divine experience of union spiritually speaking. Vama, the path of beauty in the erotic sense is transformed into and uplifted within a higher Vama or beauty of Spiritual Love. It does not cognise the idea of sinfulness but elevates one type of love into a higher type of Love. This is very honest and healthy for the human soul.

Tantra also boldly embraces both tradition and no tradition as a choice of spiritual discovery. There are Tantras which adhere to gods, goddesses, gurus and religion. And there are Tantras which go past all tradition and clear out the content of all dream material as mental cognitions on what in Truth is our Spiritual Experience. That is why this path of Anugraha Tantra, is the most very refined spiritual grace (anugraha) of ever continuous expanding and extending consciousness, understanding and love (tantra).

But again, this path without fear directly addresses and deals with the darker places of the human psyche. Those self-created karmic circumstances that people have generated out of the tamasic force of the psyche. So it gives some frightening techniques for dealing with these dark methods of the mind. For one, Kali Herself can appear terrifying so much so that She will eventually remove all terror from the mind. Also Tantra does not take anger and hate like other religions, into a religious justification of destroying other people who believe differently. But Tantra says yes the human mind has these negative forces and they are the source of all our fear and so gives remedy methods of taming these negatives into skills instead of being tamed or driven by them. One such method is stambhana which is to render the efforts of an enemy useless or to cause paralysis to the body of an enemy. But as with all other elements of human experience the Tantra elevates consciousness from there, the inertia of the psyche (tamas), to the passionate power (rajas) of the human psyche and then to the spiritually balanced state of consciousness (sattva).

If we go on with an honest surveillance of reality we will find that some systems are non-deluding about their mythological fabrications and others are not. For example, in the sacred books of the Hindus we find Vasishtha teaching the God-man Rama the Advaita Vedanta doctrines. And later we find the great illuminator Buddha Siddhartha who unleashed Advaita (Non-dualism) for the world out of pure Love to remove the great fright, teaching that same Vasishtha the *Cinacara Tantra*. How can this be? Buddha lived five centuries B.C.E. Krishna (the God-man and the consort-lover of the Goddess-woman Radha) lived three thousand years B.C.E. and Rama, I have read, lived two hundred years before Krishna. So did this Vasishtha conquer physical death for a least a few thousand years? I don't think so. Maybe one is historical and the other mythological. But the story metaphor raises consciousness out of delusion and dream and does not increase or augment delusional dream material.

You see, the facts and beliefs effect the response of the psyche in study, experience and research. For example some scientists have reduced the origin of the human race to the part animal ape, part human emergence in the Eve woman animal of Africa. That is biblically influenced research compensating the "Eve idea." The Chinese and Mongolian races claim their origin from the Peking Man. And why could not the Ramapithecus be the source being of the Indo-Australians? Why can there not be various sources for present day human beings? For plants and other animals there are various life sources. It is but a thought to consider, though not scientifically accurate according to the collection of present day facts. Who knows? There could be the bones of prehumans buried under the Polar Caps or the Gobi Desert yet now undiscovered which would change our entire perception of human origins. The thing is that in any arena of thought, if you look through the lens of science, then science is all that you see.

Also, we wonder if there is life out there, in the universe, in our home galaxy, among neighboring star systems. Most probably. But keep a rational perspective. Even if you could travel ten times the speed of light it would take you forty years to get to Earth from the Seven Sisters. The light that is reaching the Earth today left the Andromeda Galaxy, our nearest galactic neighbor, when human beings were still in the prehuman state. How humbling it is, when all we see of the stars and galaxies is what was, not what is in the now of their existence. We perceive but the ghosts of the past! The largest star yet discovered in the history of our galaxy has now been seen. There could be hundreds of planets around it. How convenient that would be for exploration of planetary habitats. But what people fail to see is that everything that is out there is already within us. We have been to the Moon. But we often do not realize the intelligent life that we brought back from there originally came from within us. The blessed nuisance of the computer. We imagined it and created it out of mathematical and mechanical genius. To me this is more amazing or as amazing in itself as if we were visited by fellows from other star systems. Everything is like that, all anomalies. We pull them out of ourselves. Just a few decades ago the computer weighed tons and tons and was filled with vacuum tubes and did not even have the capacity of a pocket calculator. Now there is Deep Blue, a computer thought to be more powerful in intelligence than any human being. But the question of ethics and feelings may still bewilder us in regard to our intelligent mechanical alien friend. What shall become?

All conditional concepts are just that, concepts only. But they effect us. The thought that the human being is merely an intelligent animal, as purely physical in nature, is a depressing thought, but can be liberating in some ways. But nevertheless it does not show what we completely are in our true nature. But in the development of intelligence, especially in regard to our religious experience, it is important to realize the real condition of the world and the naturalness of our spirituality freed from myopic mythological superstitions. I personally believe deeply in Spirituality. I cannot say to myself that Sakti (Spiritual Power) or Chitrini (Goddess Consciousness) is an anomaly. Perhaps this is my fanaticism or personal doctrinal exclusivity, but in the end I certainly realize the importance of pure experience free of all cognitive formations in the experience of that Consciousness.

This entire text was inspired by two words spoken by Swami Aseshananda (1899-1996) in his statement of how Reality is experienced as "Felt Awareness." For me, he was one of the great souls of the modern age. I only saw him a few times, but a few times was enough to see this being who was one of the last living disciples of Sri Ramakrishna's wife, Sarada, the Holy Mother. I have had dreams of Swami Aseshananda since he left his old body behind. In one dream it was a grand birthday celebration. He was as he was, very old. But he looked quite young. Perhaps this was a dream impression of him because when he used to speak he would instantly become quite young and vital in his appearance. Many of those who knew him were at the table feasting and taking leave of him. Would this not be a symbol in my dream mind of the feast of physical life itself which Swami has now left? Swami said one thing in this dream, "I don't want to talk anymore." And then he left. Perhaps this dream reflects my own subconscious feeling about his leaving the body. I enjoy living in the subconscious domain for there is more honesty here in the dream material with oneself than with connections with others, due to the distortions that occur in communication with spoken words. Love has no words. It seemed that the spiritual energy of Swami's sakti held on to his body by sheer will force. When the time of death came, Swami just let go of the body when the moment to meet Kali and Ramakrishna arrived. Beautiful. A spiritual being's death is a blessing to all who fear what is just past the mortal frontier. I realize that the dream was just a dream in Consciousness, the dream came and went, but Consciousness remains.

I dreamt of my own death. Is it anymore real or unreal than what actual death may be? It is just in Consciousness, the dream, but also, death is just in Consciousness. A boat capsized. All were dead. I saw them. Then from above, looking down at the boat upside down in the rushing water of the river leading to the ocean I said, "Look, look, we are having an out of the body experience." I repeated it twice. Then I found my beloved wife Sally looking for me. She was sitting by a river. Tired, sad, sorrowful. Her eyes were blackened by her sorrow. I came up to her to embrace her. She could not see, feel, nor hear me. I said, "I am fine. See?" Then I realized that my death had come and I started chanting, "Sakti, Sakti, Sakti..." A very loud harmonious chorus accompanied me. Further on, the Origin of the river beckoned to me. A dream no different than death, but only an experience in Consciousness. Excellent! When mind is still in the subtle condition, coming out of the dream state, practice with singular intensity, the Energy of Identity with *This Consciousness,* before the mind acts in assuming the waking state form of consciousness!

One day I had such a simple pure experience. I was resting and during my rest I was entertaining such thoughts as what if there is no spiritual meaning to life, what if we are all just evolved intelligent animals, what if when we die it is indeed as those fools say, but dust to dust and when we are gone we are gone and nothing more. And so as thoughts affect feelings I became quite depressed. But at that very moment my blessed beloved came up to me and simply kissed me. She did not know what I was silently feeling, but as she greeted me I inhaled her breath, the fragrance of which ignited in me the Power of tremendous Love. I thought to myself even if the thoughts I am entertaining are true this Love that I feel at this moment makes it all filled with meaning and absolutely worth everything. That is the simple sweet Power of Sakti as Love removing all doubts. For Love is the Pure Essence of what is Spiritual.

Ramakrishna would sing the poems of the Kali Poet Ramprasad who lived before him. "Hedge it about with Kali's name if you would keep your harvest safe; This is the stoutest hedge of all, for Death himself cannot come near it..." Ramakrishna stated in regard to this poem, "The world is not impermanent if one lives there after knowing God." Indeed, the world itself is not impermanent. Things come and go, but nothing comes nor goes, since it is all Kali. There are only great cycles of Life, Energy, Consciousness, and Love! Then it is illusion's illusion to say the world is illusion, impermanent. Realizing Kali, is this state of Pure Permanence. What Vedanta negates as illusion, Tantra affirms as reality.

Because it is ever present, one must embrace what Sri Ramakrishna called Yogamaya (the illusion of union). You see, there is no union for the Atma (Self), Atma is always Atma, so the idea that union takes places with the Atma is an illusion of maya, the greatest conscious illusion, the total struggle of all life and the divine game of the Goddess. Ramakrishna, "You see, such is the power of Yogamaya that She can cast a spell." And this spell is the cognitive power created in the amazing idea of the anomaly of dual separative consciousness when all the while it is the one Consciousness in which this imagination or spell of forgetfulness is happening. In regard to the subtle body, this Yogamaya may be the divine and spiritual yet subtle feminine projection in the internal psyche that both feels the distinction of the karmic "I" separation and then as the wondrous Kundalini

Sakti which as the subtle body is nothing but this Sakti, even so the gross body as well, that ultimately as the amalgamated moving dynamic power of the Goddess Herself, recreates for the internal psyche the illusion of enlightenment. Both are Yogamaya. So, what can we do but surrender to Her and embrace Her as the Sakti of our upliftment into the understanding of Love! As the Yogamaya of Love's upliftment comes to view, the first stage is like the maiden, the second stage is like the mother, the third stage is like the crone, what is the fourth is Mother's sweet mystery, to become, as Sakti rises, as She uplifts!

Ramakrishna says again, "Chaitanya, too, worshiped Sakti." That is he worshiped the Divine Power of the Goddess. It is actually said by the enlightened that Chaitanya was the embodied manifestation incarnate of both the Radha Energy and the Krishna Energy in one being. He started the love path of adoration of this Goddess-woman and God-man as it is more commonly known today. But it most certainly existed in other forms for thousands of years. There are Tantras devoted uniquely to the practice of this chosen spiritual ideal.

Indeed, Ramakrishna himself may have been this very same soul as it is believed that he was also Rama and then Krishna too. A great and powerful Tantrika, one named Gauri of Indes declared, "Does Vaishnavacharan call you an incarnation only? I should consider his estimate very low. My conviction is that you are He, from a part of whom the Incarnations come down to the world from age to age to do good to humanity, and with whose power they accomplish that work of theirs." Others have believed that Sri Ramakrishna and Sarada were both manifest incarnate beings who in their very innermost essence were and are the Goddess Kali. But you see, to mentally divide the spiritual principle of the Atma is a pernicious stance in consciousness. Ramakrishna clarifies, "What a crude idea! Know that it is your chosen Ideal alone who manifests himself as Kali, Krishna, Gauri (another name for Chaitanya) and all others. Hold on firmly to the conviction that it is your chosen Ideal who has become Krishna, Gauri and other Divine manifestations."

The Worship of Sakti is extremely old, going back to the very root and source of human life on this beautiful planet Earth. It is most sacred. Ramakrishna would assert that Gauri, the Tantrika, would worship his own wife as the Goddess, Sakti, the Divine Mother Herself. This spiritual method closes the gap of dualism and brings to the light of consciousness that non-dual realization, where the once dual barrier of what is felt to be humanly different and what is Spiritually ever at One, no longer puzzles the mind or what is also called the subtle body. Ramakrishna practiced this method of worship with his wife as well. In fact, in his remarkably pure mind he perceived all women as embodiments of the Divine Goddess. A perfect Tantrika. Great power comes from this spiritual method. Again Ramakrishna tells how Gauri could hold eighty-two pounds of burning wood with his left hand and perform the fire worship ceremony with his right hand, This ritual takes a long time and Ramakrishna says he saw Gauri do it. But even with his great powers, Gauri was fond of argumentation in his arrogance, but that vanished in the company of the gentle surrender and humility of Ramakrishna. Gauri did not want to return to his worldly life so one day he took his leave of Ramakrishna who out of his great loving concern inquired of him, "How is it, Gauri? Where will you go?" Gauri said he would not return until he realized God. For a long time they searched for him. But no one has heard of him since.

One last thought, Ramakrishna once said to the amazement of those who were with him at the time, "There is no outsider here. The other day, when Harish was with me, I saw Satchidananda come out of this sheath. It said, 'I incarnate Myself in every age.' I thought that I myself was saying these words out of mere fancy. I kept quiet and watched. Again Satchidananda Itself spoke saying, 'Chaitanya, too, worshiped Sakti.'" It is fascinating. No outsider may mean no dual feeling. This sheath is this body and mind. Ramakrishna always referred to his personal self as "this" as the expression does not increase the sense of the karmic "I" identity. Beautiful. But how can Satchidananda come out of the body, the "this?" Perhaps that Existence, Consciousness and Bliss, the Atma, is never in the "this", as body. Or perhaps it is a death-like experience where Ramakrishna's own sakti momentarily left his body to reveal a secret. But he is so humble that he questions his own possible words as fancy. Who is the Atma? Are we not all that Reality, that Saving Principle of Pure Spirituality? That Satchidananda! Then with all humility he spoke to M., "I saw that it is the fullest manifestation of Satchidananda; but this time the Divine Power is manifested through the glory of sattva." Yes, the sattva, that is the divine harmony. Perhaps other incarnate beings have not given us such a gentle truth with the harmony of all spiritual paths. Rama and Krishna were both warriors. Even the Buddha in his early days had to struggle with the questions of worldly life. Ramakrishna never struggled with those questions. Though he had the spiritually passionate burning to become one with the Goddess Kali and that beautiful enthusiasm led him, by the sheer force of its momentum, through the barriers of various religious and spiritual paths, into the Pure Experience of Advaitic Consciousness, Ramakrishna's Nirvikalpa!, Advaita!, without mental cycles, the perfect thought, the body astounded, the mind amazed, out of which was produced the unique and sweetest of doctrines that all paths may lead to Truth.

Blessed Sakti! I will not save the past, nor shall I borrow from the future. Answer my selfish prayer by the Power of Self, the Atma, shining in the sushumna as Chitrini Consciousness. Your Self, My Self, no longer a dualism! Give me the vital life energy to finish what You brought me here to finish. Complete my journey Mother! For to really *See* what Maha Maya (the Great Dream) is, is to see Advaita (the Non-Dual). Bless me Sakti, that I might see Birth, Dream, Prajna (Deep Sleep) and the Consciousness of Turiya, (the Fourth State), wherein Love is the Power, Consciousness is the Insight and Being (Atma) is What Exists in all situations. So with complete Humility I fully Surrender to Sakti, not retaining one thread in the weave of ego, for even that, but a single thread of ego is enough to begin the cognition of the tapestry of misery. I pray to the Goddess that this text will be the last spiritual stone in my living house of Tantra and Upanishad, where Ramakrishna dwells, filled with Sakti, She who is my essence, my answer, and my conclusion!

Anomalies In Consciousness
(Or, Seeing Serpents in a Rope)

I shall now proceed in a slow, definite, and pure way to expel superstition and confusion pertaining to some very curious, puzzling, and profound anomalies in Consciousness. The clarity of Vedanta and the mystery of Tantra will be employed in this task of love working its way to remove fear. For in fear is where confusion starts and then the mind loses its perception of the spiritual principle.

It seems to me, in my experience, that Truth is always the most honest, simple, and direct interpretation, not only of itself in its own experience, but in the perception, cognition, or encounter of an external or internal event. Truth as experience is a "felt awareness" (Aseshananda) not an execution of bare intellect. The after-effect of such experience is one of awe and beauty, reverence and humility. For I hold to Truth in the simplest way as the truest of the true.

For what indeed could be more miraculous than that one may live within this gigantic immense universe without a trace of fear? What is more amazing than to be loving and forgiving? What is more extraordinary than that one may see oneself in others? What could be a more pure and blissful phenomena than that Consciousness itself does witness the cycle of waking, dreaming and deep non-dual sleep, without itself being disturbed? What would be a greater marvel than that we may be happy though body and mind are rushing to extinguishment in the flow and flood of space and time? And what greater wonder could there be than that we may contemplate this pure and perfect simplicity of reality with the Power (Sakti, which is pronounced Shak-tee, and sometimes written as Shakti) of our minds? We confuse ourselves seeking the complex demonstration of 'something' greater than ourselves. We seek what is more than natural as a proof of what is most natural to us. Love!

So let us proceed to descend from this Peak of Beauty, deep

1

into the delusion, in order to remove, expel, expound upon and extinguish that delusion.

Consciousness As Witness

Advaita (Non-Dual) Vedanta presents the most extraordinary idea of what is perhaps the greatest cognitive delusion of all. It is that Jiva (the soul) has imagined itself to be distinct from, dualistically divided from Isvara (the God concept). This has become so apparently by the great force of Maya (cosmic measuring). But even though the imagination entertains this dualism it does not mean that this dualism is real. It is truly an extraordinary reverse miracle. What is Unalterable (the Non-Dual Oneness) has become altered by the power of cognitive imagination and from this point the entire spiraling fantasy of world delusion descends.

It is like the mental phenomena of staring fixedly at a painting, after a while, motion, or movement, or the appearance of a life force in the painting begins to take on that quality. This is a spiritual and psychological phenomena. The painting has not changed or moved. And in like manner some reports of so-called spiritual visions have been heard. But in reality they are nothing but cognitive emanations of one's own mind.

I am not here to deny God. I love God. I love the Goddess. I love Reality and Truth. It is all here, as that makes life bearable in this world, in the mind, in the human spirit. But what I seek is a greater comprehension of the Divine, the Spiritual, the Awakened.

You see, Consciousness as an aspect of what God is, divested of the masks of God, never changes, never becomes dual, divided, nor distinct from itself, for if it did then how could it be worshiped as the Eternal Constant Principle. But as life moves in its movement of waking and dreaming states in the shapes of the human being and human spirit, this Consciousness at that creative point assumes the characteristics of the Divine Witness. That is the watcher, the looker, the observer. But from the higher non-dual reality, even this Witness of the waking and

2

dreaming states is an illusion. What could the God Principle watch or look upon but God? As it is not a divided state.

In deep, dreamless, slow-wave sleep where even the slow waves of calmest thought have stopped, there is no condition of active thought as we have in this waking state, nor any dream cognition, as again the dream state is in reality nothing but thinking, so there, as it is said in the Vedanta and the Tantra, we all have an unknowing experience in the bliss of the non-dual. But as the dream mind comes out of that state, somewhat like a wave comes out of water, then there the Witness is activated to watch the dream mind, but as it is Consciousness and remains simply and purely the Witness, it does not lose itself in the dualism of active dream thought.

Here at this point begins the most amazing Power of Belief Cognition, that is between the two, between the Witness and beliefs in the dream mind, later to become the waking mind. Out of this dualism of Witness Consciousness and waking/dream mind consciousness, the most amazing and incredible phenomenal anomalies are produced. It is the reflex power of this Witness Consciousness reflected in the dream mind itself that gives the mind the power to create all these extraordinary anomalies and phenomena.

When the Power of the Witness Consciousness is reflected like a light into a mirror, on the innermost perennial space of deep sleep, there the causal identity point starts of the unconstructed dualistic ego thought. It is still a non- dual condition and so all is not lost just yet and the descent into deeper delusions has not started The Witness is reflected on the darkness of prajna (deep sleep).   Can it be said to be darkness only in that there is an illusion of the absence of light? Or that it is darkness in only that there is no waking or dream state light reflected there? No. Prajna means wisdom.   What is that Wisdom within each and every soul who ever enters into the dreamless condition of consciousness?   That Wisdom is the innate and inborn spontaneous knowledge of non-duality.   The inner spiritual essence which makes each of us, even though buried in the ego, still a splinter of light from the Consciousness

3

of God, Goddess, Reality and Truth!

One cannot underestimate the spiritual value of understanding what is the depth of this deepest sleep before consciousness begins to manifest the anomaly of dualism. Not only that it is profound peace and serenity in that the mind complex has slowed to tranquility and stillness, but that it is also said that the one who can comprehend the identity of deep sleep within their self, may measure all from within that state, may cognise all from the place of self in that free condition of natural born wisdom, and also from that position of consciousness which is freed from the dualism of active thought in the states of waking and dreaming, will realize the true nature of the altered anomaly of world phenomena (to wit, waking and dreaming) not yet as to be seen as the Consciousness which *IS* and which invokes the Reality of Goddess, Self, Truth and God!

Ultimately, Truth, Reality, never sleeps the sleep of dualism and ever remains Non-Dual, One, and the All never lost in the all. But God, as this idea in personal concept (I am using the word God here for the sake of most minds which are accustomed to this concept, even though my spiritual taste prefers the flavor of the Goddess) may indeed somehow fall asleep to become the soul in dreamless sleep. The God within you. So then the dream state is just God dreaming and as it is the result, it is God who is awake in the waking state as the wide awake world. Is this a divine cognition? It is the maya of realization and it is why some places and things are thought to be sacred and why some people are held to be holy and that that holiness and sacredness should never be forgotten. But know that the Witness is not the personal God.

Thought does not effect the Witness. What does it matter what thoughts are in your head or whether you are awake or dreaming or whether those thoughts are filled with light, active with passion or dragged by inertia? The Witness remains undisturbed. Its Existence is not changed. Its Consciousness is not excited nor depressed. It is Bliss and Bliss is not effected by ecstasy or joy, nor changed by sadness or sorrow. Bliss is serenity, peace and tranquility and because of this, Bliss is empathic to all joy and sorrow.

As it is, the Witness just watches the reflection of mind in the dream state, but watches more closely than a mirror watches the image in it. For the seeing or perception of the Witness is non-dual. The dream state is the activity of the subtle body when the waking or physical body is at rest. This subtle body is of course arrayed with the spectrum of sense perceptions, for that is why we see and hear and so forth in the dream state. But it may be more the thought or memory of these perceptions. The subtle body is nothing but mind, intellect, the ego connection and memory. The Witness witnesses these functions undisturbed by them. To know or keep aware of the Witness when the subtle body functions is a high understanding, a beautiful non-dual connection with the Pure Divine undisturbed. When one can do this the result is a knowledge that knows what is Real in everyone and everybody. The equality of each soul is understood by directly realizing the dream nature within each being. Their natural phenomenal cognitive dilemma. And so this person possessed of this understanding treats all beings equally and to that precious person all treatment towards that person is perceived equally for it is nothing but dream itself, the inner conscious movement in identity with one and all. So why should one react, this way or that way, since it is only the energy of the dream state which is equal to all beings. By this attitude, during dream, your consciousness retains the Witness Power and so does not become involved in egotistical corruptions, distortions, projections, or unaddressed questions that may arise as perplexing dualistic paradoxical symbols in dream consciousness.

But even when the physical body is active in the waking state, it is the same subtle body that is functioning as before, as it was in the dream state, but now the waking condition has been reactivated. The Witness now sees the mind (dream) and the body (waking). But even in their presence the non-duality of the Witness cannot be denied. For even when your consciousness appears or has the illusion of separating from that non-dual peace that was experienced in deep sleep, it is really not so.

5

This ananda or bliss still remains, but the active functions of the subtle body or dream mind and the physical waking functions make one forget that bliss which is innate within every-one's consciousness. If you behave (live and be) as if you are always in deep wisdom sleep then you will be free of the spell of that forgetfulness! Putting this to practice, one experiences the All-Pervasiveness, the First and Primary Principle, within every person, that is, the common feature of the Real Self within all people. By this feeling of the First and Primary Reality addressed non-dualistically within each and every living being, the satisfaction of all desires fulfilled also is enjoyed as that empathic condition is a high spiritual state.

But even as one comes out of wisdom sleep, and thought reconstitutes or restructuralizes into the dream mind, that thought itself becomes the unconscious potential as a memory of the peace experienced there still remains in the mind. This is ananda (bliss) vasana (unconscious potential). It is unconscious because it is yet to be recalled or recognized in the dream mind and waking conditions. It is potential because Bliss is the divine potential in everyone as the most potent experience of pure spiritual Reality undisturbed by the restructuralized signatures of thought.

Once, coming out of wisdom sleep back into the dream mind my higher self spoke in a voice to my ego consciousness saying, "This way or that way, I got it." Meaning whichever school of thought I embrace, that of pure natural spiritual independence, or that of traditional sects and their followers, the Witness remains, in me as the real Me, as it is the same for any and everyone. The innate Truth cannot be changed by any dictates of the outer world, society, culture, history, religion, psychology, science, the presence of self value and confidence or the absence of any of these signatures in the mind.

For what does it matter anyway? Disintegration of elements, thoughts, energies, forces, and feelings occur at death. The body mind complex is gone. Though some retain the idea that the subtle consciousness journeys forth, even so, even as this may indeed be true, a deathless element of the Self is unfailing, even then, as to where the Witness Is, not engaging the consciousness of the subtle body. Does not the Witness even observe this phenomena of consciousness leaving the physical body, as that consciousness does in the dream state, but now as a natural phenomena of not returning to the once waking physical body? So, if you have the Witness and the functioning consciousness that is witnessed, does not one idea depend upon the other idea for its existence and continuance? If there is total disintegration of the body mind idea then how can the Witness still exist as a reflex, caused by that idea upon the mirror of the Witness Condition. The body mind idea has amalgamated itself into the Witness so the dualism is now gone. This is what is experienced in deep sleep so it should not be strange to you. It is the natural condition of spiritual freedom free of any form of dependent dualism as to the nature of the Witness and its reflection in the consciousness of the mind and so also the body which you now think is your permanent home.

Upon returning to the ego complex there are two wave impressions (vrittis) that may either contaminate or bless the mind. The contamination comes from the outer ego complex itself and is the persistent hold on the anomaly of dualism which from the position of the non-dual is an unnatural view even though humanity is mostly possessed by this misconception. It is ajnana vritti, the wave impression of ignorance which is simply the ignoring of knowledge (jnana). But even in the presence of this dualistic anomaly the Witness still shines upon this wave impression. And so jnana vritti has every opportunity with every thought in consciousness to select for itself the blessing of knowledge and wisdom upon itself where thought once again spontaneously amalgamates with its Source, the Witness.

Bare intellect, active mentality, engaging the emotional and vital arena, or the simple physical body will not get it. Bliss is deeper, higher and further behind all that. Bliss is dead still, dead calm and dead to the anomaly of dualism. So ego, memory, mind and intellect are bundled up into the Bundle of Consciousness which works for our sake as the Witness ever calling us to return to its source. But the beautiful idea of Chidabhasa, the reflection of that Witness Consciousness (Kutastha: immovable, immutable, being in the highest place, being in the midst of, or Sakshi, also meaning Witness, in the sense of having or being the power to overcome, be united with, have communion with, or to enjoy, belong to, and be near) is ever present without a break, whether bare intellect and the rest are there or not there, as in deep wisdom sleep or death. Chidabhasa is the overwhelming spiritual presence of Consciousness in our lives no matter what goes on in the waking or dreaming states, and this reflection (Bhasa: this luster, to illuminate, to shine, to make evident, resplendent, to become clear in the mind, to manifest oneself, and to cause to stand out) of the powerful Witness Consciousness (Chida) is also what we experience within the silent peaceful depth of deep dreamless sleep. It is the very Wisdom itself that is within that state within every soul! It is pure Bliss, nothing but Bliss.

The mind has the strange tendency of thrusting so much external importance on events, things, ideas, and particulars when to the Witness, is it not all the same, equally, as to importance or non-importance? Really, the anomalistic view of the ego in dualism is nothing but a memory held in the subtle body arising at some point in the condition of the dream state. Even so, a profound insight on the two modes of the Witness Principle is given in the *Sarva Upanishad*. Sakshi is stated to not be involved or curious with the anomaly of the appearing and the disappearing of the three states of consciousness. This Sakshi Consciousness is not interested in whether the three conditions arise or sink back into Consciousness. The Kutastha is then the pure consciousness of the Witness Principle which is dynamically and actively involved as the power of conscious intelligence within the appearing and disappearing of the three states. If you meditate on the Witness Principle as a ball, a sphere or bundle of consciousness, one may think that one side of this ball of consciousness is only *facing* Self, and the other side of the sphere is consciously engaged with *facing* the function and cycle of the states of waking, dreaming and deep sleep. Both of these two modes of the Witness Condition are still superimpositions on the exquisitely Pure Advaita (Non-Dual) Principle.

Maps of the Mind

Maps of the mind are maps of Identity. There are many. They are transient and ever changing. But what happens when the maps are destroyed. Nothing. That Identity stays the same. This is Consciousness to which no map may describe. But these maps are ever attempting to do so. How many maps we have in a single lifetime and how many there are in the world around us ranging from the primitive, archaic, superstitious, and religious, to the modern psychological, scientific, holographic, quantum, astronomical and even purely spiritual. If one loses the map, one will not, nor does not ever lose the Consciousness to which the maps points.

The quality of the map reflects in the mirror of the mind the perception of Consciousness in that mind. If your map is a depressing one then the perception will also be so. If your map is an exalted or ecstatic map then the perception will also be so. The world appears as tragic or beautiful by the nature of the map. Consciousness, the Witness, is not changed by the map but the reflex of perception off the Witness State back into the mind certainly makes the perception either joyful or sorrowful, fearful or loving, etc. So it is good and excellent to continually feed the mind with newer and better maps so that perception will change and the cycling or rumination on old maps whose response reflexes are tired and have no solution will lose their power. It is a matter of relearning what your map is and changing it by positive cognitive energy. It is the power of the psychic energy reflex off of the Witness Consciousness that enlivens these maps so that they appear real, meaningful, potent, and actual to you at the moment you engage them.

These maps are gates. Some gates go into delusion. Some gates open into the pure free space of sweet spiritual Consciousness. These gates manifest in the mirror of mind during the liminal border of consciousness before the maps are made and then fixed to the ego feeling of the solid and specific thought maps in the waking condition. Ideas, beliefs, etc., are experienced in Consciousness alone. The body/mind, waking, dreaming and deep sleep are experienced in Consciousness alone. And when they are experienced, Consciousness acts as Witness of that phenomenal wonder.

The Near Death Experience
and the Movement of Kundalini Sakti

This is the way in which spiritual conditioning or practice changes us, or rather changes our map perception of that Unchanging Witness Consciousness. It is Self, as it is, watching self (in phenomena). The Unchanging Witness Consciousness is the Great Light of disembodiedness. As in the Near Death Experience (NDE) phenomena, it is the True Self watching the death of the little temporary self as it leaves one incarnation. People who have experienced near death most often come back with extraordinary new maps. They entered a world that for centuries has been hidden to most of us and deeply shrouded with mythology.

You see, the NDE jars loose the kundalini sakti, that powerful consciousness that is so magnificent, She has created the body mind complex itself, and has covered Herself there assuming the deepest identity of every individual. When this becomes loosened She returns to Her Source which is the place of Her Own Self, Consciousness (the Great Light). Yet, to the Witness, the event of embodiedness or disembodiedness is the same, but a serpent seen in a rope, a cognitive superimposition upon the reality of Consciousness now released in one's mind of all signatures of designation pertaining to the embodied or disembodied state. The common report of the tunnel experience in NDE's is but the kundalini power moving up and down the central spiritual nerve (sushumna) which runs from the spine base up out the top of the skull. It is a nerve in the living human body, but also a subtle and most refined spiritual channel of the powerful cognitive energy that manifests and creates consciousness in the experiences of deep non-dual sleep, the dreaming states and the waking conditions of temporary physical life.

This cognitive force is so potent that the yogis and yoginis who engage this are said to be able to not just visualize, but to manifest the living existence of the deities and deitesses along the chakra course of this spiritual nerve of non-dual consciousness. Curiously, the word "sak" from Sakti means "to be able." These spiritual poets working with this cognitive energy, manifest identity with these gods and goddesses along the sushumna course. This is not unlike the experience of meeting God, saviors and teachers, loved ones and ancient souls within the tunnel. In fact, I think it is the same experience only manifested in different mythological imagery. It is a skill in forming, shaping, directing, and surrendering to the divine control of that spiritual energy, which shapes everything that is experienced in the waking and dream state. An analogy or another map to explain this is prana which also means energy, vital living energy. It is thought that this prana is the very condition of deep sleep itself, when the dualistic influx and out flux of consciousness or prana of the waking and dreaming condition have come to rest within the non-dual spiritual nerve. This leads us to think of the beauty that is here. What is life, that waking and dreaming, is but Prana manifest. And so the state of non-dual rest, the slow wave or waveless state of wisdom sleep is but this powerful sakti kundalini as She has come back to what should be called the womb of consciousness. This is the Prana of deep sleep, the source and origin of the energy that cognises the states of waking and dreaming. When you enter deep sleep you are at rest in your own energy, the power of your own prana, which, when coming out of the "womb" creates the visualization, experiences, manifestation and even the assistance itself of all those deities, deitesses, helpers, saviors, teachers, loved ones and so forth, which appear within the sushumna.

One may think of this phenomenal anomaly as a diversity of

manifest maps of personality, of the yet one true personality of what we may call the reflex power of the higher spiritual self. Is there a rational explanation to spiritual phenomena? Does it detract from the wonder of those amazing anomalies to explain them rationally? I think it is more amazing, more a greater wonder to realize that this wonder is what is within you.

Also I must mention with praise, the work of Dr. Kenneth Ring, at present, with the study of people who are blind since birth and the NDE phenomena they experience. They can actually see and then describe physical objects that they have never seen before in their lives, during the NDE experience. Dr. Ring's study here is shattering previous ideas contained in old and now outdated mind maps. What does this say? Simply that it is Consciousness which is the True Seer (Witness) of things. Not the optic lens and nerves, not even the brain or the mind which are shut down during the NDE. And this is what Vedanta and Tantra have always said. Consciousness is the Witness-Seer, and none other!

Chitrini Sakti
(The Innermost Consciousness)

When Kundalini Chitrini (Kunda from kundalini = womb power, that is the prajna condition of deep sleep, the well source of manifest consciousness as this creation, and Lini = when that consciousness is coiled up into the manifest body/mind complex experiencing the three states. Chitrini is the divine consciousness of the Goddess as the saving movement, as in spreading, expanding, or salvation, of that consciousness = chit.) begins Her movement in the sushumna, an awakening of deeper and deeper maps of consciousness begins to take place. You see, the idea is there that as long as She sleeps in the root center (muladhara chakra) of the microcosmic individual world, one simply experiences the waking, dreaming and deep sleep states in an ordinary way. That is you simply wake, dream and sleep in an unilluminated way. She is asleep in you and so you are asleep. But when one begins to direct this cognitive energy toward the Turiya, or the fourth state of Consciousness, one begins to wake up in a spiritual way. It is said that Chitrini begins to move up the sushumna, or starts to pull within and deeper. Sushumna means the very gracious and this is the essence of spiritual grace itself. It is also called the sahaja nerve or the innermost channel of natural spontaneously born bliss. And also referred to as the avadhuti, which is the spiritual nerve of the avadhuta, the one who has shaken off the dust of world dualism.

When consciousness is directed here in the spiritual plane, not to bodily nerves or mental channels or road maps of the mind, that consciousness (Chitrini) is making Her movement through the finest spiritual fiber of consciousness back into Turiya. With this very gracious movement of consciousness, this natural sense of Her being born within you, this conscious power of being able to shake off the world delusion with all its miseries, one then begins to see that the states of waking, dreaming and deep sleep are not ordinary at all. Indeed, they are the magnificent production of Chitrini, witnessed by Her when active and fully realized as the potential of Consciousness in the Turiya State.

If one thinks of the sushumna as an organic biological nerve or even as an intense, tight or refined spiritual channel in the mind, it is almost, but not quite right as to Her real nature. She is the one who bestows spiritual grace from beyond the complexities of the body and mind. It is a gift of Her grace that one would start to experience Her movement toward spiritual consciousness as a conscious cognitive movement. People blow bellows of breath, torture their bodies with difficult postures and sing loud songs making great and tremendous efforts to awaken kundalini when it will never happen until one's focus of love is directed toward what can only be called the divine. This is pure consciousness, pure love and pure being as this is *what* Turiya is! Then that Chitrini moves as the kundalini through the sushumna. She is really always doing this but until the spiritual principle is put into the formula of the three states of consciousness, those three states of consciousness appear to be merely ordinary conditions of the mind. The principle spiritual power was always there carrying one's consciousness from the three lower chakras of the waking state, into the two upper chakras of the dream state, and then into the sixth chakra of the mind merged in deep sleep (prajna or ajna chakra). But when the seventh or pure Consciousness is left out of the mix, that mix appears ordinary. Though it never was ordinary. The spiritual nature of the human complex is never ordinary. But as long as consciousness only moves back and forth, up and down through the gross, subtle and causal planes of the six bodily centers confined to the waking, dreaming, and deep sleep cognitions, that beautiful spiritual consciousness remains asleep to the ongoing movement of our conscious cognitive processes and so we ourselves remain asleep to the spiritual potential within us. But Chitrini, as Her own ever awakened, most very gracious, spontaneous non-dualistic consciousness is ever aware of Her own self, only waiting for us fools to turn and look within into Her kindest and extremely awake gracious spiritual movements within the deepest channel of the sushumna.

She is always shining luminous within the deepest layer of the sushumna. The steady state of spiritual innateness is always there ever present within every living being. It is said that the sun and moon are swallowed in the sushumna at the occurrence of enlightenment. What does it mean? It is also said that the substance of the sushumna is the sun, moon and fire. What does it mean? Also the awakened have reported that the sushumna is of the substance of the three gunas. The sun and moon are the solar and lunar nerves of dualism. The solar nerve leads consciousness to the waking condition, it is the path of death, hot and violent. The lunar nerve leads consciousness into the dream state, it is the path of life, cool and sweet. When these two, the sun and moon are swallowed into the sushumna, it means that the dualism of life current and death current, waking and dreaming states are swallowed or devoured into the non-dualism of prajna (deep sleep) at first, as the unawakened, or yet to be awakened condition of consciousness. Later Chitrini reveals or uncovers the Turiya Background which is ever present

14

as Her gracious conscious self awareness.

The substance of the sushumna as sun, moon and fire is again nothing but the three states of waking, dreaming and deep sleep. It is metaphorical and actual. A literal and living reality. These three conditions of consciousness are swallowed into pure Consciousness, as the sushumna is an analogy for that Consciousness without fetter, otherwise called absolute Consciousness, as ab-solutus in truth means "freed from." That is, freed from the limited conditional idealism that the three states are ordinary when in reality they are nothing but pure Consciousness itself in its finest and most refined spiritual essence. Ever Present. The substance of the three gunas or qualities of force or movement are inertia as gravity (the down pull or backward force), activity or passionate movement (the forward or upward movement of consciousness and energy), and the energy of harmonious balance or spiritual tranquility between these two other forces where the pull towards Consciousness occurs in the mind. With all this inside the sushumna we get a multi-faced picture of many maps of consciousness. So much so that one might become lost within these many faced metaphysical maps of the mind.

But the meaning that all these three fold designations are in the sushumna or are the substance of that sushumna and so forth is so beautiful a spiritual map, for it simply shows that none of these three states, conditions, qualities, or movements of consciousness are ever outside, separate or dualistic in their condition from that divine and spiritual consciousness as Chitrini Kundalini! It is the effortless movement of Her ever present current of grace, always, perpetually, and continuously moving in the three states, manifesting Herself as the energy (prana) of pure dream free, dualism free sleep, where all opposite currents in their motions as consciousness, energy and matter are hushed within silence and peace. As She is in and as the very penetrating and reflecting consciousness of the dream state, going back and forth from that condition, to and from the material condition of consciousness reflected down into the physical elements of the waking state, but as itself, that is in

15

itself, that consciousness is never actually bound by those physical elements, only lost in the reflection of those elements, energies, and cognitive motions.

By and by, to these chakras (wheels or circles, centers of consciousness) are assigned numerous maps or designations of consciousness. And these are, by Chitrini Herself, previous to spiritual experience itself, swallowed within the sushumna. There are not only the physical elements of the waking state, the subtle energies of the dream condition and the cognitive motions which merge in the deep sleep state, but there are multiple diagrams of consciousness (yantras), divine letters and words as designations of particulate states of conscious awareness and awakening (mantras), and there are female and male deities and deitesses, gods and goddesses in blissful union associated with and laid out along the chakra schematic as metaphorical images expressing states of power expressed in what is simply mind and matter as the non-separate or non-dualistic manifestation of Chitrini, which is the divine dynamic state of pure Sakti. Matter is ultimately in the mind, mind is ultimately in pure Consciousness and this Consciousness is Sakti, the Goddess Kundalini.

Further Illustrations of Spiritual Maps in Visions, Encounters and Experiences that Arise out of the Cognitive Power of Chitrini Consciousness

So, we come to the impasse, that when consciousness travels along the nerves (nadis) that extend outward through the physical senses and body extensions, that consciousness as the power of Chitrini, produces the experience of the waking state. When this Chitrini consciousness withdraws, so to be now unaware of the nerve pathways that extend to the waking experience, that consciousness now moves internally along the nadis (nerves) withdrawn from the sensory message of those externally extended nerves. This is the movement of Chitrini as the dream state of consciousness. This is how Sakti Chitrini

16

moves or travels along these nerve maps. Beyond these nerve maps she goes into the non-dual current within the central nerve (sushumna) to experience deep sleep. Beyond all these nerve maps of consciousness is Turiya, where Sakti Chitrini is in Her Unstirred State, from here the reflection of Power coming out of Consciousness as Witness enlivens these maps of the mind with living cognitive energy, so they appear real, meaningful, etc.

It is said the divine image of the Goddess Kali was introduced by Krishnananda Agamavigasa (15th - 16th century C.E.) in his massive text, the *Tantrasara*. "Introduced" does not mean that he made, or created this image of the Goddess, it means that he wrote down the description of Her which I am sure without doubt goes back in time to the earliest formation of spiritual consciousness in the history of human beings. Nevertheless by writing down the feature in the consciousness of this divine image of Her called Dakshina Kalika, he crystallized that very image into the minds of many people. One of these was Sri Ramakrishna of Dakshineswar (1836 - 1886).

Ramakrishna worshiped this divine form of the Goddess in a statue of Her which to him was a living reality. He had waking state visions of Her as a living being. Amazing. And he experienced mystic visions of Her, as one might in the spiritual context of the dream mind. He also experienced Her as nothing but Consciousness, absolute (freed from) of any signature of the dream or waking mind. To him, She was the Ultimate Reality.

This Dakshina Kalika is the one of Her standing on the chest of Her Lover Shiva who is portrayed as that sleeping consciousness which we have been writing about. You see, until this Sakti Chitrini stirs him (the principle) to awaken, that principle of enlightenment is sleeping. He is dead to spirituality until She awakens him, and this death of the mind not awake is what death is in truth, if there be in reality anything that could be termed death. And since Consciousness (Sakti Chitrini) is beginningless, endless, wonderfully and beautiful beyond words and certainly beyond the thoughts of this fool who is writing about Her, then how can there be death. Death is a delusion in dualism. Death is an anomaly, a non-event to the Consciousness

17

in the most sacred function of Witness. What indeed is embodiedness or disembodiedness to the Witness Consciousness. And as Kali is the dark of the Non-Dual, She consumes all colors in the spectrum of consciousness or all dualistic maps of the mind, even so, the color of that spectrum called death, the most difficult map of all to comprehend. The *Kali Tantra* brilliantly states a high insight into the Divine Goddess, "At first, one should reflect on the Consciousness alone, then one should think of that as their Real Nature. 'I am alive, I am dead'; such thoughts are evil (that is, wrong notions). The Self has neither birth nor death. The grief of separation from relatives is false; it is only a distortion of Consciousness."

In the Tantra, one will find the most illuminating linguistic symbol of what all this means. Shiva is Shava without Sakti. Shiva, as the symbol of Self, is but Shava, a corpse, without Sakti, Kundalini, Chitrini, Kali, who is represented by the mystic letter "I" in the name Shiva, so without this divine letter in his name, that consciousness of the Self becomes but a corpse, a shava! For without Her Life Giving Spiritual Power we are all dead, as it were, or asleep within the ordinary perception of the waking, dreaming, and deep sleep states. For from the spiritual point of view you are dead until you have experienced the movement of Chitrini Sakti pulling your consciousness into the awakened state of Her Grace where the Turiya awareness covers the three ordinary states. It is here that the higher Sakti of Turiya is brought down into the lower three states to awaken the Real Potential of what is within us, as we are but sleeping corpses without Her! As the *Ananda Kalpa* (Bliss Cycle) *Tantra* states, "It is through Her Grace that He (Shiva) has overcome death. She is the Supreme Goddess having no God to guide Her."

It is important perhaps to ask how old is this divine image? But does any image take us back to the primordial State of Chitrini, before any image of this Consciousness was produced in human consciousness? I think perhaps all images might be capable of this but none do completely. For images must be left behind at the threshold of consciousness before one's consciousness consciously enters the Domain of Pure Chitrini. As it is magnificently stated at the height of spiritual insight in the *Kula* (Sakti or Family) *Cuda Mani* (Crest Jewel) *Tantra* , "In the Primordial State, She, the Goddess is hidden in absolute Chidananda (Consciousness Bliss). In it there is no creation, preservation or destruction. There is neither Creator, Preserver nor Destroyer, nor any other deities. In it there is no attachment, no suffering nor liberation; neither piety, theism, atheism, japa (prayer/mantra), guru (teacher), nor sishya (student)." This profound absolute insight is again augmented by the *Kali Tantra*, "One who, giving up names (that is all cognitive identities) and forms (that is all waking or dreaming designations), resides in the eternal and motionless Great Reality. Salvation is not attained by japa (prayer repetitions), homa (ritual oblations and sacrifices), or fasting. One who *feels* "I am none but the Great Reality' is freed. No images of God (human, divine, or otherwise: teachers, deities, deitesses, or anything), mentally imagined, cause salvation. It is like one who becomes a king of a kingdom obtained in a dream. No purpose is served by worshiping images."

Nevertheless, besides all this, what is so interesting is the cognitive power of Chitrini running through Ramakrishna's mind that could produce the experiences that he was blessed with and privileged to have. Not only that, but he made Swami Vivekananda (1863-1902) also see and have the same experiences of the Goddess that he himself had. Waking visions of Her living reality, dream like visions of Her in the mystic mind and of course, the pure direct experience of Her as Absolute Chitrini. Such is the power of cognitive potential in one's own mind and the effect of that cognitive wonder as a cause in itself, to the mind of others! Extraordinary! As it is stated in the *Jnana Sama Kalini* (Equal Knowledge of Kalini)*Tantra*, "The individual soul tied by wrong notions, remains an individual soul. Freed from those notions, she/he becomes All Knowledge. You yourself are the cause, you are the effect. This perception is the Highest of all. Still, people roam about thinking, 'this is a holy place.' One, who is ignorant of atma

19

tirtha (the holy place in oneself) cannot get salvation."

But of course, you see, the state of Sri Ramakrishna's cognitive power was so finely tuned to the spiritual that he saw God, the Goddess, the Atma (the True Self), Brahman (the Great Reality) in everyone and in everything all the time. His life and the condition of his consciousness were perpetually experiencing the high state of Consciousness ever tuned to the pitch of Divine Wonderment! He had visions and encounters not only with the Goddess, but with the Mediterranean Man of Love, Jesus, and with Sita and Rama, Radha and Krishna, Allah, Buddha, and many more too numerous to mention. And not only this, as easy cognitions of the spiritually beautiful, but that wondrous consciousness of Sri Ramakrishna perceived the Face of God, the Goddess, his Chosen Ideal of the Great Reality, in the most wicked people as well, which surpasses common understanding in the general realm.

Thus it is a fearless condition of consciousness, *ab - solutus*, freed from even the prejudiced idea of wickedness, for in truth, wickedness is born from sorrow, the fear state of separation from what is Real and True. It is tragic for those who retain and hold to this idea with its endless spirals of pain. So, who indeed, or what indeed is there within us that might shed compassion, pity, love, and charity upon the tragic condition of those who suffer spiritually, psychologically, and physically, even as they cause pain not only to themselves but to others. Who manifests any real creativity with the problem of sorrow, suffering, pain, evil and wickedness? Religions, which just toss the problem in a box, deny it, ignore it and separate it from inclusion within the wholeness of our real experiences, failing to resolve it, offer no lasting solution to the problem. Not until this gap is breached, will loving enlightenment be reached. But wisdom is here, we are not naive. One may see God in everyone, the virtuous and the wicked. But, "So you must hiss at wicked people. You must frighten them lest they should do you harm. But never inject your venom into them. One must not injure others." Ramakrishna.

You see, when one deeply realizes that prajna is Brahman,

then out of that prajna anything may be seen, anything is possible as a manifestation of consciousness in the sixth chakra center (the ajna chakra dead center in the forehead above the two eyes two inches inside the skull). It is one of the Great Sayings of the Upanishads and the constant drumbeat of the Vedanta. That is "Prajnanam Brahman". "Consciousness is the Great Reality." But analyze this with emotion and find that this Consciousness is prajna, that is, the *name* of consciousness in the deep sleep state. A direct cognition of your own consciousness in deep sleep is stated here to be the Great Reality itself. Beautiful. And where is the location of this in your individual being? It is in the command center, the ajna chakra, for ajna means the "command of wisdom", and it is wisdom that commands the manifest consciousness of everything that is seen! It is the ajna chakra which is the location of the Witness Consciousness. And it is this prajna condition of consciousness out of which the Witness is born to be an observer, a watcher, a perceiver of the perception of dualism that manifests in the consciousness of the dream state and then the waking state.

It is also in this prajna consciousness that the Witness disappears, for there, in that condition of consciousness, there is nothing but the dark depth of non-dualism. The Great Reality itself, ever present within self (atma), yet covered by this prajna, this wisdom sleep which has within it the potential womb power of giving birth to the realization of the Great Reality, or, as it may also be, to give birth to the dualism experienced back in the states of dream consciousness and waking existence. So prajna is the Womb of Consciousness. So much so, that sometimes the name Prajna is substituted for the name Sakti and Sakti is the Consciousness of, as, or in Goddess Power, being able and capable of anything as a manifestation in the entire cosmic psychosomatic field of consciousness or the birthing of Pure Reality within one's very self being! "Pra" means Supreme, and "Jnanam" is Knowledge, so this womb of consciousness within your own forehead is the place of giving birth to Supreme Knowledge! But the Heart is where this Knowledge lives as Love. Knowledge is nothing without Love and Love is a fool, a runaway train of emotion, without Knowledge.

The Imagination and Projection
of Psychic Reality on Star Clusters

My personal illusion is to have no illusion. But this in itself can only be an illusion for the mind dwells on what it wishes not to be. In great thoughts, in high thoughts, those inexpressible thoughts of understanding where one can really not find any words to express what one feels at that moment, Here, you are in your True Self and this is Insight so direct it cannot come back down into the agitation of consciousness manifesting as thoughts, words, speech, or cognition associated with anything from A to Z.

Whatever gets mind there is the Thing! Perhaps the No-Birth Doctrine of Buddha (That is Nirvana Ajata which is that Reality remains ever *unborn* to delusion and the Tatha Gata Garbha which is That Reality Thus Gone to the Womb of Suchness) or the Spirit Most Holy (This is very interesting, the Hagia Sophia or Holy Wisdom, a Divine Feminine Principle, and the Hagia Pneumato meaning air, breath, spirit or Holy Spirit as also the Holy Ghost. You see people of old believed that souls or spirits when departed became ghosts in the air and from this one arrives at the cognition of the Holy Ghost) of the Christ. But even here there are illusions associated with these two fabulous doctrines, for any doctrine is a map of the mind and once it has fallen to the level of the mind, the high essence of it becomes lost within the inadequacy of expressible language. It seems to me that everyone speaks a different language and that most real meaning is lost in noise, once the mouth vomits its sound. What you mean, what I mean and all the rest is usually misinterpreted as blundering comedy or outright confusion.

At times, everything on this Earth seems so absolutely stupid, absurd, meaningless! I use that time to raise Self above the ridiculous! Forget the hours of that down conscious time, the A to Z agitations of the mind in the consciousness betwixt

22

waking and dreaming, the unreality, the non-reality of dream worries where one is imagining that they are seeing serpents in ropes. This is the metaphor which beautifully expresses how the mind sees or thinks that it sees the world appearance upon the surface of true and real Consciousness. The seeing of the serpent is the anomaly. The rope is the consistent and real Background Principle upon which the serpent is imagined.

It takes the powerful forcing of the reestablishing one's psychic energy to Consciousness, pure and simple, each time the mind returns to the waking state. It is strange how one finds new mentalities, then forgetting these, one finds one's mind downshifting to old mentalities, but then upon the powerful reminder, one returns to new mentalities. Who knows? Perhaps it is because of galactic gravitation on the circle of the Milky Way, that our minds now tend to negative mental force that we find ourselves thinking three thousand negative thoughts a day and only three positive thoughts within that same time frame. And perhaps when the Milky Way turns our location where the galactic gravitation pulls more to the Grand Center of the Universe, we shall find that our thoughts are more to the tune of three thousand positive ones a day. Do you believe I just said that? Do you honestly believe such a thing is possible? It is no doubt an interesting Universe in which we now find ourselves dwelling, but let us not be fragmented from sober and clear thinking about our position here!

Certainly there is beauty in the harmony of the psyche when one feels a cosmological connection! Even more so when this cosmological psychic connection expands to include oneself within an identity with universal processes on the grandest scale one might imagine. But even here, if you feel you are run by it, then it is morbid dependency on ideas within a lower mind gate leading to depression, because you have lost or have actually given away your own Spiritual Power and Trust in Greater Things! Things even greater than the Universe's movements which are never still.

You see, astrologers, psychics, fortune tellers, and so forth, are playing a hit and miss game with cosmic principles. When they hit the mark they feel egotistically uplifted in a power they feel they have over you as a person. It is an imagined idea of their divinity or intuitive spiritual sensitivity to your state of affairs. When they miss the mark they do not admit their fallacy, they blame you for not living up to the conditions of your astrology chart and tell you that you are not evolved. This is psychic abuse outright and ego manipulation downright.

Astrology creates a cognitive process with the introjection of the principles it describes. The principles in themselves are quite interesting, but the introjection process creates limited designations within one's mind. It is also a consciousness projection of character content and karmic events that comes out of one's mind into the surface personality and upon events that arc continually arising in this world. It is surely strange how the ego experiences a fixation on zodiac signs, when each of the twelve signs describes the ego at various stages or in various moods. But people love their own stupidity and so they think an Aries is an immature egotist and a Pisces is a mellow fellow. But I know Aries that are very mellow and Pisces who would burn the world down. It is all a projection of imagined psychic reality upon star clusters. Then the introjection of conscious potential becomes fixed and limited by the given designations.

You see, astrology deals with a set of principles that describe the process of birth, living and dying in a beautiful circular way. The twelve signs with their character content are meant to show an example of stages and moods. The twelve houses of our common and collective experiences through the course of living and so forth give an order to the events we experience. The Sun, Moon, and planets are each associated with such principles as individuality, personality, mind, intellect, love, passion, religion, karmic fate, inventiveness, imagination, insight and so forth. Then there are the major and minor aspects both benefic and malefic which supposedly bring about fortunate or tragic karmic events. But I ask you, are not all these principles universally experienced by each and every soul that is born on Earth. The astrologer limits you by setting into your mind certain fixed designations. Your mind naturally gravitates

24

to the beneficial. But one's subconscious gravity pulls toward the astrologer's suggestions of what is negative in life, as mind, out of fear moves toward that fear of karmic doom. It is dangerous thinking and how much of it is self created misery. Life is just life. Everyone goes through everything. Even with astrological theory, every month the transiting Moon makes every single aspect with every other planet, in every house and sign that exists in the designation of astrology. This means that everybody experiences everything each month. So, the hit and miss game can be easily performed by the function of the astrologer. Even more so, the progression of the Moon does this same diagrammatic movement with all astrological formulas every twenty seven and half years. So, no one is fixed in any particular experience. Life just happens, whatever is happening to the body or the mind, and of course, all our experiences greatly vary and are not set to a framework of astrological time tables.

Another most curious thing is that in support of astrology many of those practitioners quote from Carl Jung's original experiment with three hundred married couples where he came up with a synchronistic relation between their astrological configurations. But either through stupidity or shame these astrologers do not say that Jung did the experiment again, and with greater numbers, and as such found nothing of synchronicity. Synchronicity is a psychic state which corresponds to an external event as I understand this thought. From this he came up with a greater and much more encompassing thought, that this synchronicity is just a particular instance within a wider and more comprehensive principle termed *acausal orderedness*. This is just what it sounds like, truly even a quantum explanation, an event may occur just because it is so, and needing no cause. Acausal Order (Like God making a Universe just because) has always existed, but synchronicity is a psychic creation in the field of time. He then considered that his first experiment was itself effected by the psychic creation of the experiment itself.

But the astrologer uses this collective knowledge in this

contained process and so by it, contains you within a limited potential. It is a terrible way to think of oneself. Besides this, it is all where the psychic emphasis is placed. The Tibetans go by Jupiter's twelve year orbit as the main focus of sign influence. This is the same as the place mats and calenders you find in restaurants which describe Chinese astrological signs. But we in the West think the Sun is most powerful. While the Hindus believe the strongest astrological influence is focused in the Lunar Mansions or the twenty seven Nakshatras, which are a division of the zodiac into lunar time tables rather than twelve star clusters. The Greeks called these the lunar asterisms. Also, the strangest thing is that with the retrograde shift of the Vernal Equinox, the Zodiac is off by more than two thirds of a sign, so people in reality are often born under a different star cluster in the sky but they will, in their psychological ignorance, insist they have the qualities of their seasonal sign. The point is that if astrology was actually valid there would not be so many contradictions of emphasis. A particular focus or system would stand true above other ones. But it is not the case.

In the *Tantraraja Tantra*, the Royal King of Tantras, it states in answer to this anomaly, that the Planets rotate through the circle of the Solar and Lunar Mansions and that their gravity churns or effects the five elements of earth, water, fire, air, and ether. Then it says that there is nothing more to it than that. Really it is describing the science of gravity and physics, the pull and push of energy, but it is not saying this energy motion is effecting human personality, or character content, nor the Pure Consciousness that dwells within the human being. It does not endorse the illusion of a body and mind being *born under* these influences. And this expression, "under" profoundly signifies the restrictions to the psychosomatic and spiritual limits astrology gives. But this Tantra does attach importance to the cosmic beauty of these astronomical symbols or sky illustrations, though only in a way of metaphorically associating the principles of the signs and mansions with higher spiritual principles that are found in the Tantra itself, as a way of making the mind meditate on these principles in greater and more profound interpretations of Self Reality and its realization, which is, to make it real to you.

The question arises, where is the responsible power of persuasion? I have heard and seen people do terribly abusive things under the premise that it is in their astrology chart. What fools! Abusive idiots! If emphasis is projected on to the astrological system one will find people not taking a significant and genuine participation in responsibility for their own lives and how they treat other people. If the emphasis of one's psychic reality is placed on the true and real Consciousness within, then we find people living up to the authentic honesty which makes and brings forth the best in the human mind and spirit.

Astrological study of the principles within this art is good if it is taken as a metaphoric cognitive equation in the context of humanity on the Universal Scale. It connects us together with each other and the Cosmos. But astrological principles in themselves and at their best, are mere metaphors within the paradigm of cosmological cognitive projections and the appearance of mind maps of astronomical structures in the human psyche as a psychological cause and effect equation. This is the dissolution, creation and re-creation of mind maps reflected within natural cosmic cycles. The harmonious occurrences or conjunctive correspondences within these cycles are most certainly a beautiful aspect of the human psyche moving side by side with universal motions, but to cognise a belief that you are under their power is not a free and liberated state of mind. It is non-real. Nothing more.

Multiple Personality Disorder
as a Psychic Gate
to Higher Cognitive Skills

It is to the extreme of sadness that the cognitive power of fear in generating negative psychic complexes produces so much tragic, regretful, and traumatic states of anxiety in this world. It is out of the superstitious sense of psychic separation from the

Great Reality that so many of these negative mind maps are created. Some of it may be due to the fear of being watched from above or of being killed or hurt from the outside, but nevertheless, our negative conditions of mind are produced from fear.

You see, of course, that if a very young person, out of horrible organic fear which stimulates the psychic content to develop protective personalities, as in the phenomena of Multiple Personality Disorder, in order to defend the psyche and the feelings from abuse and trauma, then why cannot this be so, out of the cognitive power which responds to tremendous Love, as Divine Force, instead of fear? It can be so and the tragic suffering of MPD demonstrates this to the stubborn empirical mind, if one can come to understand the psychic mechanism discarded of its traumatic side!

Simply consider the dream state where one's mind functions in a greater way. In the state of dream consciousness we create for ourselves the most elaborate mazes of meaning, we speak in the dream mind with a language of such symbols of self potency that the waking mind hardly ever recognizes. In the dream state the psychic self is speaking to the true Self in such a way, with such honesty, that seldom occurs while awake. That is why it is thought that in this dream state we may penetrate the veil of what is thought to be illusion, delusion and spiritual imagination. Spiritual imagination is of course the veils that we thrust over the true Self in order to make the mind accept this true Self at the level that the dream mind is prepared to handle in the dynamic sense of an understandable conscious awareness of Self to that degree.

In dream we filter the meaning and the mystery of Self in a functional way that makes sense to us. We create different dream personalities out of that one unified psychic self that is most deeply placed or built within us. All those dream scenarios are playful experiments of the psychic self. We dream of gods and goddesses, of fears and desires we want fulfilled, of magic and mystery. Dream is Chitrini Sakti moving in the form of that state. It is but consciousness dancing on the mirror of

28

Consciousness. And out of the power of consciousness there is the production of numerous identities which all have as their central and most primary axis of real identity, the Real Self itself which we may call for practicality's sake, the true Personality.

It is really extraordinary, the higher skills that some MPD's manifest. One protective personality may produce somatically, on the body, the appearance of scars, yet when the psychic shift to another protective personality makes its change, those scars disappear. What does this say about the healing power of the psyche's cognition and its potential under benevolent circumstances? Also, one personality may actually create an illness of diabetes so much so that insulin is needed to tame the diabetes, yet again when the identity of that personality shifts to another identity the insulin is no longer needed. Is it not a phenomenal anomaly, a miracle of healing? And is not this and manifesting scars, the same anomalous psychic mechanism as in such religious phenomena as stigmata?

What it all says is that the potential of Chitrini in the form of thought is extraordinary and that what is considered miraculous is really quite ordinary. It is fascinating to realize as well, that in the MPD, one personality may be quite naive and simple, and that another will be highly educated to the degree of the genius level. What could this indicate for us in the development of higher learning skills and cognitive powers, in methods of practical education and spiritual teaching. It is really an amazing phenomena and opens a key gate to potentialities within the psyche.

It is very strange really that most of us are so bound by the early imprints upon our neural maps that these maps cause us to be the way we are in such limited ways. In the first two or three years of life we are given an emotional and psychic response map that just follows us on our whole trip on Earth. What we were given in that time karmically propels us on its limited, predictable and expected way. To me this is a total tragedy to our spiritual potential. And in some way the gift of insight into not only MPD, but also NDE, may help us break the boundaries of these cognitive power maps that bind us with their binding

29

power of mental signatures.

How do we discard these old maps of the mind? Simple. Replace them with new maps. More powerful maps. Maps which speak more Truth to the reality and potential of the human Spirit. We can unplug from the circuitry of the old mind maps and plug into maps that are greater than the old mind maps. I do not know why people want to get in touch with their inner child, go backwards to those earlier neural formations and keep up their excuse for behaving the way they might do in the present based on the functions of old response systems they will not move out of, and then get on with life in a forward motion. Of course, I am all for understanding one's karmic mechanics and psychic formations, but once that is done, please, lets get on with it and move ourselves forward into what awaits the human Spirit!

You see I have a friend who is such a remarkable example of this beautiful power of the human Spirit. They are now self healed of the MPD that they developed as psychic protection from sexual abuse in early life. How great that is that they not only released themselves from the organic and psychic pain of sex abuse, but that after developing the psychic protection system of MPD, they also overcame that anomaly and reintegrated themselves back into One Identity. That is, into one functional true self, or true personality. A living, loving, compassionate, intelligent and understanding person.

My friend had developed four distinct personalities. Two masculine identities, one an adult and one a child. And two feminine identities, one adult and one child. It is fascinating, not only the innate capacity to identify with the dualism of gender identities themselves, but also in the inner feeling of their mind, that one gender may handle or protect the psyche from a certain set of feelings better than the other. Also, that there should be a mature personality and a child personality identified with both genders indicates an extraordinary, even though tragic realization, that the maturity of the higher wisdom of the adult was brought forth before its natural unfolding in time to nurture and protect the two wounded children within.

This was borderline MPD, so there was an awareness in consciousness of the coming forth and sinking back into consciousness of any of the four personalities. In deeper MPD there is no recognition or memory of one personality from another, or there is partial recognition and memory of selected personalities which may relate, respond, work with, or identify with one another. What is most interesting here is that there is a conscious threshold that accesses and addresses one personality projection or another. In that threshold of consciousness there is a smooth place in the psyche where this fluid change may take place, where access to another dimension of self or self identity may be possible. If there can be a shift from one personality to another, then why not more simply and more easily, a shift from the old limited mind maps of ego/personality consciousness to that Consciousness of the true Self, the Great Reality?

My friend said that once the four disturbing and yet protective identities of their psyche were understood by one another, that is, understood the maps and responses, the feelings and emotions, the identities and the purpose of these identities, their reasons for being projected out of the psyche, then they became free to choose who they wanted to be. They could form and choose the new and whole person that they wished to be. And they formed and chose one of the most dear and loving people I've met in my short time on this Earth. To me this is a key to the psychic gate of cognitive potential. To choose. To make a psychic decision and then to become that. Indeed, even when we are growing up, how many personalities do we try on by imitating others in their capacity as mentors, influences, and those one looks up to? My friend dealt with four different wounded persona's within, and healed all of their wounds to become a fully integrated, unified functioning person, while most of us are still complaining about our one little wounded inner person with all their pathetic problems and complaints!

In that borderline of consciousness it is the Witness Consciousness that is there as the undisturbed and un-fragmented state of Consciousness itself that is observing the phenomena of not only psychic divisions of self into diverse protective personalities, but the return process and the taking back of the psyche into the Witness Consciousness itself. What of other lives and what of life now? The Witness has watched those previous personalities come and go. The Witness has watched our dream states come and go. And the Witness, as it is Self, has watched the self, play upon Itself, waiting for the choosing of that psychic play to make the choice of re-identifying with the greater connection which is none other than the Spiritual Decision. You see, I beg you to consider in conjunction: the psychic cognitive potential of what MPD speaks to us, of what those who have experienced NDE have brought back to us, of what Spiritually Beautiful experiences are within our reach, ever there within the inner conscious current inside the Sushumna, and how all this is witnessed by the true Self in the function of Witness Consciousness.

The Production of Bhava

It would bring me great pleasure, if now, in the lucid clear daylight of Consciousness freed from the night illusion of superstition, delusional psychic states, and spiritual or religious imagination, that you would realize that you are this Consciousness itself. Jump into the River of Life, stop the denial of an isolated ego where you are defending yourself from participating in real experience and feel this with that "felt awareness." Every time we die and then return, as it were, to a physical, subtle or celestial plane of Living, do we not create or recreate a new personality, one that we feel will protect us better than the one before, from the suffering that is experienced in any of those three relative dimensions?

When death comes, or when ego consciousness is displaced there is sudden and momentary awareness of the Great Light in Turiya, that Pure Consciousness undisturbed by the activation of the three states. It may last for half a second or for a thousand years or more. But as thoughts tend to reignite, one's consciousness enters the divine ignorance of deep sleep. This charges up again the reflex of dualism as an identity stirring in

32

the beginning as the causal source point of a new life in consciousness. In the womb of deep sleep, this new stirring of life and energy occurs in the darkness and innate non-dualism of that state of consciousness. Then Consciousness begins to watch the phenomena as Witness, which will never lose itself in the phenomena of this process. As the dream state begins to ignite itself in your consciousness, there is the stirring of more diverse and yet subtle manifestations of thought forms taking on the cause and effect relationships of signatures within the psyche. One begins to imagine a high and a low (gods, goddesses, heavens, hells, etc.) and all the diverse manifest conditions of these dualisms. It is imagination, it is your own thought power and nothing more. As what is freed from imagination is the pure Spirituality within you, the true and genuine Self. When this consciousness reaches the waking state, that consciousness has probably now found itself to be within the embryonic stage of returning to life (having descended from the Pure Light, through the reflex of consciousness on that Pure Light, into the realm of subtle energies and now back into physical life), the new life, the new personality has begun, and all because of the dual reflex in the causal psyche that was born out of the womb consciousness of deep sleep. This process of returning seems to be as natural as sunrise and sunset. Yet if deep sleep is freed from the spiritual idea of the womb cognition, as to what it genuinely is, which is pure wisdom power as consciousness, prior to the stage of causal return, one may find oneself in the Great Light for a longer time, relativity speaking, or perhaps even permanently. As this is the source of each and every persona, or psyche covered by a projected personality, it is the true and original identity of each and everyone. That is Consciousness, which is our true spiritual origin. Endless, as It is. Beginningless, as It was!

The pure prajna of deep sleep is disembodiedness before the concept of it being a "womb" ever stirs within the depth of that state of consciousness itself. Turiya is never embodied as it is pure consciousness never covered with the imagination of embodiment, of course, this is from the absolute plane of consciousness. In truth, even deep sleep never contacts the condition of mind and body, that comes when consciousness reaches down into the dream and waking states. Embodiedness or disembodiedness have no meaning to the Witness Consciousness and of course, the dualism of being in or out of the body and mind means nothing to pure Turiya Consciousness where even the idea of the Witness Principle has vanished back into the Consciousness of Turiya.

Bhavas are mood cognitions of a very powerful order created and generated out of the divine power of Love. The production of these bhavas is a tremendous key to the cognition of spiritual realization. They come out of the tremendous love for the Spiritual Ideal. Four phases and then beyond the cognition of four into One Great Bliss. When your consciousness feels that it is Chitrini who has become the waking state in all its consciousness and manifestation, you have stabilized Chitrini in the "same plane" as your own. When your consciousness sees that it is Chitrini who is every manifestation of cognitive force within dream consciousness then you have reached the "same form" as Chitrini. To know Her this way as the consciousness of what deep sleep is in reality is to feel the felt awareness of the "same power" as Chitrini. To manifest the cognition of "same union" or "independence" in Chitrini as the pure force of what you are in your real Self is to regain Chitrini in Pure Turiya. These are very powerful bhavas and the sweet mystery is that they are all brought forth out of your own Chitrini Sakti! The spiritual mystery is that you have given birth to yourself (physically, psychologically, and spiritually), as it is your own Chitrini that has done this. That Chitrini as you, produced your own states of independence, power, form and plane, which are Turiya, pure prajna, dream and waking as the plane where we live and die. From this High Insight, it is You in Your True Self, in Your True Power and Form, that creates your own life and creates your own death. Which in a manner of speaking is an exit (into life) from Pure Sakti, and a reentrance (death) into Pure Sakti, since birth into form, and then the idea of the abyss of death, in themselves distinguish us as a conscious duality, from Pure Sakti. But the Witness as Pure Sakti never enters below Independence into the Plane of living and dying, as one who experiences the terror of birth or the wonder of death, except as the power behind and within the force of those experiences.

The question may come to you, and I hope that it does: can your disembodied consciousness be aware of the three states; waking, dreaming and deep sleep? The answer is yes. Turiya is what your consciousness is and it is from Turiya that the three states are generated. To think that it is not so is the illusion of non-dualism. One wants to believe that the three states are extinguished in Turiya. They are not extinguished, they are Turiya. So from this vantage point, "*the nothing but Turiya state*" is cognised, as it is, then the entire field of the three states is no longer ordinary, and so they have reached their divine status as the original Turiya. You have shaken off the dust of dualism and now you are free in the truest sense of freedom or being now freed from the delusion of imagination pertaining to what the three states of consciousness are in their real truth.

Pure Chitrini Turiya is the Sakti within you, as you, being you, and who is You, who awakens as She so Desires, to bestow by the movement of Her Grace upon Herself within the very gracious sushumna, the Bhava of Her Pure Chitrini. "To really grasp what the ego is..." A dream teaching came from the depth of Consciousness into my dreaming mind. Ego, is but a memory of the subtle body in the dream state, where subject-object, knower-known dualism starts in the intellect and mind. But to think of this is not to be thinking of Reality. It is still thinking about ego. Everything is dream material, all the intricacies, formulas, meditations, even the ascent and descent of Kula (Sakti) Kundalini, all are dream material. If one is in Sakti Bhava or Chitrini Bhava, one is not in the bhava of the three states of consciousness. To think of waking, dreaming and the deep of sleep is to not be in the Bhava of Pure Chitrini, as it were, but this Turiya Bhava, or even the deepest deep of Prajna Bhava has no dualism, no dream material. A person who has become aware of the true nature of Sakti, in this Bhava of Pure

35

Chitrini, spiritually undiluted by any dream material, is said to be a *Kulina*, one who has *become one* with Kula (Sakti).

Dragons, Demons and
Unidentified Flying Objects

You see, I am hoping that this essay may remove some of the fear and fantasy that covers Reality, the pure Consciousness within our minds. I do not wish to destroy the wonderment of the miraculous, but to bring that very wonderment down into the ordinary, for you see, the ordinary itself is most miraculous without any superimposition of extraordinary content placed over the experience of being here in this life composed of amazing physics, phenomenal psychological processes, and the deepest of spiritual experiences. But if that spiritual experience is layered with superstition, well then, what do you have? It is to discard the ideas of sin and miracle. There is but one miracle if it is such and that is Life and Love. There is only one sin if that be so, to hate and to hurt!

To me it is the most amazing miracle that here on this Earth there are beings who out from the Consciousness which they ultimately are, they can experience the felt awareness of this Consciousness and then out of this felt awareness the subtle ideation of thought stirs and that becomes cognate and then this cognate stirs into language and words that are spoken to one another and those spoken or written words in turn effect the capacity to understand the Consciousness out of which all this has proceeded.

The untapped versatility of the human mind demonstrated in MPD and the extraordinary Direct Light experiences of the NDE, in conjunction with the awareness of how powerful the reflex of consciousness on the Witness State is in its pure condition, all point to a potential which is yet to be fulfilled except in a very few remarkable beings. It is weird and wonderful no doubt, in the way that some people who have been struck by lightning experience a transformation of psychic changes in the aftermath of that experience. Is it really the lightning, the electric charge that struck them or is it the incredibly powerful reminder of life's brief passage that reminded these people of the dreamlike quality of life itself and thereby they charged up some cognitive potential to manifest within themselves? Or what of the very rare anomaly of spontaneous combustion? Some have theorized that this is the premature unleashing of Kundalini's fire in the Sushumna, and that there is no other explanation for this phenomena.

Let us consider the three archetypes hidden deep within the conscious threshold within us. These are the creative, the preserving and the destructive archetypes which propel us in our thoughts and cognitive processes and in our feelings of love and our deepest of fears in the course of life. For the mind to reach the consciousness of Chitrini in Her free state these three archetypal forces must be addressed and then released from one's consciousness, otherwise they will return again and again to bring the mind down into the anomalies of consciousness. The causal power, the subtle form and the physical plane of these anomalies distract consciousness by their sportive obstruction with conscious cognitive views which are other than pure Consciousness, but that Consciousness itself acts within the very gracious tunnel of the sushumna to liberate consciousness or make it turn and recognize itself as Consciousness. This is the conversion experience at a high level of pure Spirituality without religious or psychological coloring.

The creative archetype is the love of making life. It is simple to understand within oneself. When it is blocked we feel we are dying and in a sense we are because the spiritual sakti of creativity is obstructed within us. When it is free flowing we feel we have purpose and meaning to our lives. It is the power of fulfillment and takes any and every form imaginable, any expression of this archetypal psychic force, which is natural and non-harmful brings joy into this life. The development and expression of this power in any human being at any age of life is necessary for their happiness. It is the freedom to live free and be who you are, not blocked by negative self-identity, nor the negative expectations others may have in one's life or by society.

The persevering archetype is just what it sounds like, to preserve and keep, to hold and maintain what one has created. It is the life sustaining energy of the mind within us that holds or attempts to hold a sense of order and harmony in our lives which gives purpose to what one has created. When that sense of order is felt to be so it is really a divine high in its own way for at that time one feels the harmony of Consciousness expressing itself in one's life. It is the divine sense of cherishment and of wanting to keep as long as possible what is loved in one's life. That is fine, but if we do not realize that this too is a passing archetype or that always what is created and preserved only has a limited expanse of time to exist within, then fear, out of the sense of the expectation of loss will come into its wake. This is ever present though usually hidden deep by denial of its reality, within every person's consciousness. That fear is created by focusing on the outside preservation of consciousness and by not realizing that the inner spiritual consciousness is what has the element of eternal preservation. It is the same principle of liberation behind the creative archetype, we become arrogant and egotistical, thinking we have created something when in reality it is the Spiritual Power which has created everything, even the inspiration within us that drives us to create, but then you think it is your ego's power and with that you die.

You die because you have not understood the consuming effect of the destructive archetype and its function within the psychic cognitive manifestation of the mind. Mind is a temporary anomaly. Deep down we all know this is true, but we do not address this terrifying depth of the spiritual psyche. This causes the power of that deepest fear of termination to distort us in such ways that reach the state of startling impossibility to describe. This paralyzes us from moving forward through this deep barrier of spiritual life. To deny or to believe that you (as a body and mind) will not die is to ignore the Spiritual Power of death that tells us and tells us that we must release ourselves from ego, or not identify the ego as the Consciousness which has produced this threefold archetypal expression of creation, preservation, and destruction. The deeper you deny this archetype and the longer you put off from addressing this power within your life, the weirder and weirder, less loving and more selfish and hateful you will get and the longer is your extension of suffering due to the distortion you have on the true spiritual purpose of life, which is simply to learn to love and to realize consciously the expression of spiritual love in one's life. It is Love alone that knows no death. Love is the finest most powerful intensity of Chitrini. Love is Her Pure Reality that never leaves us and as Love is within us, it is the one feeling force that knows the true and liberated Chitrini Consciousness.

In the outward facing of these archetypes the cycle of cognitive expression turned outward to the world will continue. With this movement the creative archetype is reborn, even resurrected, as it were, with the power to bring back to life what has been destroyed. This is not breaking the cycle, it is continuing it. With the movement of inner facing, the *full power form* of what at first appears to be three separate powers is realized as one expression of Consciousness, ever speaking to itself what it is. That is, ever directing consciousness to look within and observe the phenomena from the Witness Position of Consciousness. This is Chitrini's ever present grace working on the mind content, once fragmented into three divisions and now brought back to the Original pure power of the Division-less (Advaita).

It is the non-recognition of this Power that when projected outwardly, produces amazing phenomena, or so-called anomalies in Consciousness which reach extraordinary proportions. And why should it not be so, for there is within and without, in this beautiful universe, 99.9 percent of the energy that is here that goes undetected by the human eye, which gives the optic information to the brain, becoming a mind map, then sinking into the Witness Power. What little we know! Only one/tenth of one percent of the energy field is seen by our eyes. But what does the Witness Power see, as the Source of all Energy? Let us embrace a few more of these and try at the same time to clear our minds of distorted cognitive explanations that may be associated with the interesting processes of these anomalies.

There is a process in consciousness that explains away many visions, encounters, and experiences as mere cognitive phenomena, or as not being real, or as being only as real as a dream, and what are we but creatures of dream. Three principle functions must act. The function of exciting cortical stimulation of the brain core. That of depleting emotional exhaustion. And then a conversion experience takes place, if conjunctive with other stimuli. For example, experiments have been done placing people in confined rooms for long periods of time. On the walls are pictures of churches and crucifixes and so forth, medieval religious chanting goes on and on. Before you know it, after these three functions kick in, the people are having collective visions, encounters and experiences with the cognitive spiritual forms of this religion. What is interesting is that when pictures of Earth, the stars and the galaxies are substituted and spaced out new age music is played, after exhaustion of the emotions and excitement in the cortex occurs, conversion experiences begin to take place. But instead of religious images being cognised, you have visions and encounters with UFO's, space beings or space people.

The fascinating thing is that the outer suggestions of sound and image produce related cognitive manifestations in consciousness. Accordingly, one could produce almost any cognitive related phenomena in these experimental rooms, either abusively, or for the arousal of higher cognitive skills. I suppose that would depend on their spiritual ethics, or fanatically religious morals and belief systems, or just deeply dark and demented purposes. But nevertheless, this is not the point we assume to illuminate.

You see, phenomenal anomalies are produced when a concept from the psyche is strongly deposited as a fixation on the Witness Power. Instead of just looking at the Witness as it is. When you hear someone say such things as, "God is watching y'all," this is what they have done. Strangely, one can deposit any focused concept upon the pure Witness Power: a god, a demon, a dragon, a space being, as that image will

40

produce the corresponding anomaly. These things happen as manifestations in consciousness because we do not recognize the Power that is within the Witness Consciousness.

A very curious fact is that after big hit movies on space alien encounters the swing in statistical reports of encounters with space people or seeing space ships goes up off the scale. Between these excellent movies the reports of these anomalous experiences goes way down. What indeed does that tell you about the power of suggestion? Are space people really visiting the Earth and impregnating women with their genetic code in order to save their race from extinction by producing a hybrid race of new children, part human and part space person? And then, after this, they fly off, ducking behind Jupiter or Neptune for a few years before they must come back and check up on the new being, to take that baby back on board their space craft so it may grow up in their nursery? I am sorry to say, but this seems very suspect of a large scale divine child complex! That first these beings are deified, even though as the reports go, they cause a great amount of psychosexual pain to those they abduct. Then out of this, the chosen are made special through the cognitive delusion of self importance, that they should usher in the new race. This is a terribly sad but fascinating manifestation in the human unconscious for the need of new religious inventions and fresh divine images. And the deep problem of this anomaly is projecting that divine importance on space beings and consequently their psychosexual contact or communion with those who claim these experiences. Also, another causal psychic dynamic that comes into play with this phenomena, is when the powerful thought fixes in people's heads that they just don't want to be here in this world, accepting this world as it is. So, they create an image in their minds of a way to be transported away from this world: its pain, its confusion, its unloving manners, its harshness, and its suffering. This fixation is also found in the obsession with rapture mentality, which thinks you will be taken up into the sky.

I truly believe that the three or four little alien space beings supposedly found at Roswell, amidst the rubble of shiny foil and tinsel, were in fact surgically altered and shaved chimpanzees. It was a brilliant distraction created by the government in order to take social focus off the horrible and immoral atomic testing which was being done in those days and the years that followed. Also, from the Wright brothers to the little Mars Lander has only been about a hundred years, so I think more highly amazing military crafts have been developed than is known publicly and sometimes people see these and think they are UFO's.

I certainly believe that we are not alone even among the nearby neighboring star systems and certainly out there in the beautiful amazement of our Milky Way galaxy. But I do not think as of yet we have been genuinely contacted or visited by a race of beings which have the technology for such travel or even radio contact as of yet. The distances are immense (even between the star systems of our own galaxy, where, between other galaxies, the distance is so great it would seem only God could make the leap) and traveling at the speed of light is almost incomprehensible for a physical object, a craft. Someday I hope it will be so but I don't think it has happened yet.

A few centuries ago, when all that popular fuss was about demons as the scapegoat images for trauma, abuse and religious confusion, there was an epidemic of people who would swear up and down, from hell to god, that they were being raped by demons in their sleep. Is this not similar to the people of today who report being raped by space people. The traumatic psychosexual manifestation is the same, the invasive psychic image is different. But the intensity of the cognitive manifestation is the same in that both sets of people feel their encounters as absolutely genuine. Another factor in this is the potency of cognitive distortion that occurs in the hypnagogic and hypnapompic stages of sleep/dream/waking cycles in the psychically disturbed. The distribution of that psychic energy creates cognitive experiences which they feel are genuine. This also occurs in other phenomena, some more sad and tragic, deeply needing our empathy and compassion, and some quite benevolent, innocent and sweet, even though they are still steeped in the quality of participating in mystic illusion.

That illusion taken for reality comes out of the deepest superstitious coverings that are placed on these anomalies. The beauty within the anomaly is certainly unique, spiritual and special in that it shows us the Power that is within ourselves to awaken ourselves to the Wondrous Greatness of Life and Love. But those that hurt and harm, and generate fear and superstition, I will seek to divest of their power of illusion until the day I die.

Did St. George really kill a dragon? Did dragons really exist and if so why have archeologists not found some of their bones? Did the Komodo lizard dragon somehow make its way from the islands of Southeast Asia all the way to the Europe of just a few centuries ago without other reports from other cultures between the two places? Of course, the dragon is a metaphorical unconscious symbol of the dinosaur, metaphysically within the primal psyche as an image of great spiritual power. So what did St. George slay to become a saint? Maybe nothing. But slaying dragons was good for business.

The archbishop of Notre Dame de Paris spat out some prayers at something that emerged from the river Siene and it went back down in the water after scaring everyone. Later they put the exaggerated image of this thing, probably an alligator or crocodile placed there by less than purely honest church conspirators just for that purpose, all over the magnificent carvings on this beautiful church. This was also very good for business. The church, like any other function, does not always tell the pure and actual truth, it will also exaggerate events and experiences in order to further its believed cause. We should not be so naive as to think that pure honesty would be so wonderfully portrayed, not by any religion. All have bent the truth a bit in order to serve their plan and purpose.

We are not always told the truth outright when it comes to the dualistic anomalies of the miraculous and the demonic. These two extremes are usually kept alive in their delusion for the sake of keeping our hope alive and for keeping our fear in tune to the music by which others wish us to march. The true miracle is Love and the only demon is hate. Tibetan Buddhist psychiatry has clearly explained this, but what of things a bit

43

closer to home. It is easy to understand in light of what has been explained, how the sweet little children here and there in this century have seen visions of the beautiful Mother Mary. Certainly, this is a wonderful manifestation of the beautiful cognitive potential directed toward a spiritual image and then manifested within the confined dimension of the individual cognitive experience of each child, for these visions and dialogues of a spiritual dimension were seen and heard only by them, not others. But what of the spiritual apparitions of Mary that were seen by thousands of people atop the little chapel in Zeitoun, Egypt back in 1968? Was that a collective manifestation of the type of phenomena I have been speaking of here? Or was it a trick, a holographic laser light show done with the church's intent to inspire not only fear of impending apocalypse but also hope and love? Magicians have made thousands of people see the Statue of Liberty disappear and reappear, but since that is just magic displayed over the Goddess of Liberty we do not attach much importance to such explainable phenomena. Also, as many now believe, the woman Mary was a Priestess of the Goddess, so her sweet child was indeed and truly, a child of the Goddess. Also, if one reads and studies one will find that Jesus is said to have had brothers and sisters born of the same mother. So then where is the divine virginity? Is it not a cognitive perfection?

I seek a Love of Truth and the Truth of Love filling me, and freed of all and every trace of superstitious dualistic fear. Is it the problem of evil that makes fear or is it fear that produces evil? Evil may be just the projection of the dark side of the unconscious which has not been directly addressed, that is confronted within oneself, as a psychic pattern of imagination when the ego is left as a passive observer or victim of that dark imagination. When the ego begins to participate as an active and directing force in the imagination directing the flow of fantasy, then that fantasy may be brought to the level of conscious interplay with this problem and thus reduce it to zero, at least within one's own personal dimension.

With UFO's we once projected the principle of good, even

the principle of salvation upon them and the beings we have imagined to inhabit these wonderful crafts. Then there was a shift in consciousness projection, due to disappointment in the projection of the saving principle, and the popular projection shifted to one of disaster and invasion, to wit, evil. For people have yet to take that energy and transform it within themselves into Love. This was true with Dragons as well, a few centuries ago. But with the cognition of the demon idea we create more problems of procrastinating on the confrontation with *"where"* the only evil comes from. It is generated in the unloving human heart and this is a deadly force in this world. Always, it is the same demon, hate, but wearing a different mask.

It is said in the *Yoga Vasishtha,* that it was from Consciousness that Vishnu with his four arms and weapons of love and justice emerged, and also, that it was from this very same Consciousness that the demons that He slayed and killed emerged. What is this? A duality that has come from a non-duality. This is a tremendous anomaly in Consciousness. How can this be so? How can the force which kills the demon mind and the demon mind both emerge from the same source? Is it simply Love and fear?

There is only One Consciousness in Reality, and the idea that some "other consciousness" can enter that One Consciousness is pure delusion and hallucination. Anything below this One Consciousness is pure imagination, but people give that imagination a reality through the projected force of superstition. For the cognitive power is a great one. Only one body/object (physical, subtle, or causal) may occupy the space of that body/object. Only one thought can occupy the space of that one thought. Only one consciousness occupies the space of that consciousness. And this is the message that is being conveyed when you see Gods and Goddesses dancing victorious upon the heads of demons which are nothing but metaphors for dualistic ignorance (hatred).

The idea that other subtle bodies, ghosts, spirits, whatever, may jump into your own physical, subtle, or causal body is pure delusion. Ghost jumping? No way! The only metaphysical technology that would explain this insane anomaly would be that some other consciousness could enter the innermost condition within your own sushumna. This is absolutely not possible, for the sushumna is the most refined abode of Chitrini, which is the ever extending, always expanding and continually spreading Power of Consciousness as the Saving Grace of the Goddess Sakti! That is absolutely Her Place and there is no other consciousness there but Her Own! How could it ever be otherwise! Only a fool trapped in dualistic ignorance would ever imagine it to be so!

But once again, demons are good for business. In truth if someone is so sick to think that a demon has caught hold of them it is a tragedy that needs great love and empathy. Not ritual abuse which ignites in them a cognitive worsening of their condition by the techniques of that ritual itself which often may make their state compound into a deeper problem by hammering them with all those ideas that there is something inside them that needs casting out. Much of this may come more from the fear generated out of the one who is doing the casting out, rather than from reality, what is really going on. But the other side of this is that in primitive emergences, cognitive and ritual methods might stimulate the innate psychosomatic healing process. Or, on the more benevolent side of this process, as it was with Mother Mary's kids, who out of deep spiritual faith in the guiding power of grace, brought this healing process to life in themselves, like turning on a light switch, and this in turn ignited the light or fire of this process in other people who experienced, here and there, spontaneous healing. Yes, it is beautiful!

The idea of being possessed or held by something else is a strange one indeed. Can someone else have you, hold you, or own you? It is the slavery of the mind to think this is ever true even in the most oppressive circumstances. And the slavery of the mind responds to all the vicious input from the external world. Christ! Just look how depressed one gets from watching and listening to the news! So what of the incredibly toxic thoughts that are generated by those horrible movies, particularly that one sick piece of film that had everybody and

46

their brother, their dog and their grandma thinking they were possessed. The gross exaggeration in cinematic expression certainly distorts our sense of reality.

But let us consider the tragic conjunction of numerous psychic and spiritually generated complexes that might come into play in order to be thought of as being possessed by another consciousness. Once again, since demons are so good for business, I have to believe there are some church lies about the whole thing. First of all, only sixty cases of what has been called possession have been reported by the Catholic church in nearly two thousand years. That is nothing compared to UFO reports today. And these conjunctions of tragic anomalies are explainable in a clear way that removes superstitious fear regarding this phenomena. Let us proceed.

First of all, you never ever hear of Tibetan demons possessing Catholics, nor of Catholic demons possessing Tibetans. So it appears to be a culturally confined anomaly. In other words, it is not a cross cultural ignition of psychic content. Let us imagine if one were a demon flying around in the astral plane, would it not be more fun to such a morbid soul whose job is to stir up confusion, to jump around and possess people of different religious faiths? I would think so. But this does not happen. Really, this is as absurdly crazy as catching rides on UFO's and then ducking behind Jupiter to make babies. Or blaming Medieval demons for one's psychosomatic sexual repression. The fascinating thing though, is that this demonstrates the power of negative cognition within the framework of one's belief system.

Another example is that in so called "cases" of this phenomena, in the structure of the Hindu's cognitive system, ritual readings about Christ and his belief system have no effect on the poor sick person. But read and recite to them descriptions of the sweet supernal love play of Radha and Krishna, and they will get well! What does this say about the deep cognitive gate-keys of Healing? We respond to the substance of consciousness that touches us most deeply. So you could bring in all the Christian prayer soldiers you want and it would not effect the

Hindu.

In reality, we are superstitiously afraid of these sad and very sick people, when persons such as Hitler and the Nazis, or the priests of the Inquisition, fully possessed of all their mental faculties and psychosomatic processes did in fact more damage, harm, hurt and killing than all the so called possessed people put together ever did. This is a very strange displacement of fear. And proves ever more that it is the unaddressed compounding of ignorance, hate and fear in the human heart that is the only evil. It is the vicious aspect of the human heart which is the only adversarial energy that plots against or opposes us.

Now, a number of conditions could come into play to explain this weird anomaly. We must compound all these into one psychic event. First is distorted yogic phenomena, a negative release of kundalini power which would explain some of the clairvoyant and telekinetic phenomena that is sometimes reported to happen. Interestingly enough this negatively charged kundalini release is sometimes reported to happen in young people who are reaching the age of puberty where their sexual powers are awakening. It is misdirected shakti, even Carl Jung demonstrated this strange anomaly to Freud, if I remember correctly, and the old boy fainted. It is just yogic phenomena, mind over matter, and in itself is a curious thing.

Now combine this with a religiously centered hostile psychotic aggression and much is explained. And add to this mix the power of hypnosis wherein one's psyche taps into the collective unconscious where one might gain such knowledge of things unknown to them consciously; language, events taking place elsewhere, and unknown things about people and places. This is just what Edgar Cayce did, the sleeping prophet as they have called him so often. And of course if you put the Multiple Personality Disorder on top of all this and then add the tremendous cognitive power of one's culturally confined belief system, you then have the recipe for this mental, psychic and spiritual goulash, and all the tragedy that follows with it. Add a little negative self-fulfilling prophecy as the old saying goes and there you are. Held by a combination of fully explainable disorders. Then bring in your tribal psychiatrists or witchdoctor and perhaps they can separate, distinguish and then loosen and heal some of these psychic anomalies with the help of some sweet ancestral memories, cognitive weapons, lots of prayers and tons of love. It is really an extraordinary person with great spiritual and cognitive skills that can heal such very, very sick people. And it is rare.

Humility, Surrender, and the Problem of Self Esteem

We have descended deeply into the spectrum of anomalies in consciousness. Now let us make a quick ascent back to Reality. How do we gain spiritual confidence to stand on our own without a trace of dependence on distorted anomalies that keep alive the mental force of dualism? It may indeed be a mis-thought in the effort to keep alive what has been called self esteem. Where is the Spiritual Power to be placed? Above you? Outside you? Within you? All these positions require a psychic reference point to your sense of self esteem. So if you cognitively imagine the Spiritual Power above, outside, or within you it might be all right for a time, but eventually the flow in this river of life will teach you that there is needed something more. Even if that Power is placed on the Esteem of the Witness Consciousness, that will not completely do. For it is Love that is sought and Love is past all dualism, not above, outside nor within, but something more!

Time and all that is within Time is swallowed into the Sushumna, which is Chitrini's Consciousness. Esteem is within time. I do not seek the drama of self glorification, self redemption, nor self restoration. I seek the Humility to Surrender to the Ever Present Greatness which can be said to be nothing but Love!

Humility is to forego, go with, and take the ego thought *below* the threshold of life and there be exalted in, on, and by Sakti. This is what surrender is to me. It brings the sense of order as a divine high. The pure Spiritual Logic of the Tantra

49

and the Vedanta is a great help.

Humility is Below the World, the Self Surrendered to Sakti. It is the sweet condition below the three states of consciousness, waking, dreaming and deep sleep, instead of reaching for the high Turiya, for the "high" makes you egotistical, reaching for the high of god, or the high of esteem or anything. It strengthens the dualism of ego consciousness no matter which way you go! But Humility, ah, now that works!

Love comes with Humility and Surrender. Then the ego thought dualism sinks instead of rising. It sinks into Love which is its Mother. Active waking thinking. Passive dream thinking. Slow wave thought in deep sleep. Is it thinking, yet still? Does thought ever stop in the presence of peace or do we but see the nature of thought for one half of a second? At that moment Sakti is taking over in Pure Chitrini Turiya. And then the three states are illuminated to their Original Condition where they are no longer thought of by thought itself to be "three." This is simply the *Enjoyment* of the Self Presence of Turiya (Turiya *Bhoga*) pervading the apparent appearance of the three states. This is the Love of Chitrini, ever Gracious, arrived at instantly in the spiritual mood (bhava) of genuine Humility and real Surrender, which must come first, and then understanding will arrive in the form of patience which in turn produces insightful thought upon the anomaly of dualism and the non-dualism of Consciousness. Indeed, only within the state of real Humility is dualistic ego identity and all its anomalies actually Surrendered into Chitrini Consciousness to actually come alive in that Consciousness. But to get here one must have the Humility to Surrender all contact with the apparent plane, the apparent form, the apparent sense of ego power, and even that sense of independent identity.

The Gift of Death

Most of us never even bother to *Ask* what we want from Death. Most of us never even think of death this way, as a gift giver. Beautiful Kali! As She is ever in the Inevitable. What do

I want from Her? Nirvana, Heaven (Subtle Enjoyments), to Return, with the hope of becoming a better person, or never to Return to the absurd beauty of the Human Form? Death purifies us, illuminates us, tears off the ego-mask! Death (Kali) sweeps clear the momentary distraction of ego, the head in thought, isolated and dependent on its brittle identity. She holds this once thought filled head, which She has now separated from the misconception of dualistic separation, with Her Sword of Blissful Advaitic Knowledge. Thus She grants Freedom from dualistic fear and gives freely every other Joy desired and then fulfilled. She is Ever So Patiently Waiting for Us! Beautiful!

To die a gentle passage is a blessing. In the surrendered sweetness of old age as the natural deterioration of the flesh and bone takes place, when consciousness is loosened from dragging the body around, even sick in bed as this state overwhelms the vital force, is good. It is a strange phenomena, the greatest anomaly of all, and how very weird is human life that we should live side by side while watching each other grow old. But the blessing here is that in such cases you have time to cognise what you want. Would I simply wish to stare at a picture of Mother Kali? Yes! So then my thought, my essence would move toward Her!

Where as sudden death may be different. As in accident or murder or from those striking attacks from within the body's fragile frame itself. I don't know for certain, after the leaving, consciousness will also then cognise what is wanted from Death! The gentle recollection of Self will probably come after the body's death is accepted. What do you truthfully want from the Blessed Giver? We all want "Something" from Death, but most do not know what That Is! Who even considers this? Most of us do not understand what Death wants from us. That Death wants everything from Us, then once given, She, Death, Kali Sakti gives us the Love we seek from Her. Does Death want to teach us something we do not know or rarely feel as that "felt awareness" of Divine Wonderment? Or why we should not be afraid of Her? Or perhaps that we have just forgotten Our True Nature during this momentary passage we have named life and that She will Remind You What It Is That You Are?

Humility, Real Humility is Pure Beautiful Death. I have learned this through the humility of my pain. I am crushed by death, by life, by everything. I cannot tell you what Humility is. It is not a false standing on ego. It is certainly not pretending to be at peace or anything like that. The importance of "I", the word, the name, the meaning, the concept as ego, and all that goes with it, as something of importance, leaves, out of shame perhaps, a better word I do not know at this moment, in the Presence of Real Humility. I could not kill my ego with a hundred things I found in this world, but I have died wonderfully in Humility!

Who then created death and why? Why death of all things? Who created birth? Why create, why make something or someone that it or they should just be destroyed? Is it for us to learn that nothing matters but Love, that everything is momentary except Love? My body's form will go to ashes! But my Passion Continues On! I have a dream, a thought that when I die, when what I call "I" makes its last move into dream consciousness never to return, that this "I" will fly off to the foot of a great mountain and at the foot of this mountain there is a Tantric Palace resting on a great plane where one can see for many miles without a single obstruction. The sky is pure blue. Red and gold banners and flags of the Goddess wave in the cool wind. I will then go into the palace and find many beautiful luminous knowing women and gentle elegant loving men engaged in the study and practice of Tantra. There in the center of the palace is Mother Kali. I go up to Her and touch Her and at that moment She turns *formless* and I finally realize what Love Is. At this precious moment of epiphany I realize Her Absolute, freed from and above the body and mind. I realize Her Relative, as back in a body and mind. Then the One World comes over *me*, the Divine Wonderment, where and when I understand that there is no birth and no death of a body or a mind into the anomaly of the world idea! She says to me, "Poet, use the Power of My Sakti in your fresh body and new mind! Poet, use My Power to Fix your mind on *Me*. Force My

52

Consciousness into your transparent mind!"

Somehow this vision in my thought helps me not to be so afraid of death. If you have no identification with the Ideal, the Meaning will not *Strike* you! I don't live with as much fear and resultant anger as I used to. Love flows more easily now. But my Ideal is pretty much the same as I was born with, though perhaps polished a little better. Sakti is the Real Source of all initiations into Knowledge and Love, whether these come directly from the Spiritual or through some medium of conveyance, embodied or disembodied, imagined or real. Though indeed, the idea of the disembodied is also a false conception, as much so as the idea of embodiment is, in the clear face of the Advaitic Fact. Consciousness is neither. What shall I say?

Forget your waking mind! It is too heavy with the hypocrisy (dualism) of the world. Deal directly with the dream mind. Not even its associated contents. But the Essence of what is Dream! The contemplation (to survey, to observe, to consider intensively a sacred or consecrated place or temple) of dualism? No! It is Consciousness born of Womb Consciousness. Be One with Consciousness! In the waking or dreaming state, behave or comport yourself as Prajna! Be the Prajna (Womb Consciousness) even there and *See* Prajna (Womb of Wisdom), even when the dream state appears, or the dream of the waking state. This is a High Gate to Full Turiya Consciousness. I cannot emphasize this enough. If you do it at every moment, the life/death paradox will be gone and trouble your consciousness no more.

The images in the dream state create an emotion identified with the form and contents of the dream. One has the sense that this is real out of the reflection of the Witness Consciousness which is projected into the momentary dream identity. To the Witness it is unreal, not True Self, but as said just now, it has the sense of realness due to the Presence of Witness Consciousness. In the waking state, the dream state is considered unreal in its condition. In the dream state, the waking state does not seem real since its existence is forgotten and one's consciousness is not aware of its condition. To the Witness, neither are real, nor are the momentary identities associated therein. This is true not just of the dream contents in the dream mind, but also of the same dream contents subconsciously swimming in the dream mind, while conscious in the waking mind, as they may express the greatest fears or the most loving hold or attachment we may have on the momentariness of persons and things. It is all just dream materials collected by one mind in its passage through time. It is nothing in that it causes no worry to the Witness Self. To the Witness these dream materials are ultimately meaningless, no longer having any support once the ego dies, for they all go into their once and *one true state* in that Wondrous Background Consciousness of both waking and dreaming, as All Devouring Love! Non-Dual! Infinite Kali!

That we should have *Composure* with Death, is the reason I have written this. That we should have grateful greeting for Death when Her patience for us to return has worn out. Our desires blind us to what is Ever Present in that those desires stir up the endless contents of dream material. This is where work into direct Sakti is done. Work Here. Clear out the dream content by knowing the "felt awareness" that the content itself and the nature or quality of dream is naturally pure and clear as it is Consciousness. But even all that desire, powerful and cognitively potent to stir up dream contents into massive formations that we name the world, has no effect on the Witness Consciousness. And, as it truly is, when the stirring of dream contents stop, mind naturally engages Prajna (The Womb of Wisdom). The *reflection* of Consciousness in those dream materials then retreats back from, or drops contact with the dream consciousness, there and then leaving only Consciousness without any dream state material or content. This remaining Consciousness then remembers itself as and into the Original Composure of Prajna (Sakti, as One's Own Innate Self Wisdom or "Felt Awareness"). This Principle of the Witness may appear to be a separate principle from Our Non-Dual Consciousness, but this is not so! It is one's own Consciousness in its True

State. And all idea of world goes There. Then awareness, understanding, awakening, realization, all come when you remember This! Perhaps, at best, mind may reach to and attain a state of *Unknowing Trust*, not consciously pretending nor even imagining to know a definition. Blessed is the Humility to not know and to Be at Peace. Blessed is Death, as I fervently pray to Her to show me What She Is! She is death as in going into Prajna, as much as She is again coming out of Prajna as birth. She is the Witness Consciousness and She is beyond the dualism of that idea of the Witness and the thing that is witnessed in Consciousness. What She is, I call Love.

The Mind's Illusion of Departing
and Other Mirages in Consciousness

When we speak of those who are dead, who are thus gone, we say they are departed. Is it so? Even of ourselves, when we have thus gone and departed, are we really indeed gone or *parted* as we think in the mirage of the mind's illusion? The departed are only parted for us. Or are they? We say parted, passed away, they are gone, they are no more and other such expressions, but they Are Where They Are! Not parted from There, or away from There. We apply this idea to them and we apply this idea to ourselves thinking we are going Somewhere and this creates fear, when there should be the divine opportunity for Great Love to be experienced.

So what if the body and the mind fall away from Consciousness! So what! Nothing happens to Consciousness, not to those who appear to be gone in the mirage of death and not to oneself! Nothing happens, Consciousness is the same. The innermost Chitrini Consciousness does not change during the phenomena of the death process. Is it not unlike deep sleep unaware of anything but Being, Bliss and Consciousness? As it is said in the *Brahma Upanishad* on the nature of dreamless deep sleep, "He knows being the Light Supreme. Desiring Light, he enjoys the Light." Or even still aware of the dream state, or even further, still aware of the waking state, as the Witness Chitrini is now in this moment aware of the waking state. So death is the mind's illusion of parting, as nothing ever *parts* from Consciousness! The relationship of what is within the waking and dreaming states may change, but that content of consciousness which forms the waking and dreaming states never parts from this Consciousness which is the Innermost Self. It is the mirage of the mind's illusion created from the body/mind point of view.

If you have become as the Witness Consciousness which in fact you are, if you have become as this never to die Light that is the Witness Chitrini Sakti, then how can the parting from the waking body and the dream mind be a trouble to you in any way? Even if death is but black nothingness where all trace of body and mind are gone and nothing former is then remembered, still, She is my Best and True Friend, and my One and Only Love! For what other friend or lover can one have in the end where we all must greet our own Reality in the ever present *Great Reminder* which we have named death? It is the Higher Insight, all friends, all loved ones, all connections of any kind must go and will go! But you can Love them all and still be with them in the Deeper Current of the Love that this All Perceiving Witness Consciousness Knows and Feels, it is that "Felt Awareness."

But Death gives me Her Love and bears me always Her Deepest Friendship. Like you, I have seen others die and in reality very little is remembered of them as it shall be with me. People get on with their lives here in this world. For most people I have observed in this world are so absorbed in their own ego pleasure that they seldom show any care or concern for others who have made an apparent departing. Is it that deep in the deepest depths of Consciousness we all know that the departed have not departed from Consciousness? So it is with my own Blessed and Lucky Death, Most Fortunate, She does not ever forget Me!

Even of the dead so departed, even when they weep for these who have thrown aside the body and mind, it is for the sake of their own ego misery, more so than that they miss these departed in their ego pain, knowing nothing of True Love, and rather than, the true condition of our own departed souls. Even so, the soul is never parted from Consciousness! Am I wise to say this or not? It appears less so that they care for the *thus gone* state of the disembodied themselves, than for the denial of their own ego pleasure, now in ego misery due to not understanding the nature of Love which Knows not the mirage of death. Death in its *true form* is nothing but Love, reminding us, releasing us and keeping us ever near. My friend, my lover, Death, She keeps me humble to feel empathy for all people's sorrow, especially here, and there too with the departed at times, and more often sometimes, sad and depressed as I am by all this, so, nevertheless, I do not ride on a false high of happiness based on ignorance, which is nothing but pure spiritual stupidity! Do we care for the other or our Self (even in the other) feeling "parted" from Self? As of course, the mirage of death confuses us, when there is no parting, not in our own death, nor in the death of others. One can only *Love*, in *Self*, without feeling "parted" or "apart" or as if imagined in the mirage of Consciousness, "departed." Nothing and no one is ever parted from Consciousness. It is impossible! The body drops like a leaf, but where will you (Atma) go, as that Consciousness is Ever Attained and Ever Within the Presence of Love! Never dualistic, never *parted* into duality! You see, Consciousness does not die and this is the most extraordinary thing of all.

Within the Truth of my heart and within all honesty, I still welcome the Joy of Death in this joyless world. Blessed Be Death! She who keeps me in Humility, my inner refuge, that the arrogant feeling of ego in regard to body and mind may never arise, even so surrendered to the Surprise of Non-Dualism found and always found again and again within my Sweet Loving Dark Companion (the Metaphor of Kali). Oh sweet destruction inevitable, and leading to Bliss, no ego to remain, no other view to be found, the weight of the flesh which is the source of fear and the constant business of mind now gone forever. Thank You, Sweetest Companion! Oh Death, ever waiting in the Non-

Dual. Oh Death, Never Dual! I have no more expectation on this life! But great is my expectation of Death! The last form of Sakti to be embraced and to *become*! Now I can accept the spiritual and karmic conditions of what this life has been and what it shall be without question of what shall it be!

The love of loving spiritual battle must be in you if you wish to get rid of all psychic impressions (samskaras are both previous and present life impressions)) that you are in a dual condition of separation from Reality. These wave forms (vrittis) of thought are mirages in Consciousness. You must embrace the beauty of battle, fully, even the death factor most certainly. There must be a love for the beauty of this spiritual battle, for you will become exhausted and if that love is not there you will not be replenished for the work of psychic cleaning. If one's mind is clean, clear of all separative dual thoughts, then Consciousness naturally just sets into view. The Immanent World is but a reflection of the Absolute World, no, I am wrong to say it, to cognise it this way, the Immanent is the Absolute and the Absolute is the Immanent. When the Goddess said to Ramakrishna, "Do thou remain in bhava," this is what was meant. Bhava or Bhavamukha is this Mood of Encompassing both the Immanent and the Absolute as One. "Now and then I forget Her command and suffer." Ramakrishna most honestly states. Indeed, when we forget this we suffer, in fact, all our suffering is but to forget *This*, due to dual psychic impressions which make or force us to believe differently. This is the path of Love when we remember the Mirror of Self and forget the mirage in the Mirror as just a mere reflection, but embrace its Immanent Reality, and its need for Love!

This love of spiritual battle brings about an identity with Kali. Through the cognitive power of Her Image one assumes the Great Gesture of Her Consciousness which has never fallen into the mirage of dualism. It is done in one's body, in one's mind, and most deeply, within one's own sakti power! One does not stop at the state of momentary spiritual contentment which is our cognition saying to us that this is enough. There can never be enough of the Love Power manifesting within you. One does not stop at the pleasantly comfortable feeling produced by repetition of the mantra and concentration upon the Ideal within that mantra or sacred prayer words of power. You continue, you push forth, you drive onward until you reach the Great Gesture. The Great Gesture is the Mudra (pose, gesture or seal) of the Goddess. Like it is in Her natural state, one also becomes fearless, having raised the contents of the mind beyond all dual psychic impressions. It is the course of psychic battle with one's own self mirages. She is You, the Atma, Innermost, it is Her who has become You. Any other mirage-impression is a psychic lie to the Truth within oneself. The battle is against one's own personal lie, the ego. It is Kali who has become You and so You must become Her! This is Advaita, non-dualism, when no psychic impression remains in contention with the Self. One step down from *Here* begins the powerful level of battle or conflict with all the cognitive processes!

Am I not also so entitled to confusion, frustration and contradiction like anyone else? And to the friendship with these in forgiveness. Must there be the state of battle? Must one be a psychic warrior ever alert and more alert to the smallest things that ignite ego battles with flames of dualism in the forms of crisis and confrontation? Why? Why Consciousness and Conflict? So much energy is necessary for the psychic warrior. But you must have that quality to get through suffering. Do we have that much strength? One must be humble in the self work and want only Peace in Consciousness without conflict, but a portion of that energy goes into daily crisis, the cycle of waking, dream and sleep at the very least and the agitation of consciousness within this circular process of continual change and adjustment of that consciousness. A psychic warrior has to hold on, or does he (she), can he (she) not let go of that war state of the psyche, even as one who has been killed in battle may be forgotten? O Mother, I am tired of dual life, please kill in me whatever holds me from Love and the Great Gesture of Your War Free Mind!

A passive problem (comfortable dualism) may sit well for a time, inactivated, but if it becomes a dynamic problem, active again, then ego crisis arises. Why must there be conflict with Consciousness once its Peace is known? Is it because of the application of that consciousness in continuous psychic cleaning of karmic content, or is it a choice to embrace conflict? Have I ever really known anyone dualistically, successfully and really known them? Do I keep my mind down somewhere, so that it will not see the Truth of anyone? Why not let it rise to see the totality of complex conflict in Consciousness related to anyone's experience? Then, I shall see what they really Are! Is this actually a constant reminder of what needs doing? Do I understand anyone, myself included, to feel compassion, empathy and Love for them, without the need of personal ego pleasure, in humility and surrender to the Truth within Me that responds to the Truth within them. Not ridiculous little personal truth, Real Truth!

The unsure ego cognition is the one distortion that betrays this Truth! Where is Love which is the only clear sight of our purpose? Who do you think you are? Who do you think is anyone? The problem of suffering is continuous and relentless? What reason is there for its teaching? Do you not grow tired of it? Is there no rest from it but in death? Or does it continue even after blessed release descends upon us as we have sometimes been told? Even the greatest of souls must grow weary with it! So who am I and how may I bear it with Wisdom and Love? For the Sake of Peace I shall be wise to submit my ego to daily execution! For when that spiritual separation still exists, and even as we are surrounded by loved ones, the aloneness of the soul can only be extreme until one has created a contact with the most divine inner spiritual companion, friend, lover, consort! Is it True? Yes! And those relations are but also cognitions of the psychic relation of consciousness as power with the Power of Love!

Whatever is or whatever will be, the suffering and the humiliation of this world distorted, it is better to live in a battle free state without the misery of ego intrusion. Live in this unknowing trust and let death be what it is! Suffering is the regret of the ego's misery. Love ever remains above the region

60

of suffering. In heroic sacrifice where one gives one's life for the life of another, the beauty of the ego freedom to die that way, which stirs great emotion in every soul, is because of the call of Love from Above, greater than the ego which has given itself to death for the love of someone else! It is the great offering to the Goddess, so Relax in Love! You will be Here (in the Immanent) until everyone is There (in the Absolute). And it is already so from the High View of Advaita! The Goddess always works Her ways among us in Love Work! Be like Her! Become as Her! Never Tiring! Then there is no more battle. Those who seek and go for Final Immersion (in the Absolute) before everyone, are selfish, but you can indeed enjoy Final Immersion even during the Love Work!

O Goddess, all my meditations never succeed in Reaching You, Beautiful Consciousness, Fear Free, from Where Effortless Love Pours! Do I even know the meaning of a single word? I hear the words, photon or quark, atom or star, and I only imagine some meaning in the mirage of my mind as to what these words convey. It is the same with Self or Consciousness, so in my humility I admit I know nothing at all, but my ego imagines it knows. Really, I wonder if I have ever listened to what my Life is saying to me. I can no longer deny that distortion overtakes my consciousness. I lose clarity. I become confused. But lucky enough, some shape of clarity seems to return. May I be permitted to say, in humility so low that it has never even heard the word, arrogance, that sometimes, now and then, I do not forget, and then, at that moment I am Identified with (.....), I am then (....)!

But I, (Who has done this, Mother?) no doubt generated causes for return to body and mind: my attraction to sensory sensations, my not having completely dealt with the subtle emotions of fear and exhilaration, and my ego identity in that I feel the arrogance of my body and mind riding the horse of this life. It is not all Atma in me!, doing the riding of this fine steed of life, death and life again! Yet, if I am to speak Truth to myself, I realize as I think this way, that this too is a psychic mirage in Consciousness, that I am now at this moment

61

identifying with and that can only limit my own Pure Condition! In Reality, all ideas of heavenly worlds, or of nether worlds, or of returning to a body mind complex in any form: human, animal, etc., ghost, deity, ancestor, whatever, or even the idea of Final Immersion or just coming close to it, all, one and all are cognitive psychic mirages on the Consciousness of Pure Reality. They all exist within the mind maps of the Sushumna System! And this blessed sushumna is a metaphor of the Reality of the Great Ever Unbounded Consciousness of Infinity's Identity within. All other mirages simply appear as psychic energy anomalies produced on the surface of this Consciousness. They are within the waking and dreaming states which are mirage! As mirage, is one more real than the other? No! Even the cognitive idea of spiritual battle is a superimposed psychic barrier! Why must you fight for what is ever your own and can never be, nor never has been lost! Even as the Witness Power which has been your constant companion and sole source of clarity throughout the phenomenal anomaly of your apparent conscious travel away from that Ever Amalgamated Experience. Wake up and know that in Prajna nothing is ever born and nothing ever dies! It cannot be! For Prajna is Atma (Chitrini Consciousness) veiled or unveiled, covered by your ideas or uncovered!

Remember the sweet beauty that Death is but withdrawal into the sushumna and birth is but the emanation of psychic and physical forces coming out of the sushumna. Does the sushumna survive through the birth and death process of reincarnating? Probably, as it is not an anomaly of space/time, but is in itself the time-free, space-free, and cause-free principle of Consciousness. And as Consciousness is One and Non-Dual, is there just one Sushumna that we all share in some mysterious divine way, or are there many sushumnas throughout the universe manifesting consciousness and life everywhere. I suppose this is a quantum problem for those gifted in the direction of that contemplation.

I See Death beautifully embodied in all I see... waiting within, plants and planets, stars and rocks, bodies both animal and human, even there in ghost bodies, the disembodied, yes even these, even in ancestors, gods and goddesses, and deities and deitesses, none being permanent compared to the Infinite, and Death is there waiting to release them from binding form!

Does our quality of Composure with Death in the immediate last and previous experience of death effect our Composure with Death in this life? Must we repeat this process over and over until Composure is Complete? Could you be reborn again because you were not satisfied with the way you died in your previous birth before? Yes, rebirth comes for any reason, cause or desire, since it is the gift of fulfillment from Sakti. We part from the body. We never part from Consciousness. Never! It is Impossible! Let me prove it to you. The five elements of the body break down and return from where they came. These five elements of matter merge back into material matter. They were but loaned to you, borrowed by you from Sakti. But even so, the new form of matter, made out of the old is still here, and not parted, for even though these elements are elsewhere, the ashes or the remains of our physical bodies are not parted from the form of the waking state and this state is not ever parted from Consciousness. Again, the subtle mind Sakti, which is simply the Sakti of the dream state, that too merges back into Consciousness from which it is never parted! And it should be obvious to you by now that the deepest depth of Prajna is Unchanged by the death event, or the birth event for that matter. And of course, the Non-Dual Consciousness never had the thought (which is Consciousness itself) of ever parting. That thought as concept never even approaches the Reality of Non-Duality.

You see, as Chitrini Sakti enters the mind in the form of cognitive thought like thunder and lightning, the Beauty, Wonder and Grandeur of the Great Mother reveals Herself and shows that there is no true separation or dualism ever existing with the four states of Consciousness as all these four states are nothing but Consciousness, All Consciousness. This Consciousness as Pure Sakti never assumes the form of the four states and once this is seen with crystal clarity those four states take on an entirely new look.

The Unidentified Feeling

The closer one comes to *the Unidentified Feeling* the less the mind is needed. The higher the Insight the less one is engaged in thought as a primary process. With the ascent of Insight, layer after layer of thought drops away until one reaches the Innermost Consciousness which is Love in its Purest and Completely Unfettered State. Thoughts flow in such a way that cannot be described. Comprehension comes easily. Delusion, confusion and the rest, are no longer powerful. Thought finds avenues to Love which is never confused. Under the surface of every feeling it is Love which is seeking you. The ego consciousness functioning through the mind aspect no longer needs to decide that something is so or not so. The ego consciousness functioning through the intellect no longer needs to accept the form of determination on a something in the shape of limited intellectual conception and recognition of that something, as it *becomes known* by Consciousness reflected in that intellect. And the same ego consciousness functioning through memory no longer attaches the power of importance on the memories that arise spontaneously out of the stuff of consciousness within the dream material of the mind. The Unidentified Feeling becomes identified as Love and you are then free. For Love is the Truth. The dual gender free dance is that. Love is seeking you and you are seeking Love. The Radha Krishna Love Energy is absolutely equal. Both have lost ego consciousness in the One! Krishna is not larger than Radha and Radha is not dotingly dependent on Krishna. That is a distortion! You, Chitrini, Mother, are both the Dancer and the Drumbeat which cease when Love is Discovered clear and wide without end!

It is You (Atma Chitrini) who create your death. It is You who create your new body and mind. Do it Artistically! Do it with Loving Skill by your own Sakti! Once you have identified this Unidentified Feeling, you will see this clearly. It is not a complex belief system with a God above and you below. You

(Atma Chitrini) are the Center and the Circumference without a Center. Love Power is Your Own Power, which makes you, creates you, destroys you, recreates you and awakens you! Or, if you like, one may think that it is the Entire Universal Collective of All Individual Saktis together which makes and destroys all souls. This is expressed only in the Highest Understanding of Love, without the fetter of the God idea. Do you understand even the word *understand*? The "something" that is understood now is under you, and you stand over that "something." Understand? Put Atma Under You! Stand on It! Know It! Be as Kali! She Stands with Shiva (the Atma Principle) Under Her! This is Bold Knowledge having pushed past the barrier of pleasant spiritual contentment. Advaita is not a conceptual deification of ego centered dream material, subtle bodies, returning causes, painful effects, nor a Creator or Maker of these. It is Incomprehensible Love that has never even heard of the idea of dualism and so should it Be with the Innermost You! The Atma Chitrini Infinite in Empathy to the Infinite! The answer is Yes, You are the Same!

The Final Anomaly

From *Where* does the Guiding Spiritual Power come? That is the question. It may be the final anomaly for you, as it is for me, or it may be something that has never entered your mind, as you are so possessed by the ego idea which has kept you in a state of suspense where you have not learned anything. The truth is that everything in the spiritual journey is not written down, the more of it, is personal discovery, experience, and even so, the challenge of Self.

At this point I wish to address the problem and blessing of the guru function. This function can be anything: a religion, a symbol, a person, a text, anything, even as simple as merely looking up to someone or something. But is not the very condition of looking up, putting that thing or person above and outside you? This is the anomaly. Is it not false identification itself only put or placed elsewhere, to think of the guru's body and the guru's mind as Atma for they are but body and mind and so also dream material. It is a paradox in its tradition (as any tradition), rarely dealt with. The projected image of the guru distracts from the Self-Atma. But as a location within the Immanent which expands to Engulf the Full and Complete cycle of realization this function, symbol, religion or person may help as a jumping board into your own Depth.

As it is Atma that is this Depth, say Atma not guru. Like yours, since the guru's body/mind are in waking, dream and deep sleep, also, therefore a superimposition. The enlightened person is ever of independent will as the *Paramahamsa Upanishad* states, "He prostrates himself before none." No gods, no guru, no religion, no nothing. Another example of this truth is the sage Aruneyi who was taught directly by God in the cognitive form of Brahma, the Creator, as recorded in the *Aruneyi Upanishad.* So if God is within him, then from where did the Guiding Spiritual Power of his enlightenment originate? Narada too, the famous sage of Love, was taught directly by the Goddess. In the line of Power to enlightenment, Swami Muktananda Paramahamsa stated of his own experience, "From then onward, that Divine Shakti was my Guru." What does it mean in our Spiritual Life of Discovery? Sri Ramakrishna Paramahamsa was the same in his attitude, in that the Divine Kali Sakti was his Pure Guiding Power. A Paramahamsa is one who has rid consciousness of all phenomena and as every illusion of the mind has gone and so that consciousness rests in the superconscious direct realization of the Oneness of All Existence.

"Neither am I a seeker," Highest Truth is here defined very clearly in the *Amrita Bindu* (Nectar Bliss Drop) *Upanishad.* If one is a seeker one is searching and therefore has not found Reality within. "He should not have a body of disciples," here the *Paramahamsa Upanishad* says something so bold that it directly crushes its own tradition's limitations. If you have disciples then you are alas, caught in the web of being a guru and here this Upanishad says you should not do this. Does it not indicate that one should not be a guru and in fact discards the guru process as something that does not exist in the conclusion of the spiritual journey? At the level of direct experience in our Pure Spirituality, you must interpret, translate, decode, and then recode into the language of liberated personal experience, all that this phenomenal and anomalous world tells you.

All guru work is phenomena in the mind stuff (dream material), so how is Knowledge of Atma which is Ever Shining and which is indicated to be Higher and Loftier than guru work, passed from one to another one? It is in you, like in Aruneyi, for the Consciousness that taught him was in him, from the First Cause, which is not effected by the effect of the guru principle. "To him: no Mantra, no meditation, no worship." *Paramahamsa Upanishad.* From the Highest Spiritual Standpoint, You have Understood. There is nothing outside you to be gained by reciting a mantra, nothing attained by meditation and nothing to be worshiped, no guru, no god, no religion. "He sees neither "I", nor "Thou", nor all this." He sees not seeker nor teacher, he sees not anything, guru, god and so forth to be achieved by meditation, mantra or worship. At the height of spiritual declaration the *Atma Upanishad* says, "He has no samskaras. He has no samskaras." He or she of course, has no psychic impressions of duality from this life nor any previous life! For you see, those samskaras are what distinguish the "I" and the "Thou" principles as a duality. And it is that anomaly of duality itself which creates the need or feeling that mantra, meditation or worship must be done. But if you can immediately see that Consciousness has no samskaras or impressions of duality, then you are There!

Consciousness needs no teaching! Yet there appears to be an uncovering of Atma. Not to the Atma, but to the one who retains some identity or value base with those samskaras. Who does this uncovering? Enthusiasm! Love for That! This is the *Final Anomaly*! You must realize this or you will remain dependent upon the anomaly and never know as your own Truth, the Consciousness and the Love which is always and alone your one instructor, whether you are in the presence of great temples or churches, hundreds of Christs or Buddhas, no matter even

67

then, it is this Consciousness alone which is *you* and which instructs *you* in the knowledge of *you*.

It is not unlike the motion or the dance of lovers. Are they One or Two? Only Love Knows. Love has Always Known. In Love one sees neither the "I" nor the "Thou." You (Chitrini Consciousness) yourself are always, and have ever been your own guru, which is the light/dark function within you. Light (ru) attracts to the Self always. Dark (gu) also attracts, but away from the Self apparently, on the surface, but darkness exists because of light, and so comes around in the circle of this universal dynamic to the Companionship in Self. Only the non-dual Consciousness can cognise this. Always it is, in the Pure Innermost Chitrini, never perplexed by this anomaly.

The Witness Principle, the Real within you, never needs a shred of guru work, being always Free, what is called Svacchanda, Absolute Free and Independent Will, in the *Svacchanda Tantra*. So the Vedanta statement is strange, "Never take the Witness Consciousness in the presence of the guru (deity, etc.)." On one hand it may be a problem of humility before representations of deity, etc., or another, would be the psychosomatic assumption of "oneness" in or with false identification of the guru's body and mind. If I walk fifty feet away, may I then take the Witness Stand? Or it could be a tactic of enslavement for false devotion to the body/mind of the guru image to keep the theater of this tradition functioning! The same is true with churches, religions, anything which does not want you to break out of its traditional hold. Perhaps there is some sense to this advice. How can you learn from a teaching principle if you are standing in Pure Consciousness? If you are in the Atma, then where is the world, where is the teacher, and where is the student? The relationship becomes meaningless, even non-existent at the level of Pure Non-Dual Consciousness. What "happens" to you if you take to the Witness Consciousness in the company or presence of a guru, deity, etc.? You see that illusion or mirage of superimposition and all that goes with it as it is ultimately imposed over your Real Identity! "Having done away with the Shikha, the holy thread, (both external emblems

68

of holiness) the study of the Vedas, (all enquiry directed to the teacher) and all works, (any obligation, secular or spiritual, in the here or the hereafter) as well as this universe (the entire field of anomalies and all that is within it)," *Paramahamsa Upanishad*, and all that goes with this universe: gods, gurus, deities, mantras, everything! All these, the surface things are discarded, not the Deep Currents Beneath!

Still, more often than letting the feeling awareness of enlightening Consciousness and Love be our central self being, we are engaged in the process of uncovering, asking, "Who am I?" or "Mother Sakti, Who are You?" The "I" answers! Mother answers! You are not alone, you are never abandoned. The guiding image, the guiding principle, should it be worshiped? Or the Result, the Truth? What was said of Isvara and Jiva in the first section of this essay *Consciousness as Witness* is also so true with the guru and the seeker. Otherwise Vedanta contradicts itself. *Tantraloka* says that between the body of Shiva, Isvara, God and the body of the guru, the difference is unreal. But this presents a problem, a contradiction, and Truth can contain no contradictions. The problem is that it is directing consciousness to perceive the superimposition of the three states where the guru's being exists as a glorification of that guru being as God, equal to Shiva and so forth. This guru idea imposes this imposition in your consciousness and sets up a powerful duality. It is a great proclamation, perhaps only understood from the Non-dual, but then, it would include your body and mind as well, as being identical or non-different from Shiva, etc. And that might produce tremendous egotism! That is still the storm of anomaly and not the clear of Consciousness.

Why linger in the anceint memories of the false anomaly of identity when one can reach the superior Spiritual View (Witness) and be free instantly! The past stays too long, the future does not come quickly enough. Who is the guru of whom?... in the Non-Dual Conclusion which is the only conclusion. Can one not just Love and there melt to One, with all these gurus, gods, and so on as Kali Herself, Sakti, Krishna, Shiva... and so be free in mind of all this Advaitic worry

69

(analysis), besides, who can keep it up, who has that much pure spiritual intensity to not fall back into the realm of devotion to something above you, outside you, or even a fraction of any distance from the *Real You*? All so serious, my blessed fool, never forget the Humor in the Heart (Love)!

And do not forget that Love is indeed transcendent of all human tragedy and joy, ever remaining Eternal and Undiminished, yet there is no doubt that Love is felt in the somatic system and the psyche's system and this is best, for then change begins to take place in the power system of the ego, that ego giving over its illusive sense of control, to the Power of Love. This is no doubt, the divine movement of the natural current of Kundalini Sakti through the psychosomatic system, changing and transforming that body/mind system into Love itself. This is the most amazing miracle or supernatural event that can ever take place in this most curious world universe where we dwell. As simple as can be, Love is none other than the Awakened Kundalini Sakti! And so, what was once thought to be most miraculous becomes the most ordinary and natural to the reach of common human accessibility, for we all know Love in some shape or fashion.

No spiritual ideal is perfect, there is fault with every one of them from one point of view or another. But you see, that Perfection is ever Within You as Chitrini. It is this Inner Perfection that is thrust as a projection of perfection on the Spiritual Ideal. As Shiva is All-Light and Peace, and the guru is dark/light, this guru dynamic must be discarded in the End State for there can be no dual dark/light function in the All Peace State. Nothing less will do! So be it! It is stated that the realized being sees neither duality nor unity (non-duality), they see What Is, as *This* is neither existent nor non-existent. This state of consciousness is a powerful spiritual paradox. What does it mean? This anomalous comment on the nature of realization may be attacked from two directions. If consciousness is aimed at the psychosomatic system, the psychosomatic system of a human being, a guru, a god or a deity even, then we can say as Consciousness is the stuff of which these are made then they are existent. But if we realize that as temporal anomalies, that is their psychosomatic systems identified with name and form in the temporal state of space/time, then they do not exist as Permanent forms! But they are neither existent nor non-existent. The anomaly remains as consciousness continues to identify with either focus. Now if consciousness is aimed at the Witness State, then if you are not aware of this Witness State, then it is non-existent to you, but if you are aware of the Witness State, then it is existent to you. But here the anomaly is transcended, as the Witness Consciousness is not effected at all whether your consciousness is aware of its existence or not! Now, as it is said that this is neither grasped by duality or unity, again, the anomalous comment is stated from the paradoxical level of language which can never quite express the nature of Consciousness. Anything one says is automatically qualified by the statement itself.

Still, as long as the dark/light anomaly remains in consciousness, then the principle of the guru dynamic never ceases to play its function in consciousness as an explanation of Light in one's life by the memory of what one has learned. Or is it just pure Sakti Chitrini at play with one's ego play? At times one may feel that all that needs explaining has been explained, as it is with the comprehensive instruction of Vedanta or Tantra, then what shall one do? Help others? No! The idea of just doing that is ego. Except by perfecting Love in the practice of life, for Love itself, in others and in oneself. Truth is then increased in phenomena, and only there in phenomena is Truth increased, for Truth (Love) ever is Constant!

In defense of the guru system and the necessity of this mind map, many have quoted from the example of Ramakrishna and Tota Puri, who showed him the absolutely free state of consciousness (nirvikalpa samadhi). Those who cite this episode have not completely comprehended the life of Ramakrishna. Ramakrishna had already come to that state of consciousness on his own, by himself, as is clearly illuminated in this comment, "The Brahmani, Tota Puri and others came and taught me afterwards what I had heard from him previously--

they taught me what I had already known." The "him" that is referred to here was an aspect of Sri Ramakrishna's own consciousness which appeared out of the Power of Chitrini to him in the cognitive form of a young sadhu (seeker) who looked just like himself. What could be more wondrous and beautiful? The *Pure Power* of his own Self manifested to his outstretched consciousness and taught him everything, as it was already known to his Self. I cannot address with as much power as I would like, the importance and the value of this pure spiritual insight as it answers what I have called the final anomaly!

Self stands on Self. So the guru image is in the dream material. How can I say this? Until you identify the *Unidentified Feeling*, the guiding power of this principle is ever working its sweet power within you and on you, within deeper and deeper layers of the dream material, even as one is at times unaware of its workings as the slow or fast, yet silent power of Chitrini Kundalini, until all dream clouds of that material are gone and what you are left with at that point is Clear Feeling, Knowing and Being, Self, freed from the confusion of dream. It is a beautiful self sacrificing, self surrendering principle that discards itself or does away with *itself* when you come to the Self! How can I express this thought? It is a *thought* that goes where language does not! Not the guru form. Nor any deity. Self! Pure Sakti! You see, it is all within you always. Within the sushumna Chitrini moves. When She pulls up and within the sushumna in depth meditation, moments of insight, in deep sleep or when one dies, then consciousness dies to dualism. When She moves out and down the sushumna then that same consciousness is then born to dualism. It is most simple. If there is a *real guru* at all, it is Sakti, living within your own sushumna! She is the "Ru" within you. You are the "Ru," the Light! As a metaphorical and actual reality, "ru," the Light is the Teacher within you. And the principle of "gu", the dark, is the seeker within that is seeking the Light. "Ru" of guru, is the *Real You* within, but you must bring them, gu and ru, together, facing both dark and light. Then that which *Happens* when these two Unite, or when they devour each other in the Non-

72

Dual, is the exquisite and last anomaly unraveled. The mysterious key to this wondrously beautiful and simultaneously confusing anomaly is that the "gu" principle enhances the "ru" principle. The greater the darkness, the greater the light. Use your own "gu" to uncover your own "ru." Literally, the syllable "gu" means to speed, to urge, to inspire, to further, to speed onwards. Also it means cause to sound, proclaim, and coming and going. Where the syllable "ru" means to break, to shatter, howl, yell, cry aloud, hum, resound, cause to roar, resounding with a cry. Intriguingly, the principle indicates an inspired urging forth speeding onwards to shatter or break with a loud cry, that very last anomaly of dualism! Two voices within you resounding and roaring as the One Voice, ultimately, that of Love, that Voice of True Consciousness, She is Chitrini Sakti. (As I speak through the system of this wondrous mind map) Be your own Spiritual Master and never another's! Master comes from "magnus" which means greatness. Take that Greatness to your own spiritual Self in all the humility of this gift. It is for no one else but You and no other shall be your student, for if then this becomes so, then you shall have lost that Greatness and it can only become a form of tremendous ego that you think you can teach another the Self. No one but the Self (Sakti Chitrini) teaches the Self. No one is my Owner! No one is your Owner. We are owned by none and this is Freedom, the *thing* we all seek to know and to cry out within ourselves as we shatter the barriers that keep us from the roaring joy of realization!

The Flow of Love
Within the Stillness
of the Heart

Sri Ramakrishna asked M., "Well, what do you think my attitude is?" M. replied, "It is like that of a man just awakened from sleep. He becomes aware of himself. You are always united with God." Yes, that is it. To be awakened from the sleep of all these anomalies, all illusive psychic phenomena, all mental self projected delusion, all bilge and poppycock dream material which has no special significance in the final conclusion. When you get rid of this debris and rubble in the mind, this conflagration of ego material, you become aware of Self. This is to wake up. This is what I have been hammering at all this time.

It is my hammer of truth whose purpose is to shatter all fearful foolishness of the cognitive psyche which out of that fear creates the totally distorted view of other worldliness, dualism, separation, and the idea of powers that are outside agencies, external to one's own spiritual self. Your whole world is just your spiritual self and fear is not the essence of this self world. It should never be that, fear is but the simple barrier between feeling and spiritual reality. When fear falls into the sweepings and the waste, there Love rises up free and sure. Within the stillness of my heart, Love has declared all out beautiful conclusive triumph on fear. In the Name of the Primordial Power of Love, going back all the way before so many sages and kings walked this preposterous Earth!

Memory

You see, in a principle of substitution we so often seek the memory of the Original Atma, even though great emotions, fondness and so forth are joined in that memory, it is still the maya (illusive measuring) of mind. This is not only true in the chronological spiritual history of this one lifetime, but of the deep underlying memories of other lifetimes where in we may have felt the Atma. Was it the Original Experience? Perhaps! But to have Certain Experience we must go back to the Pure First State of Atma we are trying to regain. Is this not the real meaning of what all the maya of memory is indeed ever always speaking to us in our waking and dreaming states? Is not the voice of memory but the substitution for what we are all trying so hard to remember in so many ways, the Atma? Only now and then to come to the unknowing rest and sanctuary in the kindest mercy of deep sleep where all cognitive dual delusion is wiped out and Atma is blissfully felt within as the one Reality.

74

To seek Atma in memory is to limit Atma by memory. The intensity of Atma in certain memories makes us want to return to those memories as a desire to grip the Atma again. These memory mirrors of Atma can be everything and all that exists between the range and breadth of the sexual to the spiritual, since as human beings we float and flux between these two parallels. Know clearly without doubt that the morbid or sentimental romancing of the chronology of memories is a limit on your comprehension of the Divine and Immediate Now of First Original Atma, which is Unfettered Sakti. "Your own Atma is the Divine Mother!" Swami Aseshananda.

It comes to our Love level, to our Joy level, in which it seems that our early impressions of these are fixed and so these impressions keep us in the idea of a limited capacity in Love and in Joy. It is really a matter of getting through these early memory impressions, whether somatic, psychic, or religious, and therefore making more Love and Joy possible, or more Humility and Surrender, past and beyond these memory levels where we identified what these should be, when always they are more in their actuality. It is to push past the memory's comfort level, that accustomed dimension which holds one back. It comes to a wild (in the sense of no cognitive limit) free (unfettered) abandon (in that one rises out of previous limited concepts) in the feeling-mind (awareness). We tend to be like cows, we contact that early comfort level as a memory and then stay at that sentimental level, thinking that because we have returned to the past that that is a reality to be accepted by the cow mind of the ignorant human animal. You have got to move yourself harder and further until you get to a place you have never been. Work it, work it past the knot in the stupidity of the cow mind. Seek death (in metaphoric psychic activity and as an eventual reality in the course of time), seek to destroy yourself with Joy, Love and Humility within yourself in the Highest Act of Surrender to complete Joy. Let the Love Flow and Flow. There is no end to Love, so why should there be any fear?

I want to go behind and further back, deeper before the existence of memory, or of just returning to a memory of Joy or

Love, a limited memory in its level of capacity. This is the key to deeper and more dynamic joyful loving zeal and zest. We tend to think that our spiritual discovery is just to rediscover our first original discovery of such Joy or exciting Ecstasy that we might have felt at some point in early life formations of feeling and thought. And there we limit ourselves by the maya of memory. And so often life is wasted away in the attempts at psychic transference of an earlier Ideal of Love or Joy, in our present state of consciousness so often considered unattainable in regard to its spiritual height or in returning to a contact with the quality of a memory so long ago and now past. This is the maya of mind in the extraordinary permutation of memory, the psychic database of all dream material.

So then, may I present the question, is enlightenment simply to see Atma in all and every memory or is it the destruction of all memory where the one and only memory is that of Atma? And then where is memory when Atma is what is known? But memory continues and powerfully so, never resting except in deep sleep, ever active as it is in our waking and dreaming states. But if Atma is seen there in the memory function of waking consciousness and dream thinking, then memory as an agent of distraction is rendered powerless in its force of pulling one's thoughts ever back into dualism. It comes to this, to manage, deal, exist and live with the vibration of consciousness in the dream mind or waking memory, so as to learn that this function of consciousness can never disturb the innate feeling sense of the non-dual experience.

In Vedanta, there is the concept of *Bodhalinga*, the awakened subtle body. Is this awakened subtle spiritual body only the ordinary subtle body of dream consciousness, which now brilliantly and in every motion and maneuver of its substance, only remembers the memory of Atma as to what it is contained within, as an emanation of Consciousness, coming out of the Source, as a subtle body which now only knows, only feels and only remembers itself to be Atma? Or is it that the subtle body (linga) has remembered its Source, the Great Womb of Mother Sakti, Brhat Yoni, and so has returned to the gesture (mudra) of memory in Her? Either way, the subtle psychosomatic system of dream consciousness has now somehow recalled its own True Reality, the Atma. One may also say that this is Posturing in Sakti, in Kali, in the Goddess. It is to retain only the memory of Sakti as to what the anomaly of the waking, dreaming and deep sleep conditions are in reality and of course it is now known the ever free unfettered Consciousness is nothing but Sakti. We may call this Sakti Mudra, the Spiritual Gesture of the Goddess.

These gestures in consciousness are memories of the Real Self, the Atma. We learn, as times flows on, how to posture ourselves in these states or moods of conscious being. It is intense and beautiful. It is not the posture of the body so much, it is the posture or gesture of the mind which reclaims at that moment, a pure and sharp understanding of its Original State. But remember, the Original State existed prior to all of our gestures, postures, positions in consciousness or psychic stances that we have assumed in our memories in regard to the Atma which is the Original Memory of Self.

Energy

Again, if we address the high spiritual concept of Bodha Linga we must ask what is it? It is the awakened subtle body. The unfettered intellect (buddhi) has now become Consciousness (Bodha). All the subtle body knows is Atma and so the dual vibration of former dream consciousness ceases. The subtle body itself which is the dream experiencer now truly and genuinely wakes up from the sleep of dream consciousness. Beautiful! All dualistic viewpoints stop. What a wonderful perception. Explained is relativistic terms, this Bodhalinga is how *sahaja bhava* is experienced. Sahaja (spontaneously awakened) bhava (mood-feeling) is when the the dualism of separation disintegrates. Then waking, dreaming, deep sleep and turiya are no longer seen as four points of perception in Consciousness, they are seen as only Consciousness. This is the high divine meaning of Hring Sakti, the limitation shattering mantric formula for Advaitic (Not Dual) Goddess (Sakti) Consciousness. H is waking. R is dreaming. I is deep sleep. And Ng is the conclusion to all suffering which was caused by the once former perception of separation and dualism in the experience of waking, dreaming and deep sleep. Are not the three states nothing but Consciousness as the most utterly grand expression of the Power of Power (Atma Sakti). That there is any conscious barrier at all, between ourselves and the divine energy of experience no longer exists in the realized consciousness of the awakened subtle body. All is Atma and only Atma. So life and death have no meaning to one who stays at that level. But few of us can stay at that level and so we come down to the world of complex multiple associations which start with the buddhi (intellect) and continue forth into the paradoxical puzzle of the world with all its functions and energies and so on that grow out of the buddhi. So is enlightenment an intellectual process? Perhaps. But without the power of emotion that comes out of Love, that intellectual perception of enlightenment will not stick. Love gives it purpose. And Love's sorrow for the world makes that perception a worthy one. Worthy, meaning something to be worshiped in the true sense of its import. And the only thing worthy of worship is Love. So it is Love that illuminates the subtle body that thereby becomes the awakened Bodhalinga.

It is Love that is the source of true Energy. It is what gives the impulse! The Power. From where else could you say it comes? The energy of Love is what inspires and moves us all in the right direction. Is having energy or not having it as much a matter of mental enthusiasm? Kundalini? Health? Spiritual Power? One can be healthy physically and yet paralyzed by depression and so have no energy. Or one can be ill, hurt and distressed by concern for others and still magnify the showing of amazing and great spiritual energy! So the source of Energy is a place ignited by one's enthusiasm for Love as far as I can see.

Energy is a matter of choice, extension, conservation and allotment. Consciousness ignites the Energy of Love and Love ignites the Energy of Consciousness. This is our Experience to be tried and tested. This Energy shows itself without effort. It must not be for an ego reason, not even an imagined noble purpose with the idea or hope of helping. We cannot help then but making it for our sake as a matter of expecting a result or change from someone. Here so much energy is lost. Energy as the power of an active working in this world should be given out without any expectation of return to the ego of oneself. Besides, the source of Energy is not the ego. Everyone must have a choice as to the extension of their energy to others in how and where they might allot that power or conserve it. So often we have an expectation of a communion in consciousness with another person or even an ideal. Do not forget that you have the psychic freedom of your own spiritual energy to give or allot to that or not, as a conservation of that extension, or its chosen allotment.

This Energy is what gives life to forms and to thoughts. If you are at rest and then you are watching the thoughts that come to your mind, at those moments, learn to either conserve energy or allot energy to the thoughts that come across your conscious mind. Again, when one is dreaming, some dreams will be given power by the allotment of energy. From somewhere in you a reason comes up why you will give some selection of dream material the extension of choosing that material as some image of value. You have made a choice and from it the dream material will overtake the energy of your consciousness, pulling it into some select form of extension into dualism or controversy with oneself. In that extension, or choice of allotment, whether it is a waking experience within oneself or in connection to another living being, or whether it is purely in the dream state, you may feel that it is your psychic energy that is giving an invigoration to the subject before your mind, but really speaking, it is your own Spiritual Energy behind that psychic flow that is being taken for a ride this way or that. What is really happening with Energy is that everything is happening at a spiritual level. That is so, because everything is a conjunction of life and death in its response and so the learning of spiritual purpose is constantly going on. So what is the choice you will make with the allotment of Consciousness as spiritual energy that you have been so strangely bestowed with in this human existence?

Experience

They have not yet perceived Sakti! People who look here and think I am concerned with the body. Or because the eyes are open or closed they imagine that inside there is thinking or dreaming. They have yet to perceive Sakti, just yet! This is no doubt poetry, but it is true for you, as much as it is for me.

Perfectly vacuous... my body lying here in this house. No Earth below, surrounded by stars and galaxies. My body is vacuous with atoms just floating within the shape that shapes this body, as my Consciousness rests awake within! Even the idea of subtlety is just floating there! Now who shall identify with what? And why? And where?

Everything that passes over the surface of Me is but a temporal anomaly in Love. Everyone is but searching out Self, leaving their elephant at home while going into the forest to look for his footprints.

High Sakti in my body frees my mind. I can Be without thinking. Knowing deep Her Feeling. Down in the Source and Root of Me.

Dream consciousness wherein dream objects appear or do not appear is just Consciousness, when the dream objects which are nothing but dream memories are gone, or even when they are there. A good lesson to learn is trusting Consciousness behind the mind, know thoughts that need to come will come when they do.

In the wicked and the wondrous see Sakti. Sometimes life is interesting and sometimes it is seen to be the completely absurd experience that it is. Why look there any longer? Find meaning at the Source, the Root! Have no fear. Emit no fear!

Does anyone ever really want to hear about other people's intense experiences? Usually not. The ego reacts and imposes saying, "Oh I had that happen." They don't want to listen. Or the inner skeptic states, "Yea, sure." Or something deeper happens from the stillness of the Heart, where Love shines. These intense experiences should be mine, that is they should be yours and not others, or whatever has been experienced by anyone, sage or fool, may indeed be experienced by me. This is the true voice of the inner spirit saying what is real to you must indeed be your own experience, your own reality, your own energy, memory and feeling of the highest spiritual Love. It is no good for you if it is someone else's experience, except in that such experiences of others may be a guideline for your own eventual assimilation of what is the spiritual content of this life.

The Dualism of the Body Idea

Most of us never consider that the body is an idea in the mind, that is, mind as subtle body. And the subtle body is an idea within the causal body which is the experiencer of deep sleep. Finally, it is Consciousness, the Atma, which is behind all this. But most often we tend to think of Self as the substance of the waking material body, when all the while it is the subtle mind body which is doing this thinking, and then that thinking momentarily stops when the subtle body enters the non-dual condition of consciousness known in deep sleep. Again, it is Atma, the Self, that is watching and knowing this phenomenal cycle. The dualism of the body idea is what makes the human mind fear death. The dualism of the body idea is again what makes us feel separate or dual from Atma and that makes mind fear death. Of death, we should not be afraid. Mother Kali will keep me alive as long as She wants, but I am ready, not surprised by today, and celebrating like it is the last day of this precious life on Earth, but not of Life Never to end. So I walk this Earth in Humility knowing without doubt that Kali as Atma will find me when need be.

What happens when we die? The dualism of the body idea is gone. At least in the sense relation to physical terms. One can only understand what Love is by also contemplating death, even sexual love cannot be comprehended without the contemplation of death. For the closing in of death gives even

81

sexual Love its power of force on the soul which knows that the physical form does not last, so something more lasting is sought. For a love that is a real Love will seek a way to live on and continue undisturbed. It is the desire to possess Joy forever.

The Tantra describes every shape, form, position, body part, emotional, mental, spiritual state, age, stage, occupation or condition of woman, even as to the exact degree of her spiritual nature by observing the nature, level and quality of excitement or its absence demonstrated when spiritual feelings and ideas are engaged. In the Tantra there is Vamacara, the left hand path as it is called, for this method engages sexual union as if it were prayer itself. But what Vama really means is to ever see beauty or spiritual wonder divinized in all women as Goddess. It is a high calling to require of anyone, man, objectively, and woman too on the subjective ground of self perception. But metaphorically, what is meant? A saying in the Tantra is, *"To become as a woman,"* so that you may know what Love is. It is the total full comprehension of all conflict of spiritual perception resumed into the one view of Consciousness as Goddess, Mother, Lover, Friend, and Teacher, healing all distorted schismatic fragmented viewpoints. The dualism of the other is swallowed into oneself and thereby one becomes what is viewed as a duality and so duality goes. Ramakrishna *only* practiced this *divinized* path in ways no other person has done. Also, like seeing the Atma in all memory, it is the same principle here, all that is seen is seen as Sakti, so no duality is seen and the dualism of the body idea goes and with that going the constructs of psychic restriction also go and with that the mind becomes ready for advaita (non-dualism).

You see it is viewing the human state as a condition of dualism that causes the phenomena of return to that state of dualism in the body idea. If what is seen is non-dualism then there is no return to that state of the body idea, in the phenomena of reincarnating or even in just dropping down from the consciousness of non-dualism. Because of the body idea you will never find Total Joy in another person. Because, we are split apart and then humbled by Death. But since Consciousness as Atma is never lost in the body idea, it never need be humbled by death.

War, the aggressive feeling that one needs to destroy, comes out of dualism. The war of the soul. The war between men. It arises out of the feeling ignited by patriarchal territorialism and phallic possessiveness of the begotten and the begetting. Even Krishna was a warrior. Many scholars now believe that forty to twenty thousand years ago most Earth cultures were Goddess centered. They were peaceful. Then came the stage in consciousness of the Goddess and Her consort. Then the stage of the consort (God) and his goddess. Concluding with the wiping out of the Goddess ideal almost completely as She was subordinated to a nearly unnecessary position by the absurd and ridiculous idea of old and foolish patriarchs of a God who creates life without any woman or Goddess whatsoever. The loss of the Goddess ideal has tipped the world into the insane and extensive history of war and destruction. An unloving world civilization. Now the Goddess ideal is returning to consciousness in many many ways we see everyday around us. But where do we go from here. To remember the past is part of the answer, to just return to the past will not solve the state affairs.

It is said in the *Niruttara Tantra* (Without the Upper, you see, uttara means upper, higher, better, but this Tantra is titled in such a way that it is beyond or without, nir, superiority), that a woman who thinks or practices spiritual cognition on herself as Kali, can roam about, that is walk the Earth and enjoy herself like Kali, and that she among women is worshiped in the three worlds. This is the call and the cry of truth now needed. Where do we go, we go to the New Mothers. Who are they? They are you and me. It is simple. There is so much life here on Earth that needs mothering, cherishing and loving. Who can do this? You and me. Get over and forget the trap of blood lines. Go past the absurdity of family psychological lineage. True family is Kula (the Family of the Goddess). And humanity is it. You are Mother Kali. I am Mother Kali. There we now are.

Rather than the animal desire to birth another child, tell me what do you hope to find in birthing? A Self Connection from another life? A connection with this life? That is here already. And it goes on and on. A Parent is one who brings forth, we are all the parents of each other and so many of us are here now as the manifestation of the Self in All Beings. All Beings are Kula, the Goddess' Family. Living and Dead, Infinite They Are. Create your self in Kali before you create another broken and disappointed child.

It has shocked me to hear people say after procreating another child on this Earth, that they actually found themselves startled by the fact that they had to feed, cloth, house, and educate that child. They never thought of this. Can anyone be so unconscious of life? It is this kind of self righteous blind impulse to mothering that is so destructive and damaging. It is the blind ego of the mother that feels she has brought a child into the world. No. It is the Goddess who brought every one of us here. Not an ordinary human mother. It is the shame of the Earth to bring yet one more child into life and not be able to mother them to a healthy and stable sense of reality. I know no one who has escaped the damage of this kind of mothering. I am not ignorant of the creative joy a mother feels, nor of the benefits we should receive from our physical mother, that she should nourish and cherish us, physically, emotionally, psychologically and spiritually. But it is so often so far from that and I know no one who has not in some way been injured by bad mothering (or fathering).

In fifty years Mother Earth will have in Her lap four billion more human beings. It is now the responsibility of the bold and the unselfish to take upon themselves the mothering of life here and now. To blindly procreate is a hideous boring redundancy of the ego of motherhood. Mother the life that is here. We speak of ego problems but few dare to speak of this problem of the mother's insane need to create life that cannot be cared for. I heard an exhausted mother with one child say, "It is amazing that human beings have survived at all." What a statement in regard to raising just one child. And there are those who feel they must make more children, not even for the sake of the

84

child's spiritual benefit, but because they are afraid to be alone, now and when they are old. When there is so much life here and now that already needs Mothering it is absolutely selfish to follow simple blind animal physical need (or social pressure) and then not provide.

Every soul on Earth should complete the unfinished parenting of all life and all beings. One can parent anything and especially any child. Whose heart does not go out to a child who has no one? Only the vilest and most selfish soul could not feel a love to be felt by taking under their wing such a soul abandoned. To go forth and multiply was an ignorant patriarchal demand to increase the density of a religious community. This no longer applies. In fact it is destructive advice. Reckoning population and food ratios it is not out of the question that the human race could procreate itself out of existence by starvation or even food wars in the future. I cry out to the New Mothers who will awaken, please keep us from this and protect us from conventionality.

To just procreate is an insecure ego reason. But now to be a New Mother, that is a grand and great adventure of the soul and we are talking now of matters pertaining to the soul itself. The *Pancadasi* gives its warning of woe to the parents who seek the fulfillment of Self in a child. What child does not bring heartbreak to their parents? Not so much that the child does this intentionally, they are just another human being, it is the parent's expectation of seeing their self fulfilled in a child when the absurdity of it is that they were never fulfilled in themselves in the first place. And now they want the child to do it. I am sorry for the children born of such parents. I call for a Love that is brought forth out of the New Mothers, beyond blood connections, that shares the Heart of the Earth. What is this racist blood thought? Blood is blood and we all bleed red. But inside that blood is blue, the same in him, her, me and you.

I look around me and I see beautiful extraordinary Goddess women walking the Earth. But oh how their eyes are so bound, dark and tired, by the ungrateful and unruly children they are unable to care for. Always needing, wanting, crying and complaining for them. Do we behave this way toward the Spiritual Goddess Herself as Her children here on Earth? I become utterly racked with shame if I complain to the Goddess. Sapping Mother's Energy! For what, my moment of discomfort? This is a most powerful analogy for what happens by all of our foolish egotistical selfish desires and complaints. New Mothers, would you come to their rescue in the forms of both women and men, vital or old. In the divine and purely selfless non-ego centered service to the Greater Ideal of Empathy for all souls who need all this and more of this incarnating experience.

Reality and Its Living Metaphor

It may be a very curious arena of symbolism when we consider the spiritual implications of romantic love. What is vulvic? What is phallic? What is their union and their separation? Common sex dependence does not express Love. People cannot explain Love with sex. Spirituality is Love, sex is just sex, like eating. Does eating explain the taste of food and the wonder of bodily nourishment? But Love gives it life. As Love gives life to everything.

Is spirituality merely being so broken down by life that one has no other recourse than to humbly surrender to the helplessness of Love? In a way it is so. Exhaustion of the mind comes in contemplation of the Great Reality which the mind cannot grasp. Then all the barriers as those psychic signatures in the body mind complex break down. Then it seems that consciousness itself becomes exhausted with identifying in duality. It is a beautiful revelation, after exploring the world complex, consciousness wants to return to Consciousness. Like a child to the womb of the mother. This state of humility and surrender to the soul, comes of itself to the spirit, when arrogance and egotism are no longer held as realities. To think that spiritual attraction is an element of one's ego is the extraordinary deception of the ego. All attraction comes from Love itself! There is no fixed outline to this life. We constantly have the opportunity of re-configuring our consciousness of this life. No absolute definition is there. And again, by this reconfiguration of consciousness we can change the experience of the recurring world of the waking state, as well as more easily, the dream state. No one's situation is really that unique. Everyone has situations they must give in to, even if it is but the offensive demands of their own ego. The surrender of consciousness is inevitable.

Now, if a metaphor is really the higher form of something then what is the metaphor of romantic love? You see, the subtle body is called a linga. This is also the term for the phallus. What does it mean? A phallus penetrates with the function of creativity. What does the subtle body penetrate? The matrix of world matter. The waking state. But also the subtle body returns like a child to the womb, when it loses its constructed form in the dream state and reenters the womb of deep sleep, where there is nothing but consciousness. Is this the true metaphor, the real and deeper meaning behind the outside living symbols in nature's fold?

Then what is the yoni, the vulva, in this metaphor of spiritual principles reflected within nature's wondrous substance of life? The divine principle, herein reflected, is expressed as the Womb of Suchness. A term of Reality found in Buddhist Tantra. The vulva is thought to swallow and this is why it is feared by some. The vulva is thought to be receptive and this is why it is adored by others. But if we consider this womb of consciousness as the higher principle of deep sleep, then that condition of consciousness is what swallows dualism and the subtle body along with that temporal condition of dualism. Then is it not also true that the blessing of peace is ever waiting there for the subtle body in the condition of deep sleep, most extremely receptive to the subtle body's need for rest and peace from this world? But then if you come around from the other point of view it is Sakti (Mother Consciousness) that penetrates the subtle body with the creative power of Energy and Experience. So here, linga (subtle body) is the receptive as well as the one who swallows that energy and experience within itself. So who can say whether that vulvic or phallic dualism really exists since these principles reflected in the higher conditions and dynamics of the waking, dreaming and deep sleep exist within every living being.

Then beyond limitations both the ideas of root or source of life and things can be applied to both the vulvic or phallic conditional concepts. Both are limitations as they are but a part, or half of dualism. The waking body just dies, returns to the ocean of material life. But until the subtle body is unified within deep sleep and that deep sleep is recognized or remembered as the pure and profound turiya, then duality continues and with duality's continuance continues misery and with misery comes confusion and so on. So here people look for Love, especially romantic love. They seek the union of the two. But that real union that is ever so painfully sought only genuinely and as permanently wished for, only then comes as the soul returns to the higher state of Love unknown to the mind yet experienced as that "felt awareness" of turiya.

What happens when you die? Consciousness ceases to identify with the vulvic or phallic mind states. The subtle body is that one who is concerned with death or rather the conditions of itself as to what happens in death and afterwards. Consciousness is never concerned with death, only life, as consciousness never dies. The subtle body is what comes and goes and it is the one who is contained by the limitations of these concerns. When death comes, Consciousness is just Consciousness, at least for a moment. Then the recycling starts up. Consciousness as ego wants to reenter somewhere and that is when the vulvic or phallic identity cycles bust back into one's mind and one is brought down to the embryonic state of rebirth. Physical birth from the womb is obvious even to the most ignorant. What is not obvious is the birth of the subtle body out of its Source. The Womb of Consciousness. Shall you identify this Consciousness, the Atma, as Source or as Root, as both or Beyond?

In everyone there is the Radha Energy and the Krishna Energy. The two great lovers of all times. Does each individual need to amalgamate the force of these two energies into One

88

Experience, that of the Beauty of Pure Love, in order to cease the subtle body's coming and going into and out of the matrix womb of consciousness as the potent tendency to crave separation and the anomaly of dualism? It would seem so. Can one define Radha energy as tender natural? Can one define Krishna energy as aggressive natural? Is it the dualism of the tender and the aggressive that forces us into rebirth? What happens if you combine the tender and the aggressive, what does that energy then become? Tender aggression? Or Fierce love? Perhaps that is not the way, the direction to go. Maybe one should drop both the tender and the aggressive in order to reach the energy of experience which is the state of Love that knows no distraction into rebirth.

Please do not accuse me of not being tender, compassionate or loving, and for that matter please do not accuse me of being aggressively protective. Are not both egotistical concerns? Really, isn't concern for others so often egotistical, and not genuine compassion or protective love, in that one may feel superior to others in that we imagine that we make fix their trouble? It is like the feeling insight of psychic limitations in others is easy to see, of what holds them back in our minds. It is easy compared with one's own self sight on the same condition. Why? Because ego blinds the view. As we are all this Love, then who as an ego shall take it upon themselves to be tender? As we are all this Love indeed, then who out of arrogance shall seek to protect who, from what, out of aggressive force? Does it make sense to you? Has your mind reached tranquility which sees the One behind the two, where Reality is found, now free of metaphorical delusions? When all superficial gender illusions are stripped off of Consciousness, There you experience only Love's Pure Excitement! Luminous Feeling is never confined by phallic/vulvic dualism!

Perhaps there are only two languages on Earth, even throughout the universe. Male-anese and Femi-nese. When does the emotional dualism of their continuing dialogue rest in its own peace which is the experience of the energy of Love? Beyond the erotic realm, or thought attraction, or even pure spiritual energies coming and going toward or away from one another, shall one's mind gravitate toward Radha, or toward Krishna, toward both, or Beyond? Love flows and becomes the two but always knows the truth within the stillness of the heart.

Love as Advaitic Luminosity

It is Love that heals, saves, endures, fills life with meaning, turns emptiness into fullness, and comes unnoticed, unforced, and unexpected in the subtle most and most simple ways. Love is the author of this work.

Love is felt in the head as an idea arising there in consciousness, then as a warmth in the heart, and then as a weeping sweetness throughout the bone joints. Love flows down from the place of Spirituality so high it cannot be diagramed. When Love flows the ego and its pain goes. Love rises up out of the center of consciousness which is indeed the center of the world, the base bone of the central spine column. The bone balls of the ilium sockets churn out of the root chakra and Love rises up to the ajna center immediately as a blissful joyful pain stirring an emotion that is overwhelming, situated behind the eye sockets. Love rises to there and touches the Infinite and Indescribable Feeling and then it floods back down to the center, the root, the middle of the world. This root center is in the middle of the world, in the middle of all that is above and all that is below. It is where you begin and where you come back to as an agent of force and compassion in this world where you feel Self in the Self of all at the center of the universe. All that is out there as world, universe, and life is in you at the center of the world and Love is the Power moving there always.

So often we feel that life is given to us and then ripped away from us. Is there no reason for it? Is the universe that crazy? No, beyond the barrier of dualism that perceives a body of one's own possession or a body of others (relations) as an object of coming or going, there in the deep stillness of the Heart, Love is Known. And once known this Love may flow in phenomenal wonder! But not if one is still caught in the psychic net of dualism which perceives the body idea as the conclusive reality. We all know the body comes and goes, but who ever stops to ask what or who is watching this coming and going? That is the Stillness of the Heart where Atma dwells ever knowing its own sweet Stillness undisturbed by life and death, knowing all that is within and beyond life and death and there flowing as the Love which enlightens the heaviness of the world.

By our own enthusiasm we enlighten ourselves by our Love for Love and Enlightenment. Only the most ignorant fool would put a limit on Love. All relation forms in human experience contain the energy of Love. And yet Love is more, always more than the content of any relation form. To those who disparage Love as simply a concept of sexual co-dependency I say the subject of your statement comes from engaging yourselves only in the forcefully sundered position of a love which is dependent merely on the assumption that sense perceptions and sense experiences are the final state of reality. Fools, your psychological bull discardings are long gone by those who have passed over you. How sad is your confined concept of Love. It breaks my heart to see and observe people's preoccupation with the absurd, the ridiculous. How dare you designate the limit of definition in regard to Love! How arrogant! Love is the power that created your mind that is now engaged in the disparagement of Love, you foolish mass of elephant droppings. I send you my blessings. Oh well, enough ranting.

Really, back to a more gentle voice, in all relations; that of lovers, that of parents and children or to be the child of a parent who brings you forth, teachers and students and teachers who are never so arrogant as to not be students, friends among friends, or in solitude alone with deity, or to see Love in the most wicked of one's enemies, or to feel you are but nothing and no one in this massive ocean of experience we call humanity, a concept we speak of but who feels it, or to think you are the most important person on the Earth. In all these, the only reason any of these have any meaning at all is because Love inspires them with the enthusiasm of Love's energy. And yet Love remains above all these relations.

The idea that Love is dependent on dualistic relational context is only an idea and a false idea at that. Love has its own existence above all dual relation contents. It is the force behind all those dual connections and the only fulfillment to be found that is sought in those conditions. Love is the only memory we seek and Love is all the energy of any real experience. It is very funny to me that the human mind thinks that Love can only be experienced dualistically. For at the moment Love is felt dualism dies. The shining forth of the Spiritual Self, the Atma, which is composed of nothing but Love in the expressible context of our own energy and experience, is always a fresh and new experience, no matter how many times it happens, to the stranger of the human mind. Love is the Energy of Non-Duality (Advaita) in the Experience between two, where the between feeling and the thought of there being two, both disappear in that Energy of Experience. As memory is simply to remember, this is what is eventually and ultimately remembered. As Experience is simply to test or to try, this is what is discovered in that trying and testing. A Spiritual Experience is then one that out proportions all previous concepts of what a spiritual experience is, that is, anything one may have tried or tested before. It sounds dangerous, but I am definitely not speaking of worldly experiences, I am hammering at your innermost potential.

If we look through the metaphor of the Radha/Krishna experience of deepest spiritual and romantic love, some understanding may come. When Radha and Krishna meet at the moment of Love or within the continuing experience of Love, dualism dies at once. Love is all that is at that moment. No Radha. No Krishna. The death process of dualism is clearly and sweetly reflected in the metaphorical romantic love of Radha and Krishna. Our lives, living itself is a kind of courtship, romance or foreplay we have with the non-dual experience of Love. And so death as it is the extinguishing of the dualistic idea of the body, is then final consummation, or the beautiful violence of excitement in the revolution or turning of consciousness around to look back on its Source and become one with that Source at the Root, Atma. One may say that Kundalini rises at that moment to marry the Infinite Unbroken Self as Divine Wonderment.

Enthusiasm grows as the four states uncover and reveal their Nature. One cannot but help being more and more attracted to the Depth of it all (Love). All psychic signatures of the personal body mind complex go in the transiting identity dissolving into further and farther experience in the Energy of Love. The form of the subtle body dissolves. In the first stage which may correspond to the waking state one feels Love's warmth, comfort and initial feeling. In the second stage which may relate to the dream state Love's energy becomes thrill, clarity and fine fine feeling. In the third stage which may go with the deep sleep stage Love is felt as heightened ecstasy which the increase thereof is only held back by subconscious or unconscious holding to doubt, the finite figuring which wrongly believes it cannot comprehend the Infinite. The fourth stage of Love is then actually turiya where a divine spiritual revolution which out proportions all previous conceptual stages takes place in consciousness. Love is so powerful here that it might appear to the unfamiliar psychosomatic system as a violent excitement of bliss, violent only in that it is so powerful that it changes the other states or stages in regard to itself, which is Love liberated from the former finite container of the three states of consciousness. The idea that this was a dual experience only existed with the existence of the body idea that was held as a reality in the waking, dreaming or deep sleep states.

Cremating the Subtle Body
in the Luminosity of Consciousness

When you die it is Love's Luminosity that faces you. The Pure Luminous Feeling, yes, beyond all cognitive relation forms that all drop away as we enter the Luminous Feeling without the cognition of ancestors, deities, loved ones and so forth. This can be done in death, but it can be done in the waking state or the dream state. In deep sleep there is no doing.

This is not the psychic survival of self as ego. Ego must and will eventually die. It is nothing but a temporal anomaly. Consciousness has no instinct nor need for survival, for

Consciousness knows that it is all that survives the death of ego and body. This Consciousness is Love, of course.

All of our psychology or psychic functioning is in the subtle body. Subtle body is nothing but the active working (energy) of the mind. It can be a help or be a hindrance, an obstruction. Often it is more of an obstruction in that most usually reason blocks the Flow of Love. If I hurt myself I hurt someone else. If I hurt someone else I hurt myself. If I help myself, through liberating that subtle body's active working, well then, what shall that do for the subtle body of someone else? The subtle body is sometimes thought of as One manifesting through many waking bodies. This of course, is a high idea that expresses the emotional reality of shared universal empathy, or the Energy (active working) of Love.

If I learn does another learn? I know that when someone else learns I automatically also learn. If I Love, does another Love? Yes, always, at some level, even if it is hidden and buried deep down below the obvious. Even if they are hurting me, if I can be Love, in the Flow of Love, within the stillness of my heart, at some level they learn Love. For human minds are all deeply connected by the Atma, which is their essential and core Reality. It is the absolute and deepest responsibility of every single soul in existence to realize this Atma and liberate oneself in Atma. Not only for the sake of oneself, but for the sake of others even more so. This is the higher purpose of the Energy of Love. Also, at the last, a seldom thought of condition is that one should liberate oneself in the Atma so as to free any and every guiding power in any form (a rock, a flower, a person, a deity, a pure idea) that has helped you. Is it not the ultimate act of kindness and Love toward the teacher or guiding principle to show that principle compassion and Love by even freeing that guiding power of its responsibility toward you? That teaching power took on the deepest responsibility to you when it assumed the role of taking you where you might want to be. You asked that power or principle where will you take me? If then responsibility was assumed it is now your own responsibility to take in hand, realize and liberate yourself in the Atma, so as to

94

free that power, principle or person from the work of carting you where you wanted to be. But ultimately, the guiding force in your life, if it is a true and genuine one, knows without doubt where you will be taken and with that knowledge that guiding force has already been freed of its responsibility toward you. It is only for you as Atma to know the Atma and so catch up with where you will be.

In the subtle body dreams arise. Have you ever noticed how when one has delightful dreams that bust out of the comedy of the subconscious, these dreams are less often remembered for a longer time than those dreams that are negative or dark in their content? I have. And this forces me to conclude that it is so necessary to see Atma not only in the beautiful and wondrous, but equally so, within the maya of the negative, the maya of memory, of mind, ego, intellect, all this, the maya of dream. You see, the state of luminous flowing Love is really beyond the dualism of comedy and tragedy, or as it may be more often called, joy and sorrow. The two essential emotions that imprint the subtle body with the notion of dualistic experiences. That idea of dualism comes when consciousness identifies with the body as reality and from that arises the fear of death or losing that body, this is the cause of birth, embodiment, rebirth, whatever, as well as the cause of how the ego is generated into existence.

To cremate the subtle body in the Luminosity of Love is to find, discover, realize or liberate the subtle body into its renewed, reborn, freshest or most refreshed state of being. It is not death, when the subtle body goes, one then discovers what is Real, as Love has ever been the higher substance or content of what the subtle body has been seeking all this time. If something is extinguished in Love then Love the Extinguisher is what remains. As the voice eats words and then silence remains so Love remains as stillness in the Heart, but in this sense it is not the heart in the center of the subtle or physical body, but the Heart of Love behind and within the subtle body, all subtle bodies, the universe itself for that matter.

At the moment Love is experienced dualism dies and with

95

the death of dualism the subtle body is cremated in Love. And so is all that is contained within the subtle body. The flow of love is within the subtle body. The stillness of the Heart as Love is not within the subtle body, just as the hand that holds a cherry is not within the cherry. You see, the subtle body is nothing but the mental condition of identity. Emotions imprint the psychic signatures or configurations of identity. These imprints or impressions within the subtle body as to what the subtle body is, give rise to the always wrong or dualistic identity and meaning of Self. Self as Love is never dual, but all the psychic configuration make us feel that it is so and from that we live our lives in the dream world of the subtle body identified with dualistic dream consciousness. It is nothing but the spiritual somnambulism of the Atma. And in that sleep walking we do not see and feel what existed before the break into dualism.

You see, thoughts, within the subtle body, are nothing but Consciousness, in both senses of the word. That of Consciousness as Atma or as consciousness as the substance of the finite figuring mind. In the subtle body are the seven chakras, of course. These chakras are composed of nothing but thought. It is just thought that becomes all the letters of the alphabet that circle around the chakra points and with that the subtle body's self definition comes up and limits the expanse of Consciousness within the subtle body by the very force of the subtle body's limited definition. If we think of Kali's necklace of skulls, which are the same number as the Sanskrit alphabet and it is said that each of the skulls is a letter of that alphabet. So you see Her Necklace is the adornment of the subtle body that identifies that subtle body with its own meaning. So when the necklace is there the subtle body has many meanings through the combination of letters and words. But when She removes Her necklace the subtle body can have only one definition. Pure Love or Pure Consciousness which are the Atma. You see again, the necklace adorns the throat chakra, which is the Voice invigorating space and time with its power. Consciousness comes down through the Voice and is Felt in the heart. The Ineffable moves down through the Infinite, then through the skulls of Kali's necklace as the alphabetical formation of letters within the substance of consciousness and then concludes the circles of identities that we find within the experience of this immanent world. The busy multiplications of all these formations in consciousness are the power of the greatest distraction and so one comes to rest when all this description and so forth is seen to be just what it is in Reality and that is just Atma, the subtle body sees or voices itself now to be just Atma. There is known that there is no other substance to the subtle body than Atma. All psychic function of the subtle body ceases and sees only the Atma within it. Or even as psychic functioning may continue, every wave form of that functioning is felt only as Atma.

As you are Atma, you will not reach the stage of most Joyful Love as long as there is an identification of any sort whatsoever with the subtle body. In deep sleep, and as it should go without saying by now, in Turiya, there is no language, letters, ideation or thinking. Thought is still as Consciousness (Atma). Again, the letters within the subtle body are dead matter, beautifully symbolized by skulls which are lifeless as being without meaning, that is unawakened in the subtle body, until or unless the potentials of Consciousness awaken. This is the Sakti form of the bijas within the subtle body. Sakti is Love and the bijas are the real potential behind and within the letter forms that circulate within the subtle body. Each potential or bija is only Atma. One has a choice, leave the subtle body filled with the imprints of dead lifeless thought or fill that subtle body with the high power of Atma through the potential within what is composing the subtle body. This is why working in the dream material (the subtle body) brings about recognition of what the subtle body is and this becomes that Bodha (awakened consciousness) linga (subtle body).

When consciousness comes out of deep sleep, before recreating the subtle body which was extinguished in the non-dual bliss of deep sleep, that consciousness turning back on what was the energy of its experience in deep sleep, usually projects the ideation of beginning dualism on the surface of that deep sleep, in the thought form of god or deity, of goddess, deitess or the womb of Mother. This is the finest level of dualism where the cognition of a separative feeling originates. The causal body is identical to deep sleep and contains only the memory of non-dual bliss. It is in the subtle body that all memories are contained. So it is only the memory of the subtle body that must be cremated in the Luminosity of Consciousness. If you think deeply about it you must ask yourself, if the nature of the experience of the causal body in deep sleep is non-dual then how can there be any more then but One, so clearly shown at this level of consciousness.

So you see, in consciousness which was a moment ago in the non-dual bliss of deep sleep, a word or ideation stirs by some external or internal stimulation and with that stirring comes the recreation of all the memories contained within the subtle body. Do not hold to the subtle body. It is no better, no more real or unreal than the waking body. For all the dualistic conceptions are only stirred up in the subtle body to begin with and then they are experienced more concretely in the waking body. Even the idea of the seven centers of consciousness are merely conceptions held within the subtle body. It is true. Even the seventh highest center of Absolute Consciousness is merely a conception of Absolute Consciousness held within the mind of the subtle body. In deep sleep where a taste of Absolute Consciousness is experienced, there is no conception of that Consciousness. This proves that the seven centers are only of a conceptual nature, but the power of cognitive energy within the subtle may indeed create the experience of these centers.

Internally, from the point of enlightened viewing, as the Bodhalinga, is there the experience of seven center phases within that subtle body or just the Atma as the true power behind the subtle body? It is a good question. Tantra speaks of the four higher centers and of the three lower centers. Over a time, we may be born into a new waking state body, or even when consciousness descends back down from the fourth center, the heart, or above, that consciousness reenters those three lower centers which are like stone blocks in the spiritual path. At the first center there is the banality of having to make efforts for survival of the physical body. At the second is the fore of sex lust. Then at the third is all the business of the ego blown up with dualistic confusion. These are hard to get over and hard to get through every time we are born again, or when consciousness reenters those dimensions.

The fourth center is the heart and that is where Love first makes its presence known. At the fifth center is the level of Comprehension corresponding to the voice. Then at the sixth center in the forehead is the place of Inner Wisdom. And the whole thing culminates in the seventh center as Illumination in Purest Consciousness at the very top of the skull. Again, the human skull is only dead matter without the presence of the Goddess. So that is why Tantra gives these sacred practices for reestablishing the higher Powers of the fourth, fifth, sixth, and seventh centers of consciousness. But we are talking of conceptions in the subtle body and all these are only those conceptions.

But thinking upon them is certainly a help for posturing consciousness in Kali, the Goddess of the Non-Dual. This is like the Sky Gesture (Khechari Mudra) which is mentioned in Tantra Yoga, where it is said one conquers death. Well yes, the Sky of Consciousness is deathless, but not the physical body. Another yogic example is invoking the shadow body (Pratikopasana), where the shadow of the body is said to be seen in the sky. One should not take it literally. What is meant is that the subtle body and all of the subtle body's contents are seen in the Sky of Consciousness. Or that the Sky of Consciousness is seen pervading and filling those contents of the subtle body itself. It is a beautiful metaphor for spiritual experience. With this comes the thought of the Great Womb Gesture (Brhat Yoni Mudra). The created world is brought back to Original Non-Dualism with this Gesture in Consciousness. One may think it is necessary to do breathing exercises and other related yogic practices in order to bring the Kundalini back to this Original Oneness in the Yoni of the Goddess, but it is not, no one but Mother moves the Kundalini. And Kundalini is the Energy of

Love moved only by the experience of Love which is a gift of Mother. A gift which is always Here. If we believe in created dualism then are we not all Her children coming out of the same womb of Mother? But even the idea of being a child of Mother is a cognition in the subtle body. Am I Mother's child or am I that which has produced the idea of Mother upon the surface of non-dualism, which, without that surface may be boldly experienced as the Pure Free Energy of Non-Dualism? From Here, Love is Understood!

This leaves nothing to be said about the flesh and bone experience of the waking state. The waking state is experienced only through the subtle body. Of course, it is nothing but the Consciousness within the subtle body which is the Real Experiencer. When this is recognized, then there is nothing to solve, nothing to remember, and nothing to figure. The subtle body knows itself to be awakened and so Atma is known, and felt entirely throughout the subtle body. Atma is what Is. The meaning of any and every dream material within the subtle body is Atma. It is Atma alone that is experienced as Bliss in the non-dualism of deep sleep. And it is the backward projection of ignorance of the Atma upon deep sleep which is the cause of dream material. This too is the cause of the sleep character of deep sleep, instead of that condition manifesting in consciousness as the turiya of Consciousness.

If one cognises this as the Womb of Mother, then that cognition becomes the Gesture of the Great Mother. Consciousness rests in the borderline between the waves of manifesting consciousness and Consciousness at its Pure Root and Source. This ideation of a womb, a point of creating consciousness, must also be taken as a limitation to further freer experience, for that ideation will only nourish the subtle body with more dream material. For we seek its cremation in Love, not its continuation as dream material. Any ideation of spiritual conception will do this. One who adores the formless cannot allow any thought form to interfere with that adoration, an adoration which will resolve itself into Experience without the limitation of qualitative forms of consciousness. Still, in the borderline below, a gesturing or posturing in Kali, the Goddess, the Mother, may sometimes be needed.

"There is no doubt that the mind,
which is in reality non-dual,
appears to be dual in dreams;
likewise, there is no doubt
that what is non-dual(the Atma)
appears to be dual in the waking state."
"Therefore non-dualism alone
is free from error."
Gaudapada

Groundwork for
The Goddess and the God Man

The shape of our conscious cognition determines the shape of our Spirituality. For me, that shape is the Goddess. She is that Great Spirituality for me. She is the Power of that and it is from Her that all good things have come. I am nothing, She is everything. By getting into less and less of the impulse of the ego "I", one gets more and more an immediate instinct or intuition of Her in one's life. Both Vedanta and Tantra have in their systems the spiritual paradigm of the four states of consciousness. The waking state is conditioned by the symbol "A". The dream state is illustrated by the letter "U". The state of deep sleep where the dualism of mind movement has ceased for a time is demonstrated by the signature of "M". And turiya, the fourth state designated as the Self in its pure nature of Existence Consciousness and Bliss Ultimate, is illuminated by the complete and unified designation of "OM". Yet there is "something" that is even more capable of grasping this high concept and that is pure Sakti Experience.

A man named M. wrote down his experiences with Ramakrishna (1836-1886). He wrote of everything he saw, heard and encountered with the Goddess loving God man who lived in Dakshineswar, India. He recorded the direct words of the Goddess Kali as conveyed to Ramakrishna and that same Ramakrishna's conceptions and experiences of Her. All this eventually became The Gospel of Sri Ramakrishna , from which most of the quotations in this text are drawn. My other reference and inspiration is The Great Master, written by Swami Saradananda. Quotations borrowed from his book are followed by the letter S. The third source of my contemplation of this commentary comes from The Life of Sri Ramakrishna, written by Swami Nikhilananda. Quotes from there will be indicated by N. Also, it did not seem necessary to have a Sanskrit glossary, for the meanings of such words are present in context with the commentaries that are given.

In my spiritual work, I see Ramakrishna as a most excellent and divine prototype of the dynamic possibility within each living being. He was one who was given the gift of complete and total surrender to the Goddess, and one will conclude that finally this freedom which comes in the state of psychic surrender of the ego, is indeed a gift from Her, as ego cannot submit itself to something that is beyond its orbit in consciousness. For the one half of a century that he occupied in this region of mortal beings, his entire person and his personal life was ultimately a most astounding journey and innate discovery of the Goddess Experience in the shape of Kali.

I sincerely hope and pray that this commentary may be of a progressive class and so serve to help in some small way those who desire to improve their spiritual condition. Ramakrishna had a most exquisite inner relationship with the Goddess, and as Sakti is Immense, so are the relationships to Her. In this study presented for you, the Principles of Connection in Sakti apply with absolute equality to woman or man and, in truth, to human suffering and its solution in consciousness. I pray that, in regard to this equality, those who read this text will not wander into misinterpretation based on the patterns of old thinking; in other words, in the East or the West, and particularly in this commentary, the problem of woman's role in Hindu culture. In Ramakrishna's time, though he cherished and demonstrated the Ideal of the Goddess in a most remarkable way, there still existed as there does even today, the social oppression of women. It becomes a task of separating the water from the container, the spiritual forms from the social forms.

In no way do I wish to present this work as a male-oriented doctrine for the upliftment of man alone. Ramakrishna could have been born as a woman and what is presented here would be exactly the same in the principles of spirituality but, of course, the story would most probably have not reached as widespread an arena, due to this oppression of feminine factors. In fact, there was a time during Ramakrishna's life where he felt that strict identification with the male body alone was such a spiritual obstruction that he wished if he were to be reincarnated that he would be reborn as a woman who lived alone, with her garden, and who spent her whole life in the worship of Krishna. Of course, this cognitive spiritual image is culturally from Ramakrishna's world, in respect to the worship of Krishna. But that different cultural image should be of no limitation to anyone.

Mythological ideologies which have influenced social behaviors have given women the idea that their only function is to be good mothers who, for example, must care for and feed the naughty boy-king Krishna, and that their sole purpose and identity is to bring forth the boy-king. Or they identify with the ideal of the long-suffering Sita, feeling that they alone are supposed to carry the woes of the world. These ideals have created the historical situation of a culturally caged lion. Because, in truth, the inner nature of woman is more like a lion of Kali. Kali who is wildly dancing on the corpse of Shiva, for the absolute principle represented by Shiva is lifeless without the Power of She who is Life, the Divine Current. So, the good mother image on one hand and the wildly dancing liberated Kali on the other put a contradiction into the subconscious behavioral response in both women and men, from their respective views. Both think that they must necessarily be one way or the other, instead of a unified wild dancing mother in a woman or even a man, or simply in the respective and accepting attitudes of each to the other.

103

May this Prayer never Cease. May this prayer be remembered in unceasing wonder. May this poetic begging ever be effective to remove every trace of resentment, anger, or fear in regard to our skills in the spiritual Love of the Goddess through all forms of Love as those apparently solid images of waking state conditions; as the momentary emanations of dream state conditions, as the forms most personal and chosen of the formless that rise and then sink into the Self tranquil in the state that is free of dream. Can this be Mother's Turiya? It is the Goddess alone who gives birth to these god beings, whose prayers are continuous in hunger or abundance, tiredness or rest, waking or dreaming, ever engaged in Sakti worship, and so, free of the fear of death or return, never engaged in the lower disparaging mind function, and so, free to practice the Exercise of Sakti's Joy.

May the strings of my mind be tuned to the music of the Goddess, and may it first be pleasing to Her and then, second, pleasing to others. May this prayer-commentary be continuous, under the surface of life, even farther under and deeper than the poet's voice, unceasingly engaged in the purest cerebral ecstasy, filled with Love, no matter whether or not the body and psyche have caught up or not caught up with Her. Whether or not these two functions of body and mind have cooled out and have become still or whether they are continuing to be psychically hot, it does not matter, for it will come no matter what varying mood displays itself in the content of the mind current, as it might be frustration or despair, free consciousness or joy, or psychic weight, simple human redundancy or deeply spiritual insight. May this prayer commentary ever be continuous on the lowest floor of the mind, whether or not the Current of Love is awake, where Her Blessed Blissful Toes may touch the very top of the skull of what may or may not be the best in this poet, moving and stirring the Current of Love in him.

Whether or not the adornment of knowledge and its fragrance are present or absent, at the first stage or the seventh stage, may this poet ever elect to direct the force of thought and feeling that frequently and ordinarily position themselves to the left or the right, now take that current in and within the sacred midpoint of blessed non- dualism. May all this continually be sacrificed in the sweet fire of surrender ever burning up the roots of self- importance and the mental states that know not the sacred connection that this continuous prayer brings by its potential in poetic capacity. May it instantly change the mind into the mood which undoubtedly knows the real feeling of pure sweet simple non-dualism, that which is nothing but Love, being nothing else but Love. As the Consciousness of which has no definition in the mind, so mind must be continuous in its prayer of shaping itself to this Consciousness which is Love.

Within this prayer continuous the sweet vigorous poetry of our inner dialogue can never all be written down in its entirety. So I give up the efforts of doing so, except at Her powerful demand. At the conjunction of luminosity and shadow, She is indescribable in that She devours all we may know. At the moment when luminosity melts with shadow, She is what heals us of all we have known. At this indescribable midpoint, She lifts us to not suffer the misery in the strangest knowing. For She does not wake, nor dream, nor sleep. She is the One that was, before death was made. She was there long before the thought of immortality was wed to us.

The new mind may be discovered everyday. It is the state of Consciousness, pure Sakti Experience, filled with the Energy of Loving Emotion. May the Sacred Imprints of Her Blessed and Beautiful Lotus Feet ever be the shape of my mind. Could the true nature of Love most simply be Empathic Identity? For it is the Empathic Identity with Love that pulls everyone toward what they seek to be. And may it now, once and for all, please be so very clearly defined, that it is not a self-centered, self-realization. It is the Super Abundance of Goddess Experience. And it is She alone who grants this, to any who seek Her with the extreme desire to find that Empathic Identity within Her.

It is my wish that this text be dedicated

to my beloved spiritual companion,
my most cherished friend
in this journey of life,
Sarah Elisabeth Grace.

"By You Alone, the Goddess,
this world is filled."
"You are, O Goddess,
the Ruler of all that is
moving and unmoving."
"Salutations, again and again,
to the Goddess,
Who Abides in All Beings
as Consciousness."
rendered from the
sacred text
Chandi

"To my Divine Mother I prayed only for pure love. I offered
flowers at Her Lotus Feet and prayed to Her: 'Mother, here is
Thy virtue, here is Thy vice. Take them both and grant me only
pure love for Thee. Here is Thy knowledge, here is Thy
ignorance. Take them both and grant me only pure love for
Thee. Here is Thy purity, here is Thy impurity. Take them
both, Mother, and grant me only pure love for Thee. Here is Thy
dharma (right), here is Thy adharma (wrong). Take them both,
Mother, and grant me only pure love for Thee.'"
"O Mother! O Embodiment of Om! Mother, how many things
people say about Thee! But I don't understand any of them. I
don't know anything, Mother. I have taken refuge at Thy feet. I
have sought protection in Thee. O Mother, I pray only that I
may have pure love for Thy Lotus Feet, love that seeks no
return. And Mother, do not delude me with Thy world-
bewitching maya. I seek Thy protection. I have taken refuge in
Thee."
Sri Ramakrishna

THE GODDESS
and the God Man
An Explorative Study of the Intimate Relationship
of the Goddess Kali
with Sri Ramakrishna of Dakshineswar

"Hello, Mother!"

This very statement raises the question as to whether or not Ramakrishna's consciousness of the Goddess was perpetual. He greets Her. It is the communion of him as a natural man with Her, the Goddess; perhaps out of the indivisible depth of nirvikalpa samadhi he has returned to a state of mind where Her visible living presence is seen, and so, he greets Her.

"Mother, good-bye."

Can one say that Ramakrishna's communion with the Goddess was over, or is this just apparently so? For in truth, if one examines his life and the state of his mind, one will come to the conclusion that he had a perpetual consciousness of the Goddess.

"The Mother showed me that all this is verily maya. She alone is real, and all else is the splendour of Her maya."

This beautiful comment perhaps throws light on the above questions of his communion with Her occurring or being apparently over. Is there a kind of divine phasing in and phasing out? Ordinary minds would certainly understand this as such. For I, myself, as one, do most certainly phase in and phase out of, more or less, states of clarity, conditions of alertness, and emotions of love, peace, happiness, and their opposites. Whether She comes or goes, Ramakrishna has known deeply that She alone is real. The cosmic measurements of maya are but the splendour of Her coming and going, apparently.

"I used to roam at night in the streets, all alone, and cry to the Divine Mother, 'O Mother, blight with Thy thunderbolt my desire to reason!'"

Can you imagine such a state? Roaming the streets alone at night begging the Goddess to remove the obstruction. Who has done that even in the safety of their home? Who feels that much spiritual passion to want the figuring process of the dual mind content to be removed so that the direct experience of the Goddess may be gotten? The three states of waking, dreaming and deep sleep all come from and return to the Goddess. The universe is fully contained within these three states, individually and cosmically, so all reasoning processes deal only with these three states or conditions. If that process is removed or relaxed, at that very instant, the consciousness of the Goddess comes forth. If the mind is engaged in the function of intellectual duality, then how can that consciousness be openly accepting to the experience of the non-dual, the ultimate nature of the Goddess, which as a Higher Function, takes over the function of the ego?

Passing through all these states, I said to the Divine Mother: 'Mother, in these states there is separation. Give me a state where there is no separation.' Then I remained for some time absorbed in the Indivisible Satchidananda."

How indeed can the function of dualistic figuring ever enter the divine content of the indivisible experience of sheer existence, unfettered consciousness, and love that knows no boundary? Satchidananda is such. If consciousness is occupied with the process of reasoning, it creates an instant state of separation from Oneness. Oneness needs no figuring nor reasoning. Two things are needed for one to reason about the other.

"There are two persons in this. One, the Divine Mother-" "Yes, one is She. And the other is Her devotee."

Here, you may easily see that Ramakrishna could flow on the current of the Goddess from the non-dual state to the dual

109

state and back to the non-dual state. His identity seems to have two conditions, one as a mind that is devoted to the adoration of the Goddess and one that is completely and utterly identified with Her. Then the mind is gone and there is only Oneness. Nevertheless, even in the state of dualistic mentality, he would feel Her just the same. It appears to be of the nature of divine coexistence. Was this spiritual quality or sentiment innate in the self that was born or incarnated in the mind and body of Ramakrishna? Or was it purely and directly an Incarnation of the Goddess Kali Herself?

"Now I see that I and the Mother have become one."

Yet, ultimately and finally, the "I" and the Goddess are One, or, perhaps, are in a continual condition of becoming One. Whichever, Oneness with Her is the ultimate conclusion. How does this wondrous example relate to us who are simply ordinary souls in our mind/body complex? Can that non-dual consciousness be had by one and all? In truth, is any soul ordinary? If we can see the demonstration of an incarnation as a fully human person, instantly the same reality becomes suddenly and automatically reachable or experientially possible. In truth, the cognition of this innate human potential should not be confined by the effects produced out of our traditional concepts of what an incarnation is, in fact. A human being.

"Sometimes I say to myself in the Kali temple, 'O Mother, the mind is nothing but Yourself.' Therefore Pure Mind, Pure Buddhi, and Pure Atman are one and the same thing."

For me, this is one of the most amazing statements Ramakrishna gives. It is the most profoundly relaxing spiritual position. What is this, the mind itself is nothing other than Mother Sakti. As one attentively focuses the current of consciousness which is Pure Consciousness at the midpoint of non-dualism within the conscious state, the truth of this remark to the Goddess becomes clear. She is the mind and, therefore, no search or effort for Her is needed, as She is the mind itself. She is the pure mind, that which is the true conveyor of spiritual

110

knowledge. She is intelligence or intellect, the mirror of consciousness which simply reflects what comes before it (buddhi). She is the true Self, the pure Atman as the fourth unfettered state of Consciousness, free and yet within the three states of consciousness which are the waking, the dreaming, and the deep sleep state.

As this current of consciousness becomes more steadily focused at the center position of the brain core where the dualistic hemispheres meet and join, the unity of that higher current creates a revolution in the conscious state. You see that current of consciousness is always there, always has been there, and is Consciousness itself, forever going unnoticed. But as attention is directed to it, it becomes more evident as to its existence and joyful presence. Then, mind, intelligence, and self are seen, all to be but one and the same thing: the Goddess. But until the profound non-dual unity is experienced there within the conscious current, the three ideas of mind, intellect, and self-being are distinguished to be different due to the dualistic training of the mind. As mind itself is the very Self of the Mother, no dualism can exist, but this is not experienced as long as the ego impulse is there overriding or masking one's true and innate spiritual condition. The truth of this spiritual insight is the same, whether the mind as being recognized to be the Mother, is embodied or disembodied.

"But who are you? It is the Divine Mother who has become all this. It is only as long as you do not know Her that you say, 'I', 'I'."

Who and what are you? It is the Divine Mother who alone has become the who and the what that every living being is in reality. She is the True Self. The Answer within the question of who and what we all are. She is the spiritual conclusion to the question of this universe. From the clear insight of the highest flight of absolutely non-dual spiritual consciousness, it may never be denied. But as long as the impulse of "I" or the throb of ego continues, that wondrous and most beautiful spiritual gift goes sadly unnoticed. Because of ego, who you are is not

111

perceived. Because of ego, Mother is not seen! Again, the Principle described here when one does not know Her is the same, whether that impulse of ego, which is the tendency to think only in reference to the "I" and not the greater Sakti Experience, which is all consuming, as She consumes all time, is embodied or disembodied. The realization of "I" is not the conclusion. Even as the search for the Atma, which is ever attended with the idea of saving, keeping, or salvaging the ego. Many get caught up in that attempt and neglect to see the greater and more immense experience of Pure Sakti, the Goddess.

'In this state I realize that it is the Mother alone who has become everything. I see Her everywhere. In the Kali temple I found that the Mother Herself had become everything--even the wicked, even the brother of Bhagavat Pundit."

From the level of the dualistic mind, thinking proceeds with what may appear to be wicked and what may appear to be wonderful. This is the precognitive judgment of the mind state that limits us all. Yet, from the non-dual state of Mother Consciousness, nothing is eliminated from that Consciousness or is seen as not innately having that Consciousness within it. To perhaps put it more simply, if an all good power created this world universe, then how could anything all good ever create something that is distinctly wicked or not, at some level, having the innate power of good within it? Again, darkness or shadow is there only to glorify or magnify the unfolding of what is good in parallel to it. As our minds are usually involved in only one small part or definition of the universe, we do not usually see what is going on in the greater immense matrix of things. We define something and that limits us immediately to that definition. How often, if not every time, do we experience something we feel is a curse at the first burst and later discover it to be a blessing in disguise? Also, something good may happen but, at the time, we do not realize the trail of difficulty which falls in its wake. Sakti, the Mother, never curses, She only blesses. Yet, it is so that challenges appear as entanglement, enmeshment, or the embracing of a problem, individual or collective, in order to keep us grounded; to keep us from floating away into some ego fantasy or personal legend or some delusive, grandiose history of our ego.

"The Divine Mother showed me in the Kali temple that everything is Chinmaya, the Embodiment of Spirit; that it is She who has become all this --the image, myself, the utensils of worship, the door-sill, the marble floor. Everything is indeed Chinmaya."

The primary and profound experience of the Goddess in the Kali temple is described by Ramakrishna with slight, subtle turns of meaning on different occasions, as in Mother becoming everything and seeing Her everywhere. Here, She is described as being the embodiment of Spirit or as everything that is, is the embodiment of Her. Elsewhere, She is described as Pure Spirit without the idea or cognition of embodiment. Again, She is described as Consciousness immanently pervading every form and yet spontaneously transcending them. Embodied or free of embodiment, it is the Mother, Sakti, the Goddess. As the human mind cognizes the dualism of forms and the formless, it is no reality to the true nature of the Goddess. It is the dualistic mental preoccupation of the cognitive mind which has been trained to think only within the realm of dualism.

"The Divine Mother revealed to me in the Kali temple that it was She who had become everything. She showed me that everything is full of Consciousness. The Image was Consciousness, the altar was Consciousness, the water-vessels were Consciousness, the door-sill was Consciousness, the marble floor was Consciousness --all was Consciousness."

This Consciousness is always here. Yet, it is the polish of the perceptual instrument which sees that this is so. We are told that the truth is that the Goddess is everywhere as Consciousness. Even more so, that nothing exists, in fact, except for that Consciousness. The perceptual instrument may indeed see this Spiritual Current with no masking of that beautiful state. But it does most certainly depend on the internal cognitive power of that perceptual instrument for its capacity to see what is Really Here! Consciousness is present always. It is not a manifestation of a principle which sometimes is here and sometimes not. It is a matter of coming to this perception of what is always here. The phasing in or phasing out of this Consciousness does not determine whether or not this Consciousness exists. It is merely the tuning of the perceptual instrument. The mind may be heavy with gravity dragging it down, or turning continuously with its own activity pulling it up, or even calm, balanced, tranquil, quiet, and finely tuned, as it then perceives greater unity and harmony. Gravity depresses the ego nature; activity asserts the ego nature; and balance gives gratification to the ego nature.

Still, ego holds to dualism and is yet to enter the not-two state of oneness where consciousness is utterly free and nothing binds that consciousness. This is the state where consciousness is not so engaged with the energy field of the physical world, nor even embracing the balanced field of psychic equality. It has even moved past the movement of a spiritual current. It is then just Consciousness, entertaining no other thought, feeling, or positioning in this conscious state. It is Consciousness, right here, right now, in the right mind or, even better, without the concept of "here", "now", or "mind", with no defining limitation as to a location point within the current of time.

"I found everything inside the room soaked, as it were, in Bliss - -the Bliss of Satchidananda. I saw a wicked man in front of the Kali temple; but in him also I saw the Power of the Divine Mother vibrating."

Here we see that Pure Existence, that Pure Consciousness, that Pure Bliss of Love, soaks everything within the room where he was having this experience. Everything was wet, soaked, saturated, or drenched with the Principle of Reality and that includes the person who is having this experience. It also includes the person who is, apparently, on the surface, one who is contradictory to the state of Satchidananda. Though the person is not aware of what is within them at the spiritual level, the one who is at that level perceives this Reality all too clearly. It is not so hard to understand from the point of a vast overview that everyone is simply reaching for Love, for Reality, blindly or with twenty/twenty vision, from the position of their own conditioned states, cognitive levels, psychic plateaus, and so forth. The high view of the loving heart sees that no matter where another may be in the scale of cause and effect and its unfolding, there, no matter what, the Power of the Goddess is in some way vibrating, as energy, as consciousness, as the unfolding of that soul.

"That was why I fed a cat with the food that was to be offered to the Divine Mother. I clearly perceived that the Divine Mother Herself had become everything --even the cat."

From this high plane of consciousness it may be clearly seen that nothing exists except the Goddess. All dualism as to the thoughts that this is She and this is not She are gone. Nothing is left in the experiential mind but the experience of the Goddess. What a State! Nothing is not She and therefore there is nothing that is not sacred. Because She is within everything, every being, even animals, there is no distinction in consciousness as to what is sacred or not so. It is the clearest perception that the spiritual essence of the Goddess lives in every living being!

"I wept before the Mother and prayed, 'O Mother, please tell me, please reveal to me, what the yogis have realized through yoga and the jnanis through discrimination.' And the Mother has revealed everything to me. She reveals everything if the devotee cries with a yearning heart. She has shown me everything that is in the Vedas, the Vedanta, the Puranas, and the Tantras."

It is shown here that the Goddess can and does reveal everything. This means not just inner spiritual knowledge and the state of loving bliss, but, somehow, She has even shown to Ramakrishna the practical and pragmatic instructions that are given in the sacred texts of his cultural spiritual world. It may be that the Tantra, Vedanta, and Purana were taught to him by hearing, which they were, as it is the practice in India of listening to the holy writings being read, but Ramakrishna perceived everything as coming forth from the Goddess, and so this might perhaps be one interpretation for the logical mind to feed on. Yet, then again, all written spiritual knowledge originally came from somewhere within, so maybe somehow all the prior practical, technical, and historical spiritual information was indeed revealed to him by the Goddess within. New research has shown that everyone naturally has creative ideas, as, for example, in the dream state, yet some are just a little better at capturing those ideas in the waking mind. Those people surround, challenge, and broaden the waking mind to the capacity of capturing creative ideas that are continuously rising up out of consciousness.

"One by one She has revealed all these to me." *"Yes, She has taught me everything. Oh, how many things She has shown me!"*
Some of these things we will not know unless we embrace the abysmal knowledge of the Goddess, for some of these "many things" were not written down. And some of these "many things" are only shown within the intimacy of pure Sakti Experience.

"The Mother reveals to me that She Herself has become everything."
Nevertheless, whatever is learned is somehow She Herself, who has become everything. The comprehension of this principle is very lofty. Could it be that somehow She is the current of all divinely inspired thought? Everyday, my prayer is to discover more and more, how Para (Highest) Sakti (Power) works for us, in us, and around us. She is the work, the focus, the creativity, the high rapture, the purpose and pleasure of insight, connection, communion and realization.

"She is formless and, again, She has forms."
Who may know Her with the limited body and mind in the form of the waking or dream state? Who can bring that

knowledge of Her into those conditions? Yet, in the formless consciousness of the deep sleep condition, there is ever present within everyone the non-dual and formless bliss experience of that state. Yet one must not forget that the pure Sakti experience goes far beyond even the experience of the fourth condition (turiya), as pure consciousness in the bright evidence of one's own conscious spiritual experience. Can anyone ever really know Her as She is? The human mind is so conditioned to think only within conditions, but one cannot doubt that a genuine sentiment of Her presence rises up every now and then.

"She will let you know Her true nature."

Most profound, for it is She who brings forward the pure Consciousness of Sakti Experience. In the deepest depth of deep sleep, non-duality is experienced, for no dualistic vibrational content operates within that state of consciousness. In the waking and dream states there is the function of dualism within the consciousness of the mind. You see, our perception is trained so strongly to generally see only dualism and rarely to be alert to the non-dual, but it is here within us all. She brings that non-dual consciousness forward so that we may have direct awareness with the existence of its reality. She brings it forward into the conscious state so we may have knowledge of this reality which both permeates and transcends the waking, dreaming, and deep sleep conditions. Her nature is expressed in those conditions always, but Her true nature is never confined by the boundaries of those conditions; nor do the concepts of dualism and non-dualism really define Her. If you say She is non-dual, well, the presence of the dual world before us contradicts that statement. And if you say that She is dual, well, also, that statement is contradicted by the evidence of non-duality in the deep sleep condition. The mind is conditioned to think either in oneness or multiplicity. But this conditional thinking does not grasp that She is, as a fourth possibility; the Consciousness of pure Sakti Experience. The consciousness that makes up the mind is capable of knowing turiya, the fourth state, but in both turiya and deep sleep there is no mind as we

117

know it in the waking and dream states. However, there is consciousness. That consciousness is Her true nature, but She is so much more than just that. Simple turiya consciousness is like going to the ocean and taking one personal bucket of water, whereas pure Sakti Experience is more like an astronomically vast absorption in a dynamic living spirituality. Where the other state, turiya consciousness, is like a single burning star.

> *"That which is Brahman is Sakti, and That, again, is the Mother."*

Words turn on themselves redundantly, trying to express the Feeling of Non-Duality. This has always been a problem of poets and people of realization in those moments of ultimate sensation at the supersensuous sphere of comprehension and the experiential sentiment of the spiritual. Sakti is Divine Power. Brahman is Divine Absolute. They are both the Goddess, the Mother. She is within the manifest world and beyond, totally past the realm of dualistic words or logic.

> *"I always say to the Divine Mother: 'O Mother! Thou art the Operator and I am the machine. I do as Thou makest me do, I speak as Thou makest me speak."*

Sakti, the Divine Mother, is Brahman, the abysmal and indefinable Infinite. She is the Operator! We hold the delusive conception that it is the ego that does, makes, and speaks, but it is She who puts life into the machine. Once this is felt, the dualistic sense of ego as a separate activity is lifted off and differentiated consciousness goes with it. In all truth, it is simply the memory of duality or the memory of ego, which as mind has attached itself to the complication of all other memories. When one becomes exhausted with this, then consciousness and feeling naturally return to what Is! Satchidananda, pure Sakti Experience comes when one lets go of the hold on memory-ego dualism. One no longer needs to assert the ego in order to feel or to affirm one's own Reality. The dualistic apprehension or inconvenience with agreement (friendship) or disagreement (enmity) in the mind content, or any relational connection, no longer exists as an ego triggered spiritual stumbling block. Truth exists, whether you agree or disagree with its Reality, it still exists. Truth is, whether ego sees it or not. Ego is a delicate tendril of Sakti. She has made the ego, so its substance has originated from Her. It is, at any rate, a strange phenomena, that the ego, with this Great Power behind it, is still so easily wounded. Squelch the ego and it screams, placate it and it expands, suppress it and it get louder, give it permanence and it dies, restrain it and it breaks loose. So it appears that this ego is satiated only when it becomes sweetened with Sakti.

"Whatever names and forms you see are nothing but the manifestations of the power of Chitsakti. Everything is the power of Chitsakti --even meditation and he who meditates."

A most astounding statement. If one understands this correctly, you will realize that it is Sakti Consciousness that is doing everything, has done everything, and will do everything. The release that comes with this understanding brings about tremendous and absolute relaxation. She is you who meditates and She is all your meditation. All activity or manifestation of consciousness is Her work, not yours, not the ego's, for it is but a player and She is the director. Even ego is a form of Chitsakti and so is the name associated with the identity form of the ego. What a wonder. This is the way of the kitten who has totally surrendered to its mother or, even more so, never needed to surrender, always knowing without doubt that the mother cat would do everything. The opposite metaphor of spiritual attitude is that of the monkey who must hold with great intensity to its mother, out of the fear that she might leave the helpless ego all alone. But that too is a manifestation of the power of Sakti Consciousness. Nothing is outside Her. She continually sings this truth in the breathing process of every living being. The inward and outward breath never ceases to proclaim the chorus of Her ever continuous perpetual presence. Saham, She (Sa), am I (aham) voices itself in all life. This is the song of the cosmic prana (life force or vital energy) as the voice of Her vital energetic living joy in excessive dimensions, boundless and with no end. Indeed, the outward breath is the manifest waking state itself and the inward breath is the dream condition returning. So, the calm stillness of deep sleep is the suspended breath where there is no dualistic movement, as in waking and dreaming activity, moving inward and outward as names and forms and conditions; or as thoughts in meditation, or feelings that the one who meditates may have. It is all Her. She is always here with a nod and a smile affirming the reality of your existence in non-duality with Her. She is all that is packed into the river of life. Even all subconscious imprints within the play of dream activity, or the conscious prints within the waking mind, are all, one and all, the charge of Her Energetic Power. So, what was resistance in the shape of memories, moods, thoughts, and conditions; now becomes assistance, benefit, and comfort, causing one to stand with the Goddess in the unsurpassed vigor of Her spiritual intensity. This understanding becomes indelibly printed in both the subconscious and conscious mind, so that whether one is in the state of waking or dreaming, the sight, mood or memory of Sakti is not lost. It is She alone that is born as you who are the direct awareness that is ever-present as Her!

"The Mother showed me that there exists only One, and not two. It is Satchidananda alone that has taken all these various forms."

The cognition of the human mind is so accustomed to thinking in terms of dualism when, in reality, what Sakti is, Is just the One; so simple, so utterly simple, such sweet simplicity. She is the non-dual One, and the "two"' and all the "various forms" that come later; yet the mind consciousness so often seeks the diagrammatic complex of technical, mystical, metaphysical, and spiritual principles to satiate its hunger for an answer; when all the while, the answer sought is the sweet experience of simple happiness. You see, the neuronal network is constantly remapping and readjusting itself to catch the experience of Consciousness in the Single State. Eventually, the nervous system, the emotions and consciousness in the waking and dreaming conditions, clears up or tunes up to the Single Un-throbbing Pulse of Living Sakti Consciousness. Then, there are moments when there are no fluctuations or needed adjustments to catch the "One", as a visceral and innately instinctive experience. It may be something akin to laughter. A split instant after the comprehension of something comical, the brain sweeps itself clear, with an electrical impulse, and then laughter arises. It is the experience of empathic simplicity and honest universality, wherein the beauty of oneness or non dualism is recognized. Others may attempt to explain this state by the full function of the neurotransmitters, grasping the unique human condition; when serotonin, oxcytocin, endorphines, dopamine and the newly discovered anandamides (related to ecstasy, joy, bliss: the meaning of ananda) are all on full alert. It is food for organic thought, if your mind tends to that direction, and, of course, an intriguing potential that exists innately within the human system.

"We can go into the inner chamber only when She lets us pass through the door. Living outside,we see only outer objects, but not that Eternal Being, Existence --Knowledge --- Bliss Absolute."

It is this diagrammatic consciousness of the external outer objects, the association of images in consciousness, instead of the focus on the simple consciousness which makes up the various images, that keeps us from passing through Her door. Within the "inner chamber" is pure Sakti Experience. She lets us go there when consciousness comes to the conclusion that this consciousness is, in reality, free of all images and diagrammatic associations and is never actually bound by these conditions appearing in the waking and dream states. The mind, ever engaged in the current of circulation with dualistic thinking in the waking and dream states, cannot enter there. But Love is allowed to do so, even unbidden. Then again, the mind itself is nothing but She in reality, so everything is reduced to the sweetest simplicity of the Sakti Experience, which is nothing but

Love. Therefore, one does not have to repeat the lesson of life over and over until it is gotten right. Love alone knows how to live, cherish, and be; how to answer the question of self to other people and to oneself. And Love alone has not fear of death, for Love knows not what death is. The body and mind are what is afraid of death, but Love never has the sentiment of termination within it; for Love is not an emotional configuration which calculates the measure of time against the phenomena of apparent death; not true spiritual Love. Even just the ordinary emotion of Love usually sees the experience of life with a greater perspective. Love is the inner chamber of the infinite precious moment of now. Love, as spiritual knowledge, understands what has gone in the past. Love, as spiritual trust, knows and feels automatically, how the future is to be lived. Sakti, keep the state of my mind, always, in the high soaring current of Love, for only from there may I see what Life Is! All else is blindness of the heart.

"Have faith. Depend on God. Then you will not have to do anything for yourself. Mother Kali will do everything for you. Jnana goes as far as the outer court, but bhakti can enter the inner court."

Here, God is mentioned. Though words must be used to speak, Ramakrishna did not differentiate Goddess and God, as most of us do so powerfully in one way or the other, giving priority to one of the two. It is fascinating to note that the Old High Germanic, Icelandic, Dutch, and so forth, words for God, such as Gott, Godh, Gudh, etc, originally meant a Supreme Being, a Supreme Power which did not have the ideas of sexual gender conceptually attached to it. It was only after the misshapen distortion of Judaic- Christian thinking that God became a masculine syntactic form, completely eliminating a feminine concept of Spiritual Power. As words go deeply ingrained in consciousness, this particular limited definition of God has become a deeply prejudiced problem in the mind of most people in general. But for Ramakrishna, the words were interchangeable in their use and absolutely equal. Mother, God, and Kali, all the same. The syntactic arrangement of words did not trouble the mind of Ramakrishna.

"Reason, mere intellectual knowledge, is like a man who can go only as far as the outer court of the house. But bhakti is like a woman who goes into the inner court."

Cognitive reasoning can never enter into the pure spiritual dimension of unfettered Reality. It can only go as far as the outer court. Love, pure and non-dual, is what enters the inner court of the Goddess. Love is the only part of us which may go there. Even the Vedantic process of eliminating the unreal from the Real is a routine methodology of the dualistic intellectual sifting and reasoning through the ego mind. It only goes as far as the outer court. Even the finest impulse of ego is still ego, even with the highest noble intent, and so, will bind Self with action, when all action is the Working of Her Power.

"Bhakti may be likened to a woman who has access to the inner court of a house. Jnana can go only as far as the outer rooms."

Love is the Current that runs Deepest in every one of us. Love (Bhakti) goes directly into the chamber, the inner court of Reality, as the finest expression of Truth as the Self. Pure Feeling is easily allowed into the spiritual chamber without any interrogation of the mind whatsoever. Love goes from ego mind immediately to the Goddess. She is Love, formless and yet within and beyond forms. The mind cannot get it. Love alone knows how to completely surrender. Complete surrender takes place when the ego mind realizes that it has no control. It is the complete letting go of that idea. It is difficult for the ordinary mind to grasp the fact that even the apparent process of decisions and choices is due to the karmic set of circumstances which have been instilled or ingrained within the ego mind. It appears that one makes a personal choice out of free will but, in reality, that choice is based upon a preexisting set of causes and effects to which the mind is actually a slave. The flow of life goes on and people do not realize this until death approaches and the ego mind wakes up and says to itself that it has no controlling power of its own. A form of last ditch effort for spirituality then arises in that ego mind which has now accepted its helplessness and prays to a Great Help for assistance. How unfortunate that this beautiful spiritual condition does not take place at an earlier time where it could be enjoyed for a longer period of time. That again is the question: can the ego mind control the events in time or space due to causes and their effects?

"The Divine Mother gives Her devotee Brahmajnana too."

As patriarchal thinking has ingrained within most minds that things feminine are secondary, it comes to the light of truth that this is not so. It is She who gives, bestows, or makes a gift of the Primary Knowledge of Absolute God. That Brahmajnana is none other than the non-dual state of nirvikalpa samadhi, where all dualism is gone, even those primal and powerful dualisms of thoughts that this Primary Experience is gender-defined. All barriers broken, one sees that She is beyond all dualism. Then one Loves the world as the Goddess, and so world is not world; it is Her, from the highest altitude of pure spirituality. For God has become what we are and we are what God Is. Non-dualism is a state of Consciousness that occurs when the diametric paradox of the dual stops. There is not even a coming or a becoming to it... no God, no us, no arrival; because there was never a departure. Dualism is to presume that the ego and God are forever two principles. Qualified non-dualsim is to see God and ego as one; yet there is still the retaining of ego identity. In complete non-dualism, ego is gone, and so are all ideas about its existence. From this rapturous apex of advaita (non-dual) jnana (knowledge) there is no confusion, no conflict, no dependent relationship, no connection, no formulas of thought, no other stages of emotion, nothing hidden, and no discovering. It is Love, in Love, in the Goddess, with no world problem at all, the ultimate zenith of pure dynamic spiritual solution. It is the Love that has always been felt within every living being, innately and unceasingly here as the essence of human nature. Love is what this delicate created being Is, and what it seeks. If there is a need at all, it is to allow oneself the Gift of Love. She will give this Love to you, once the maya, or measurement of thought has turned or folded back into the Ecstatic Love of pure Sakti, by Her Power, which alone extinguishes the conflicting paradox of dual thinking. Indeed, is there any thought within dualism that may reach Her exuberant peak of mood cognizance, the stature, esteem and sagacity of what She really is?

"That which is Syama is also Brahman."
"Brahman is Sakti; Sakti is Brahman. They are not two."

She is not the wife of, nor the mistress of, nor the handmaiden attached to, nor the mother of, nor the consort joined with Brahman, the gender-neutral Infinite. She is the Infinite. She is Pure God, if you wish, divested of the mask that we think of as God. And so, She is profound Bliss, the Divine Power of Excessive Joy and the highest Loft of Contentment beyond all words. She is the Lady of Rapture and Ecstasy and that is Her Gift to us. She is the one Divine Power indicated by the root word, 'Sak'. It is that Power of Hers which has in turn become both the nirguna consciousness, which is free of modifications, and the saguna consciousness, which has modifications. She is both Chit Sakti, the Goddess as Consciousness Absolute, and She is Maya Sakti, the Power which manifests the modification out of that same Consciousness which we name the world, the universe, or the play of life. Syama is Mother in Her original primordial state of Absolute Non- Dual Darkness, where not even a secondary shadow is cast, not even an emanation of light.

"When there were neither the creation, nor the sun, the moon, the planets, and the earth, and when darkness was enveloped in darkness, then the Mother, the Formless One, Maha Kali, the Great Power, was one with Maha Kala, the Absolute."

A description of the absolute non-dual reality, before the appearance of creation itself or any dual existence whatsoever. Consciousness perceives and experiences no difference between "Power" and "Absolute". Truthfully, consciousness was not even created then, so the concept of a perceiver or experiencer is inapplicable at this point before any dualism existed as a perplexing question over the face of the deepest darkness of the abysmal, infinite, non-dual, formless oneness. It is the Goddess Herself and so knowing this there should be no fear of the abysmal, that which has no bottom, no top, no start, no finish. Because this is the very nature of non-dual existence, we must admit our surrender while we acknowledge our joy, our ecstasy at the wonder of what is finally indescribable: your original spiritual nature. This is placed upon the conscious surface of pure Sakti Experience with such words as ineffable, effulgent, luminous, infinite, and so on. Somewhere deep within the core of our being we remember this as the reality which is, for from it we have come. It is the great (Maha) state of Sakti Experience before time (Kali) and the timeless (Kala) became separated, along with the extension of spatial identity in dualistic consciousness. The great wonder of this Sakti Experience is to contact the remembrance of our original being and live not separate from this within our daily cycle of life. The impulse of ego now quietens down into the Immense Current of Sakti, where Real Power is found, discovered, without ego, its identity, or the contest of conscious thought. One is no longer compelled nor impelled by the ego identity, to rationalize, analyze or intellectualize Experience away, nor vitiate this feeling by the process of contending cognitive reasoning. The current of thought is now sweetened by Sakti. And so, the process of thought is no longer antagonistic to Direct Experience. One no longer needs to struggle against the thought of this Experience, for one comes to know that the substance, the essence, and the true content of the psyche, is Love, which transcends all that is considered to be rational. Love is the Feeling that Knows without thinking. So, from now onward, the return to the cognitve process only appears on the surface to interrupt Experience. Then you and I both may Live what these words are saying.

"Thus one cannot think of Brahman without Sakti, or of Sakti

without Brahman."

And it is that very thinking itself that creates a sense of duality, as if Sakti and the Infinite are different. Yet, as one begins to think with the Sakti Experience that She is all, all thoughts, everything, then ones sees and feels that Infinite within the perception of everything as Sakti. A smooth, flowing perception becomes the nature of the movement in living.

"Brahman is verily Kali."

She, Kali, the Goddess, is the One Infinite Unbound Most Absolute. What could be more simple? Or, if we say, Kali is truthfully Brahman, then does the high Brahman idea somehow keep us from knowing or hide from us what pure Sakti is in the dynamic, immediate, living Kali Experience? Can the concept of an Absolute so high disguise from us what is our immediate experience? She alone is Real and Brahman alone is Real and yet, they are not two. Dualism confuses. Is it She, as the Luminosity of Brahman, that removes the darkness covering Brahman? Kali is that very Brahman, the Great non-dual Infinite! All logic turns on itself as the current of conscious conception slowly stills. If one thinks of one thing as real, then, automatically, something appears in the mind covered with the thought that it is unreal or illusory, and so consciousness will continue to try to interpret Reality with dualism. In pure Sakti Experience there is no unreal; turiya, deep sleep, dreaming, and waking experiences are all Real, all Kali Incarnate!

One then may come to the question: were Ramakrishna's visions, communions, and living connections with the Goddess cognitive projections from within his own mind content or perceptual insights into what is really there? The mind is nothing but She, whether those experiences are inspired by natural phenomena, such as a sunrise or watching seven birds fly in perfect unity, the spiritually uplifting power of one's own thoughts, or, indeed, the perceptual insight into the existence of the actual Deitess as Chosen Ideal. When Ramakrishna was about to leave his body, when he was about to die, the tone of "Kali, Kali, Kali," was spoken by him three times. Then he dropped the body. From the dual position we say that he returned to Her. Yet, from the non-dual state we realize that She then returned to Herself. (If we can even say "return", for there is dualism in that thought.) His wife was sad, for she felt that the Goddess Herself had left her. But she had an experience hearing her husband's voice, "I have only passed from one room to another." So beautiful, but still, what shall we do with the conscious current that continues to differentiate, even as one room being different from another?

Again, in this concluding phase of his life, we read that he distinctly said, " He who was Rama and Krishna is now, in this body, Ramakrishna--but not in your Vedantic sense." What indeed does this mean? If we interpet the comment from the Vedantic point of view, it is easy to understand that all beings come from the One Existence Consciousness and Bliss Ultimate. But that is not what he meant. Yet, if we realize that Avatara, an Incarnation, comes from an aspect of the Goddess as Tara, the Compassionate Mother, and Ava, to Descend, well then, the statement becomes easily comprehended. But even so, there is no real dualism between what is described as the "Vedantic sense" and what the True Nature of Kali is. Also, when his wife, Sarada, asked him how he regarded her, he said, "The Mother who is worshiped in the temple is the mother who has given birth to my body and is now living in the nahabat, and it is She again who is stroking my feet at this moment. Indeed, I always look on you as the personification of the Blissfull Mother Kali." In his mind, Kali is stroking his feet, which is a fantastic barrier breaking perception of spiritual potential. Could it be so, that She adores us as much as we might be able to adore Her? But this was not one sided, for Ramakrishna worshiped his wife Saradamani, as the Goddess Herself, during his practice of the highly sacred Shodasi ritual.

Also, it is Hindu custom, that the feet are symbols of where the Goddesses and the Gods have left their imprints, charging the very dust of the ground with the divine energy of Sakti. The act of touching the feet is one of tremendous humilty and surrender to a Greater Power than one's ego centric configuration. For true spiritual energy comes from the surrender of the ego into humility. Ramakrishna would even take the dust of others' feet, for there was no illusory pride in him. It is not an act of bowing or saluting a human power. It is a sign of greeting the Sakti within everyone! He would say, "As for me, I consider myself as a speck of the dust of the devotee's feet." This shows two things dramatically. A genuinely illuminated being is more humble than... dust, and that their purpose for existing is to help others. So you may see that there was no aspect of life or death that was dual from Kali as pure Sakti Experience. Kali is Brahman, Brahman is Kali, so he was never dualistically different from Her, from Kali. The four phases of his life: birth and spiritual exercise to get to bhavamukha, the attainment of bhavamukha, living from the high plane of bhavamukha and his work and death within bhavamukha (the Goddess' unique spiritual gift and high command), were never separate from Her. All that was demonstrated, spiritual mechanisms, methods, techniques, and realisations were all for the sweet, potent, beautiful Simplicity of the pure Kali Expereince. His entire person and all his personal life were but the incarnate Love which is pure Sakti.

"Kali moves even the Immutable."

That which is impossible to understand, She makes possible to understand, for it is She who stands over all that is, and so it is all under Her. Even the Immutable. That is, Sakti can stir that Principle Absolute which cannot be stirred. She can change the Unchanging (Brahman)! Is She not Brahman Itself? She can bring or move this Birthless, Deathless, Infinite Consciousness into the finite experiencing of the changes of birth and death. What else is here to experience those changes if not what is the Real, when all is said and done? She can make for us what is Inaccessible, accessible as human experience. If She can move what cannot be moved, then She is more Powerful than the Unchanging Ideal. Human experience is constant changes. When does it rest? It is of the nature of time and space, movement and feeling, cause and effect. So, that Unchanging

Height, distant and transcendent, is brought down into our mutable experience by Sakti. She alone can move the One into the Immense, or the Immense back into the One. It is She who makes the One accessible to the Immense, infusing that Universal Immensity with the Vigorous Power of the One. This is a most dramatic and dynamic statement by Ramakrishna.

"O Mother, Thou art verily Brahman, and Thou art verily Sakti. Thou art Purusha and Thou art Prakriti. Thou art Virat. Thou art the Absolute, and Thou dost manifest Thyself as the Relative. Thou art verily the twenty four cosmic principles."

From the highest spiritual position of pure non-dual Sakti Experience, nothing can be found anywhere that is not She. It is She who is all this, so non-duality is proven by this most evident and obvious fact. She is the Infinite. She is the Power. She is the one purusha soul and She is the prakriti matrix of all that manifests as the natural universe. And She, Herself, is what becomes that universe (virat). She is both the absolute and the relative, so She is something more than these two principles combined, divided, or at one with each other; and it is She who has become the twenty-four cosmic principles; the four states of the psyche as conscious current of mind, intellect, ego, and memory; the five senses perceiving touch, smell, taste, sound, and sight; the five instruments of hands, feet, mouth, anus and sex. The five subtle energy states or quantum forms, which are in turn the background dimensions of the same five physical elements of nature, namely earth, water, fire, air, and ether (the substance which makes up the space/time fabric itself).

"He whom you address as Brahma is none other than She whom I call Sakti, the Primal Energy."

Sakti is Real, and so all conceptions of Her have value and validity. The conception is one thing and the Reality is yet another, or so it seems. The conception arises out of a reflex in thought that tries to bring down into the mind a memory of Her Primal Primordial Power. The conceptual form of Her formless Power may take numerous novel shapes unique in themselves. It may be Brahma, here mentioned, as the Creator God, or Vishnu, the Preserver, or Shiva, the Destroyer. Also it may be Allah, Buddha, Krishna, Christ, or Rama. The same Spiritual Principle is designated by various names. One sees the Spiritual as one thinks of the Spiritual. The trouble and botheration that comes from the conflict of different opinions is due to the egotistical clinging to one ideal of Spiritual Reality to the exclusion of all others. Ramakrishna never felt that way. His heart was universal and all religions and paths were to him but their own unique efforts to reach the Great Reality. He knew well that lovers of God, Sakti, Truth do not belong to any distinction that limits them. Religious thought systems which have come up on our world presented no difficulty to his spiritual thinking. He saw them all as shapes of Sakti, so he harbored no intolerance or resentment to any of these. Whether they arose from India East, the Orient, the Abrahamic systems, or the Primal, Aboriginal, Native, and Earlier Prehistoric systems. This is demonstrated by his spiritual practice. He, in his brilliant assimilation of spiritual experiments through history, held them all in deepest regard as manifestations of the Goddess, whether or not he had the opportunity to practice those paths. He knew all too well that, in the end, all religions are but symbols of the Self attained in the state of non-dual consciousness, when mind completely plunges into the Great Cause, which is that non-dual consciousness, and those many symbols are like poems trying to describe what cannot be described.

To get to Reality one must have real thought, and address, with genuine and honest frontal confrontation, one's true and real feeling. In this light it is most absolutely important to clear the mind of all cognitive distortions; allegorical, mythical, legendary, and historical, in regard to the great figures of religion, for in their attempts at descrbing a Reality of their own concept, or in the posthumous glorification of their personalities, they may have certainly given us some very unrealistic and untrue views of life and death, the true nature of the body, the divine barrier of death, how the world really came to be and what the truth of immortality is in reality. And most utterly important it is to free one's feelings of the poisonous thoughts generated by the attitudes of what can only be called intolerant spiritual racism, or that some select group may acquire divine profusion and others may not. This bias and bigotry, this confining narrow parochialism and ignorant provincialism kills out any teachings of Love in this world, and that is tragic.

"Yet Brahman and Sakti are, in fact, not different. That which is the Blissful Mother is, again, Existence --Knowledge--Bliss Absolute."

At least to what appears, as far as we can Be (Existence), Know (Knowledge) and Feel (Bliss) in terms of these words. The Blissful Mother is "again" Existence--Knowledge--Bliss, but what is She before the appearance of these conceptual conditions of that which Her Reality is as pure Sakti Experience?

"Water is water whether it is calm or full of waves and bubbles. The Absolute alone is the Primordial Energy."

As long as you believe that the Primordial Energy of the Goddess and the Absolute as the Goddess are two conceptions, you will still experience the dualism of dream consciousness. Dream consciousness veils by the vibration content of the dream current, and yet also unveils or liberates duality from itself as a binding factor within consciousness itself by none other than the bright moment of melting change that comes during wave currents of the dream state, as during waking up from or slipping into deep sleep. This is the mind nature of the conscious current of conception, and this also applies to the states of mood change. As most of life just seems to be the redundancy of getting up from sleep, as being unconscious of the Great Undivided Goddess, the mind becomes alert. We then take account of our spiritual worth, resulting in immediate joy in the Goddess. Also, ego is a bubble, waiting, even wanting to burst, so that it may return to identify with what it originally was. Ego, in the stages of the waking and dreaming conditions, is what illusively or superficially divides wave and water, yet in Reality it is not so.

"The Divine Mother is always playful and sportive. This universe is Her play. She is self--willed and must always have Her own way. She is full of bliss. She gives freedom to one out of a hundred thousand."

We are talking of the Goddess. She who rocks the universe to sleep. She who rolls all life along, within that same universe. It is all for Her Great Pleasure. Of course, numbers are metaphorical, emphasizing that "freedom" is very special. At the beginning of the Common Era, there were only about a quarter of a billion people in this world. At the turn of the century, there was about a billion. Now, there are an extraordinary six billion people in the world. Even though it is a frightening calculation, it is still the Goddess who is rolling all this forward.

"That is Her will. Her pleasure is in continuing the game."

Even as She is the mind, coming out of and expressing the Divine Current, ever revealing and ever uncovering that Current in every moment of life itself. As it is Her pastime, spiritual enlightenment may be simply an entertainment to Her as the Power already enlightened. As a game, can we of simple human minds say to ourselves what the achievement of Her objective is in reality? Could it simply be the pleasure of illumination? In reality, it is She who gives us our feelings through the conditional karmic reactions within cause and effect. It is She who says "yes" or "no" to things beyond the delusive idea that human ego has the thought of control. She is the one who wakes us, slowly or quickly. She is destiny already done! So, mind is already done!

"It is as if the Divine Mother said to the human mind in confidence, with a sign from Her eye, 'Go and enjoy the world.' How can one blame the mind? The mind can disentangle itself from worldliness if, through Her grace, She makes it turn toward Herself. Only then does it become devoted to the Lotus Feet of the Divine Mother."

It appears that She directs everything without exception, even the advent of the sentiment of Love for Her which disentangles consciousness from wayfaring among other forms of love not directed purely into the Goddess. Pure Spiritual Love is not motivated by a need for egotistical satiation, nor guilt, nor remorse, nor unworthiness, nor even a fear of hell. The mind is not to blame, nor are human passions and desires. One cannot love Her out of a sense of shame. That is imploded selfishness. Pure Love is not motivated by the outcome of negative feeling, but, of course, the empathic sentiment for others' suffering may cause Love to rise up in the heart. The Goddess says to the mind confiding in the trust of Her divine secrecy that the mind may indeed enjoy the world, but, when world is over, mind returns to Her. She pulls it back when those desires are finished. Only from the comprehension of the fact that the ego has no basis of real control over life, death, and the events between, may this divine concept be understood. The world, creation, joy, and suffering too, are all in the sign of Her eyes, which are ever saying that it is all for the learning of Love, once forgotten. She triggers the emotional memory of Love within us.

"One attains the vision of God if Mahamaya steps aside from the door. Mahamaya's grace is necessary: hence the worship of Sakti."

All Knowledge is Within You, awakened by the Luminous Spiritual Current of Love. You need not read, learn or memorize anything, but find something of your own that continuously will stir and stimulate or excite that Current to the conscious surface of your self/being as a Living Power, a Living Reality. When that great power of defining measurements removes itself from consciousness, that same consciousness, by the excited living power of Sakti, shows to itself what it is. When She as "Mahamaya" steps aside, then She as pure Sakti uncovers the living power of the Reality which was always there within you.

134

"Then like a madman I began to shower flowers in all directions. Whatever I saw I worshiped."

This remark comes out of a most extraordinary spiritual state. It is not only what is surrounding that is worshiped; all that is inside and all that is outside is adored as the Goddess. It is the pure Sakti Experience. The worship of Her includes the body, the mind, and the "I" as a principle, an impulse, as steady formless awareness and as the infinite waves of ideation. It is not madness, it is a divinely sound condition, a perceptual sanity where all that is, is seen as the Goddess.

"There was intolerable anguish in my heart because I could not have Her vision."

His desperate pangs of separation from Her are probably incomprehensible to most of us who live our lives only at the level of ordinary feelings. Not so many of us feel that deep anguish at our apparent separation from the Great Principle. Though we tend to live our lives with an inward sublimated suffering, we do not openly and honestly address the primary problem. Who of us even loses sleep over our lack of God Consciousness? Who of us desires to tune and direct our cognitive energy to the lofty pitch of spiritual experience? Most of us carry this unrecognized wound and never address the force of spiritual anguish as its source. Who of us would even devote five hours directly addressing this anguish of dualistic feeling clearly in the mind in order get merely five seconds of Peace? It is a curious phenomena, that in the dream state, one has hundreds, if not thousands of cognitive images, and yet upon awaking, the mind in the shape of memory attaches itself to a fixed selection of these images, and that, in itself, produces a mood condition. The same physics of emotion apply to events, connections, and word or image cognates in the waking state. It is in deep sleep, where mind and memory have no hold, no existence in that state, and so are not making any type of dual measurement or comparison. Deep sleep is unconscious of duality, so here, one experiences an inner condition of unilluminated bliss, not dependent on subtle or physical externals. If waking is conscious, then dream is subconscious, and deep sleep is unconscious. So then, the fourth state is superconscious. Yet, pure Sakti Experience is clear spiritual knowing, aware and accepting of all that has been described here, and going beyond and past it all at the same time. At this level, the mood or emotion of Love is constant and perpetual, being much deeper and more powerful than the rotation of the three states of modified consciousness over the silent, and yet dynamic surface of Sakti Consciousness. The potential for this Mood Contact or Clear Emotion is inside each individual. But who will reach so deep into the anguish that addresses the feeling of being in a state of separation from Her vision, from Her Love? Who ever engages so deeply in the want, to have, such an experience of empathic identity with the Goddess?

"I thought there was no use in living such a life. My eyes suddenly fell upon the sword that was there in the Mother's temple. I made up my mind to put an end to my life with it that very moment. Like one mad, I ran and caught hold of it, when suddenly I had the wonderful vision of the Mother, and fell down unconscious. I did not know what happened then in the external world--how that day and the next slipped away. But, in my heart of hearts, there was flowing a current of intense bliss, never experienced before, and I had the immediate knowledge of the Light that is Mother."

How many of us have felt that there was indeed no use to life at merely not gaining the love of one desired as a consort? People have taken their own lives over just this in the mad passion of romantic love. Ramakrishna's desire to have the knowledge of the Goddess was ten thousand times greater than the desire to experience the return of love from another human being. He was ready to sacrifice his own body if it would bring the knowledge of the Goddess to him. He was ready to lose and let go of his mind. He was prepared for the complete extinguishment of the idea of self as ego in order to get Her to love him and show Her divine nature to him clearly. Who is prepared to do that in order to know Reality? Who has that kind of passion; vital, living, and burning Love for that form of Infinite Love? Then, at the level of this determination, he became unconscious of that very body, mind, and self, to intensely experience like never before the wondrous divine current of Her Love. This brought him to that immediate direct unfettered state of knowledge, which is nothing other than the Light and Luminosity of the Goddess. It would take such resignation on anyone's part to get to that state of illumination. And apparently that resignation of an absolute giving up, requires a view of life which has become hollow, empty, and meaningless unless the knowledge of the Goddess fills the heart. For those thoughtful people who are aware of some factors of the near death experience, they may see a parallel. He was unconscious of the external world and the passage of time during the loss of contact with the body and mind, and the overwhelming and all inclusive experience of the Light, which for him was the Goddess, the Mother, his Chosen Ideal.

"It was as if the houses, doors, temples ,and all other things vanished altogether; as if there was nothing anywhere! And what I saw was a boundless infinite Conscious Sea of Light! However far and in whatever direction I looked, I found a continuous succession of Effulgent Waves coming forward, raging and storming from all sides with great speed. Very soon they fell on me and made me sink to the Abysmal Depths of Infinity."

All external surrounding forms of the waking state occupying consciousness disappear. So, too, all subtle forms of the dream mind vanish altogether. Nothing anywhere filled his consciousness but the Sakti of Mother rushing and storming at his center of identity, boundless and infinite. It was not a state of the unconscious. It was a highly alert Conscious State, a Sea of Light. From everywhere without a center or source point and continuous without end, the Bright Waves of Mother approached with a speed that we cannot measure with the relative mind. The sensation is that these Waves of Her were coming forward at him, raging, perhaps like a hurricane or a tornado. But what is

137

interesting, what is so spiritually fascinating is that as these waves came over his center of conscious identity and fell upon that place, they made him sink, as it were, not transcend, into the deep, the depth of Infinity. It is described uniquely as an all consuming abyss, which means having no bottom or anything too deep to be measured. This is his description of the infinite. It is the abysmal infinite swallowing all dualistic consciousness which retains a separation from the state of consciousness which perceives and experiences the wonder and awe and beauty of the non- dual.

"The figure of a young Sannyasin looking like me used to come out again and again from within me and instruct me on all matters; when he emerged, sometimes I had a little outer consciousness and, at other times, lost it altogether and lay inert, only seeing and hearing his actions and words, I regained full external consciousness only when he entered the gross body again. The Brahmani, Tota Puri and others came and taught me afterwards what I had heard from him previously--they taught me what I had already known."

This is truly a most extraordinary statement of Ramakrishna's spiritual experience. It is possibly quite puzzling to even the most thoughtful spiritual seekers. One thing is that the figure who looks like a Shiva sadhu in the form of a young sannyasin appears just like himself. That is, this subtle image looks just like Ramakrishna. Psychologists could have great fun with theories of projection from the subconscious of a self-image on the screen of the conscious, or even without external consciousness in a dreamlike condition. But the sweet simplicity of this is that this is Ramakrishna's own pure mind acting as the teacher of himself; his own mind is his guru. There is great wisdom in this, for is not our mind always with us? However, a physical human guru is not always there, and so one might become deeply dependent upon the presence or absence of such a teacher. The light (ru) of his own mind is what lifted and removed the darkness (gu). This is fantastically beautiful. And if one remembers that Ramakrishna saw his own mind as ultimately nothing but the Goddess Herself, then what is this saying? Could it be that, like all things, She indeed appeared to him in the figure of this young Shiva- like sadhu and taught him everything that was later to be redundantly defined by the Brahmani, Totapuri, and the rest? If Ramakrishna says that he learned everything then and there from the self-figure of the sadhu, then it is so. The Brahmani was a woman Tantric teacher. Totapuri was a Vedanta teacher. With Jatadhari, he practiced the worship of Ramlala, and Govinda Ray was a Moslem Sufi with whom he practiced that course. But you see, they did not teach him anything new. It was Ramakrishna's Goddess as the current of his own mind that taught him everything originally. The Sakti of Tantra, the Nirvikalpa of Vedanta, the subtle plane experiences of devotional contact with the Chosen Ideal in the form of the baby Rama, and the depth consciousness of the formless Allah Ideal were already absolutely known by him previously. So, the arrival and the engaging with teachers was for some reason performed, though completely unnecessary for him. Perhaps it is more for us that, to some extent, we should recognize a degree of spiritual education but that, in the final degree, it is none other than the Goddess appearing as our own mind that is the one and only one who shows us Truth, Reality, and Love as pure Sakti Experience. This again is a type of manifestation of the Chosen Ideal expressing the Greater Reality, but in some certain spiritual perspectives, as that of non dual Vedanta, the Chosen Ideal, even so, is thought to be ultimately illusory, since it emerges out of the mind content; and only Reality is Real. So what can mind teach to the mind? We come then to a realization of the Sakti Consciousness as the one process of revelation into the Real!

"God used to dance then, taking the form of Kali."
So, on one hand, from the high plane of non-dual consciousness, the conscious conception of the Chosen Ideal as a form of God or Goddess, even the very thought of God or Goddess as that intimate ideal, is considered to be ultimately

unreal. But from the other perspective of the deepest undoubting belief that the Chosen Ideal is indeed a personal form of the Great Reality, that same Ideal may reveal Reality to that person. This all shows that the Power within the current of consciousness really knows no limitations as to its potential, especially in the matters of spirituality. God can be Kali. Kali can be God. They are not two, but they may appear as two. It is truly miraculous when you think about it.

"Raga--bhakti is pure love of God, a love that seeks God alone and not any worldly end."

This Love is the most powerful force in the universe or above it. It breaks through the frame of all conscious conception and has no limitations to its spiritual potential. It is within everyone since it is the Power that has created everything. But usually this Love is directed toward the attainment of objectives within the waking state that in turn become dream objects. Seldom does this Love ordinarily turn upon itself seeking only itself. Yet in deep sleep, that Love is in this state where no worldly end is sought. It is pure, joyful non-duality yet to be brought back into conscious conception, but each time this begins to happen, greater and greater dimensions of this expanded Love begin to take place. In the fourth state of pure consciousness where no sleep, dream, or waking attachment is given credence, this Love reaches full proportion.

"Besides, it produced in him a great love for his chosen Ideal which took him beyond the firm steel--frame of the rules and regulations of ritualistic devotion to the spontaneity and freedom of the Ragatmika form of divine love, culminating in the immediate realization of the Divine Mother."
S.

That is, the mantra of the Goddess produced in him that great love. The psychic base prints within the mind, put there by tradition and upbringing, can limit our idea of what our cognitive potential is, as the immensity and reality of the Chosen Ideal, the deepest Spiritual Concept that we hold within the core of the mind. Creative imagination generates greater and greater consciousness of what the potential of that spiritual ideal can do. The power of the ideal becomes unhindered by previous mental relations and concepts. My ideal of Kali is certainly different from Ramakrishna's ideal of Kali. Everyone's cognition varies. So it is even at the depth of spiritual experience. The experience is the same oneness, as it would seem that the feeling of Love is the same felt emotion through one and all, but when we come down to the region of vocabulary, our expressions will certainly vary from one to the other.

"The attainment of the Nirvikalpa Samadhi is not very remote from this devout aspirant who has been able to advance so far.
Thus the mind of the person, who gets rid of the belief in the existence of the external world to which he has been accustomed for an infinitely long time, becomes endowed with much power and determination. The whole of his mind goes forward with enthusiasm in the direction of the enjoyment of divine bliss, when once there arises the conviction that the enjoyment of that bliss becomes more intense if the mind can be made completely free from modifications. Or, it may be said that the very intense love for his chosen Ideal shows him that plane, and urged by it, he realizes his identity with that Ideal."
S.

The key words here are enthusiasm for bliss. One realizes that modifications in the current of conscious conception limit the intensity of bliss as pure Sakti Experience. So one develops an inspired eagerness to get away from those modifications which limit one's spiritual enjoyment. This culminates in knowing the current of pure Sakti Experience without conscious conception. Even the identity with the Ideal must melt away at this level. Those modifications are all identity currents with a physical, subtle, or causal reality; all that is associated in consciousness with things regarding the waking, dream, and deep sleep states. Out from the experiences of Sakti's joy within the conscious current, comes a God inspired zeal and enthusiasm to have more Joy, unfettered by things, feelings, identities, concepts, and thoughts within the conscious current, until nothing binds the pure Sakti Experience. Here, all chosen ideals, all dual mind contents, melt away entirely. When mind melts into deep sleep this experience occurs frequently. But sleep covers the depth of this experience and the nature of non-dual reality as conscious joyful experience goes unrecognized. Here, one knows in the motionless depth of the calm Current of Sakti, I am Free, nothing binds Me. This is the Sakti Mood of this face of Reality, but what is experienced within cannot be described nor shown by the outer expression of that mood. There, there is no writer, no thinker, no thought, no release, no return, no Nirvana, no Samsara, no Brahman, no Sakti, no this this, no that that, no stillness, no motion. So, samadhi is simply the joy, peace, and happiness that naturally arises out of spiritual focus, contact, identity, or even the final beatitude of total disintegration of all ego related mind contents into the sense of the Infinite. But ego can never define, designate, nor describe the Experience, for as it has only a finite existence, then how may it reveal, impart, or transmit something that is Infinite in its nature.

"That which is formless again has form. One should believe in the forms of God also. By meditating on Kali the aspirant realizes God as Kali. Next he finds that the form merges in the Indivisble Absolute. That which is the Indivisible Satchidananda is verily Kali."

Kali is the Indivisible. Kali is the Divisible. She who is Sakti, is indeed the spiritual midpoint where the divisible and indivisible meet and merge. That is the place or site of pure Sakti Experience. Kali is the Experience and She is the Power that demonstrates the Experience. In Her, the eternal (Ka) and the relative (Li) both exist as Conditionless Unmodified Oneness. She is the chosen spiritual ideal that spontaneously appears or comes out of the Indivisible into the divisible forms of consciousness; to show, reveal, and illuminate the Indivisible. Then She returns, as She was, to the Indivisible which is what She Is. But, of course, this explanation is all the dual mind

142

perceiving a process for its own sake, in regard to uncovering the most intimate discovery of pure Sakti Experience. The revolution or turnabout within one's own consciousness, through the spiritual ideal, back into pure Sakti Consciousness, occurs within that innate potential of consciousness and cognition itself.

"But as they go on getting more frequent experiences of that Power in their lives day after day, a strong desire to be fully acquainted with it arises in their minds."

S.

It is the acquaintance with pure Sakti that becomes more and more frequent. Day after day, the mind becomes more accustomed to the nature of pure Sakti Experience. A strong desire brings about more and more frequent experiences until the impulse of ego identity comes to a point where it causes little or no distraction from the pure Sakti Experience.

"The sudra Ekalavya learnt archery in the forest before a clay image of Drona."

It would be good to remove from the mind all superstition, fear, taboo, illusion, and fantasy regarding the guru function. Even if one does so at the level of the mind, sometimes the trace emotions caused by superstition, etc. will get in the way. It is none other than Ekalavya's own mind, the power of its focus, that caused the learning of what he sought to know. It was not the clay, it was not the image in the clay, it was not the environment of the forest. It is the mind function itself that acts as both the teacher and the image of the chosen ideal. This is known clearly when one no longer separates the two functions from pure Sakti. She is the Power within that teaches and appears as some form of the Divine. The Happiness that we seek from these two functions, as well as the Principle recognized commonly as God, starts when intellectual separation stops! Make use of an image, a Chosen Ideal in the pattern of your own consciousness and see the Goddess in that. For Ramakrishna, it was the Kali of Dakshineswar. Create your own spirituality at whatever level the mind feeling comes at!

"In the end Vilwamangal renounced the world and went away in order to worship God. He said to the prostitute, 'You are my guru. You have taught me how one should yearn for God.' He addressed the prostitute as his mother and gave her up."

You see, Vilwa was rushing to see his lover and was unconscious of the external world. So much was he absorbed in the thought of being with her that he tripped over a yogi who was meditating on God. He asked the yogi how is it that he is meditating on God and still conscious of the world, where he, Vilwa, was so deep in the feeling of seeing his mistress that he was unaware of the external forms. This is an excellent example of the guru function. It was the Light of Love within his own consciousness that awakened Vilwa. It was not the person of the prostitute, though Vilwa identifies her as "guru". She was not actively aware that this phenomena of awakening was going on within the mind of her lover. So, at anytime and anywhere, the sudden charge of realized Love may overwhelm us and carry us into pure Sakti Experience. His own yearning ignited the Light of Love within him to act as the guru function. We cannot limit when and where the Power of Sakti's Love may enlighten us.

"If you worship with love even a brick or stone as God, then through His grace you can see Him."

Here we see that the God or Goddess conception may cover whatever is there before the current of conscious conception and, by the very nature of its powerful indication, may teach, illuminate, release, liberate and enlighten the conscious current of thought itself. It is the ideal within the mind itself that illuminates. The brick or stone has no power in itself. It is pure Sakti that reveals the Consciousness of Herself. But if you need a human image, a deity, a concept, a brick or stone, instead of just responding to pure Sakti, well then, your experience will be identified to that extent. In reality, true and absolute, even the images and chosen ideal forms of Sakti are limited identifications on or over what the pure Sakti Experience is in its unfettered and unlimited fact. You see, influences that occupy the conscious current of the mind instantly create maps of response within the mind current. All education, word cognates, spiritual conceptions, waking state connections, surfacing dream images, what we read, the things we hear, even contact with high and holy people (or people not so high and holy) create an instant transient state of personal reality which is generally not the pure Sakti Experience. Better is the pure depth influence from one's own wisdom state that comes out from Sakti Consciousness, which is experienced everyday in the deep sleep state as a motionless consciousness of non-dual joy and which is then seen and experienced throughout the dreaming and waking conditions of consciousness.

"Mother, is it You or I? Do I do anything? No, no! It is You."

There are three conditions of the mind current which make it difficult to liberate consciousness of the dualistic impulse of the "I" principle: the perverse mind obsessed with complex diversity; the mind that is conditioned to the stress of perfectionism or purity and so fears what is thought to be wicked, which descends from the word *wizard*; and the doubting mind filled with procrastination which is nothing but tomorrow-ism, not embracing the moment of the eternal now. Really speaking, hesitation or spiritual procrastination is an obsession with the apparent state of self-importance, which puts off getting to humility, surrender, and spiritual gratitude. It is truly that we hold so strongly to the self-delusive idea of self- importance that prevents us from crossing the barrier of dualism and entering the state of being non-dual in the Goddess. So here one sees that Ramakrishna does not even feel that he does anything. It is all the Goddess. The beauty of this is that he realized She is his own mind and revealed everything to that same mind. Also, all this Power is given to Her. He keeps none of this for his own. It is all You, Mother, and so the problem of ego identity is left miles behind. It is ego that desires to be liberated. Liberation itself, as pure Sakti Experience, is ever always free and, so, has no desire for the state of the ego's liberation.

"She dwells in all beings."

She not only dwells in all beings, She has become all beings and, further on, She is all beings, from the conclusive overview of non-dual consciousness. She is true Sakti. 'Sa', meaning Divine Power and Spiritual Prosperity, and 'Kti', meaning Might, Strength, and utter Spiritual Ability. These two words combined give the cognitive force to the word as Power. She is the Living Power of Life and Self, not a dry thought. Again, 'Sa', is the feminine word for the True Self of Atma, so, joined with 'Kti', it gives that Self its Power, Strength, and Life.

"I vowed to the Divine Mother that I would kill myself if I did not see God. I said to Her: 'O Mother, I am a fool. Please teach me what is contained in the Vedas, the Puranas, the Tantras, and other scriptures.' The Mother said to me, 'The essence of the Vedanta is that Brahman alone is real and the world illusory.'"

Even though the Goddess Kali is supremely the original Goddess of Tantra, She is also the ultimate teacher of Vedanta, in that Her dance in the cremation field of illusory phenomena negates all that is not Her. She leaves only Herself, the Essence, the Great Infinite. After the process of not this, not this is finished, removing every limited conception of Reality, what we find is She. Blessed Be Sakti! Blessed Be the Adoration of Sakti! Blessed Be the Consciousness that Communes with Her, She who is Love!

"Mother, may those who come to You have all their desires fulfilled! But please don't make them give up everything at once, Mother. Well, You may do whatever You like in the end. If You keep them in the world, Mother, then please reveal Yourself to them now and then. Otherwise, how will they live? How will they be encouraged if they don't see You once in a while? But You may do whatever You like in the end."

What Love for others, not just for self. He begs the Goddess to reveal Herself to others so that life may be bearable. He asks Her not to force them to give up everything too quickly as human nature is well understood. But Ramakrishna knows that, in the end, what is done is done by Her wish, Her liking, Her Power alone! But what empathy for others. Not just for himself. However, he openly admits that She controls it all and not he. It is really astounding when one begins to realize how intimate was the relationship between the Goddess and Ramakrishna. He would see Her standing on the balcony at Dakshineswar looking over the night lights of Calcutta, with Her long black tresses hanging down Her back. When She would not allow him to speak of the deepest spiritual mysteries from the plane of non-dual consciousness, he would speak of Her, calling Her, "That Woman, the Mother, is surely very naughty." Can you imagine, "naughty", because She is so playful and as Mayasakti, She is like that, never being still. When She would keep his consciousness in the highest plane of non duality he would have to ask Her to please come down from there so that he could talk, function, move, and be among the world and the people in it. There were also times when he would comment how She was showing off in Her Benares sari, or that he would request Her to be still. All this shows us a relationship which is so intimate and without a trace of fear. Too fearful a respect for the Principle, the Chosen Ideal, God, or Goddess keeps one from an intimacy with the Great Power of pure Sakti Experience. A true lover of Sakti knows not that attitude being so intimate with the Goddess, the most Excelling Principle. The Living Power. The Living Reality. Or to put it from another angle of bearing, if one listens to fear or anger, psychic distortion or arduous emotional cognition coming from the voice of the body, or even the thoughts, assumptions, theories, conjectures, opinions, deductions, inducements, assessments, perspectives, recommendations, and responses from other people, then how can one listen to the inborn Consciousness of the Goddess within oneself. It is very difficult to listen to two songs at once. One Voice. One Power. One Sakti, brings you to the sweet intimate communion of non-dual rapture. Nothing else is needed.

"I say, 'O Mother, I am the machine and You are the Operator, I am inert and You make me conscious; I do as You make me do; I speak as You make me speak.' But the ignorant say, 'I am partly responsible, and God is partly responsible.'"

A most extraordinary spiritual insight to say that one's mind is not even conscious, having consciousness, having awareness, or being capable of thinking without Her. It is but a lifeless machine without the dynamic energy of Sakti which gives power to the mind and which animates with living force this entire universal complex. As long as the ego retains a partial percentage as a ratio of responsibility in this stream of cause and effect called life, then complete and total, full and pure Sakti Experience is not possible. For you see, that will only come when the ideal concept of ego is totally destroyed and what arises in its place is what was there before the ego had its existence in the state of phenomenal responses. What is that?

"What wrong have I done, Mother? Do I ever do anything? It is Thou, Mother, who doest everything. I am the machine and Thou art its Operator."

Do not be a fool about this. We live by the Law of Love, not to harm any, and that is the one spiritual law there is. But from the high plane of non-dual consciousness, at one with the Ultimate Cause, one understands the sources, origins, and effects of all conditions in occurrence. So what wrong can be done when it is all Mother? From the state of pure non-dual Sakti Experience it may be seen that really nothing is done by ego. Everything is known in Her Matrix, as what comes down the river is not seen from the shore you are sitting on till it reaches you, but, nevertheless it was there upriver, even though you as ego were unaware of it.

"On all sides he found the manifestation of the Divine Mother - the Omnipotent Mother of the universe! She was in the water, and She was on land. She was the body, and She was the mind. She was pain, and She was comfort. She was knowledge and She was ignorance. She was life, and She was death. He found

*the Mother in everything he saw, or heard, or thought, or
imagined. She was turning Yea into Nay, and vice versa. No
embodied being could go beyond Her jurisdiction unless She
was pleased to let him go. He had not even the freedom to die!
Again, beyond the body and mind also, it was She--the Mother,
in Her Transcendent , Her Absolute Aspect! She was the
Brahman whom he had been worshiping all his life, and to
whom he had been offering his heart's adoration! Brahman and
Shakti were one and the same thing--the two aspects of the same
Entity."*

N.

What can I say as a commentary to this remarkable insight?
I am just a fool, powerless but for the Power of Herself.
Totapuri was the one who acted as the example of the absolute
non-dual nirvikalpa samadhi teaching in the personal life
demonstration of Ramakrishna's paragon as a spiritual prototype.
Yet, you see that Totapuri was carried even further on than non-
dual nirvikalpa by none other than Ramakrishna's Goddess. She
took him further forward into pure Sakti Experience! You see,
Tota had reached the perfect knowledge of non-dual
consciousness in nirvikalpa samadhi, but he still retained the
idea of self-importance under the delusion of ego "I" impulse.
On this occasion he was attempting to take his life, to discard his
body because of the pain of illness. But the Goddess would not
let him do so and it was at this point that he discovered humility.
Ramakrishna's Goddess carried him further on in his spiritual
life and realization. He had acquired nirvikalpa by dint of his
own self effort and will, which in itself shows us great things
about human nature. Yet he was stuck there in that state until
the Goddess showed him more. Was this Bhavamukha or simply
Vijnana, did She show Herself to him as the Immense Universal
Divine "I" Consciousness where he became identified with Her
as Ramakrishna did? Or did She merely take him to the stage of
Vijnana as the special enlightenment of seeing Sakti in both Her
absolute formless and Her relative forms simultaneously?
Nevertheless, such wonderful potential, which is within us all, is
demonstrated here for the sake of realizing this potential itself.

149

"There is Someone within me who does all these things through me."

Someone who is none other than the Goddess Herself of Incomparable Beauty. In the slowing stillness of Her most sacred serenity, the Divine Current, the One Someone within the heart of all life, we become peacefully relaxed with delight and there in that precious moment of conscious now, there is no disturbance, no stillness, no motion. Nothing binds. Ramakrishna's Goddess is Real. She is Power more Real than anything seen or heard, thought of or imagined, mental, emotional or physical. That Power is Love. Love is the most Central Emotion. Yet, the Goddess is not just an emotion. Love is not just an emotion. Sakti Power is not just an emotion, but the Central Feeling of Love as this Power is felt as an emotion. You too can experience this potential if you see what is Real Within, as when the ego is erased. Then it is clear. However do not confuse the personality with the ego.

"You know I am a fool. I know nothing. Then who is it that says all these things? I say to the Divine Mother, 'O Mother, I move as Thou makest me move. It is not I! It is not I! It is all Thou! It is all Thou!'"

Are we all not fools, knowing nothing of Truth, as long as we hold to the impulse of "I"?

"You may feel a thousand times that it is all magic; but you are still under the control of the Divine Mother. You cannot escape Her. You are not free. You must do what She makes you do. A man attains Brahmajnana only when it is given to him by the Adyasakti, the Divine Mother. Then alone does he see the whole thing as magic; otherwise not."

That Knowledge of the Absolute, which is none other than the Primordial Sakti, is given when She brings all things together for that Experience. She gives Herself as the Absolute Knowledge to one and to all. It is the possible potential within every living being but, since ego magically identifies

150

immediately with whatever form is placed before it, Her Gift of pure Sakti Experience goes so often unnoticed by us.

> *"As long as the slightest trace of ego remains, one lives within the jurisdiction of the Adyasakti. One is under Her sway. One cannot go beyond Her."*

So when ego is gone, the idea of a binding jurisdiction is gone. Jurisdiction is the extent of power, as Her authority extends everywhere. The entire universe is Her district. But when ego goes, one sees Her as She is, remaining Absolute in Herself. Therefore, one must ask the question: is it possible to go beyond the furthest limit? Is there such an extent of Power? Or is it just Sakti Experience, all in all? Do those like myself who worship Sakti eventually return by the reincarnating path? She alone gives Absolute Knowledge, where reincarnation apparently ceases. Or does it? The Absolute idea of a non-reincarnating state, which for its sake alone is not concerned with others, may be the highest form of selfishness imaginable. There is no way to bridge the gap of personal and absolute dualism within conscious conception without Sakti. In pure Sakti Experience, even if you, as a self reborn, return to a body, the Absolute is still remaining in your experience! Therefore, the thought of plunging one way or the other is gone and Sakti takes over your current.

> *"Everything is due to the Sakti of the Divine Mother."*

She, Para Sakti, is more Real than anything one perceives through mental, emotional, or sensory perceptual instruments. There is in the end nothing that can be found which is not Sakti! This is the pinnacle of beautiful ideas to be nourished spiritually, slowly, as an embryo would grow in the current of consciousness. It is much more than the spiritual stances of faith, belief, or trust. It is the evidence of pure Sakti Experience transcending and surpassing all logic of the mental level. It is the blessing of power and skill in the Goddess Herself, O sapient one! It is absolute abandon which equals real surrender to Her as Power, as everything, as what is so much greater than the

151

little impulse of ego.

"You are what You are."

He had a living spirituality, a divine creativity that flows without precognitive calculation or intellectual separative thinking. Pure inner dialogue. Pure potent psychology of the deepest soulful experience. Pure spirituality. Para Sakti is Real. She is as Real as the fourth state of unfettered consciousness, as real as She is in the shape of deep sleep, the forms of the dream state, or that reality we commonly call the "waking condition". Analysis creates separation or dualism within the figure of intellectual activity. Love doesn't even think about it; separation goes instantly in Unified Feeling. This inborn gift of the Love Content understands Truth immediately! Her Great Power is Real! But if your reality is a conscious connection with self-importance, the intellectual figure of the ego and so forth, then how will you experience and feel and see the Reality of the Great Power, Her Current of Love which is simultaneously within both and including both the transcendent and the immanent? His experience is beyond words and it is possible, potential, and eventual in every single soul as we are all made of the same consciousness. It may seem that, at first look, this remark of Ramakrishna comes from the region of the dual mind looking at the Goddess as something other, something above and distinct from him. But if you will remember, it was Ramakrishna's divine experience to realize Her everywhere and in everything, even his own body, as even the very substance of his own mind and, even more so, as his own self. Even as Consciousness had become his own self. She is what She is! As such, She is this all- inclusive non-dual Consciousness with no exception. But you see, Ramakrishna displaces all sense of personal self- importance by deflecting the state of mind totally and completely to Her. You "are", not I. What power do I have? It is all in Her. My ego has no power.

"The Brahman of Vedanta and the Chitsakti are identical, like water and its wetness. The moment you think of water you must

also think of its wetness, and the moment you think of water's wetness you must also think of water. "

If one separates as two ideas the Infinite as Brahman and Consciousness Power as Chitsakti, one will never get into the non-dual state. They are not two, they are one. They are not even "they". No calculating idea may be associated with the experience. Does one then see the world moving as water's wetness? As long as one thinks of Brahman as turiya and the states of deep sleep, dream, and waking as Chitsakti's manifest power, the experience of non-duality will not come. The defined practice of Sakti thinking is inspirited insight and high emotion. It is like sunlight breaking through a dream. Between the waking and dream states, beautiful ideas are moving within the current. Between the dream and deep sleep states, a serenity melts through the threshold before the stirring of dream currents in consciousness. Between deep sleep and turiya, one begins to fully know the feeling that even here in the depth of pure now one is free and bound by nothing. Here, the natural impulse within us to identify the experience to the "me" idea, goes, for in pure Sakti Experience, She takes you past mere seeking of Atma consciousness into an overriding depth where nothing may bind what you feel!

"But I went through great suffering. I used to lie on the ground with my head resting on a mound for a pillow. I hardly noticed the passing days. I only called on God and wept, "O Mother! O Mother!"'

Who of us would reenter the great suffering of the waking, dreaming, and deep sleep states as the forms of physical birth and death, the confusion of psychic dualism and the darkness of deep sleep unknowing of Reality out of choice, as it would appear, after becoming free in the pure Consciousness of Spiritual Reality to experience a weeping agony such as this for the sake of others, for the sake of Love alone? How many of us will weep over death or the agony of having the body, or over romance or finance, but who would weep for Her? Who would weep for Her to give Her Divine Self to and into your own self,

153

as lovers weep to be affirmed by one another? Most of us are so contained in our own self-importance that we would never weep this way. We are so self-conscious of others' opinions, thoughts, measurements, and feelings, judging ourselves on self-based reflections of what we think others will think of us, that we will never let ourselves go into the weeping prayer for the Goddess. The training of our minds has left us with the delusive idea that we should fear the ingrained controlling cognition of hell, which is but the illusion of anger, and regret life while waiting for the distant idea of Love in a heaven to come, and that we should never let go into full surrender to the Power of Her Love right in this Immediate Now. Ramakrishna's Love for Mother Sakti had none of this negative-based ego self- reflection. His emotions poured out to Her. A Love of Pure Passion. Pure Intensity. Pure living power, strength, skill, and ability to feel the most exalted emotion for Her and the agony of separation from Her.

"Who is my Mother? She is the Mother of the Universe. It is She who creates and preserves the world, who always protects Her children, and who grants whatever they desire: dharma, artha, kama, moksha."

The Goddess gives whatever is desired, of course, within the parameters of the four natural desires, free from the context of moral distortion. Dharma is purpose or a meaningful fully functional life pattern that leads or guides one to spiritual freedom, enlightenment, and liberation, that which is moksha. Kama is the attraction to sexual and sensual pleasure. Artha is the desire for wealth, money, material security. Now we see a contradiction perhaps, at least on the surface, for Ramakrishna is famous for saying that kamini (sexual desire, woman) and kanchana (gold, money), which are simply kama and artha, are the chief obstacles to spiritual life. Yet here he says his Divine Mother grants those desires.

Kamini is feminine as "woman". If I were a woman this would certainly hurt my feelings and spiritually trusting emotions to be referred to as a spiritual obstacle because of the male sex drive. It becomes a puzzle to reason that and, at the same time, to be worshiped as an embodiment of the Goddess.

This is a very problematic puzzle for many people in Ramakrishna's teachings, for very few can maintain natural, non-neurotic, non-contradictory and effortless celibacy as Ramakrishna did, even as he considered his own wife to be the Goddess Herself. His high state is total abandon to the pure absolute Goddess Ideal, and that is Ramakrishna's solution. However if all were to live at that level and the planet were to become completely celibate, then in a century and half there would be no human life on this world. So desire has its place. Also, it is imperative to remember that Ramakrishna's celibacy was not dry or lifeless, nor devoid of appreciation, celebration, joy, and ecstasy. If anything it was a heightened pleasure of the world spiritualized that very few can ever comprehend much less experience themselves. Remember that the Divine Mother showed him Siva and Sakti everywhere, even in the coupling of a male and female dog and that he worshiped the Goddess within women, whether they were virgins or prostitutes. Obscene and vulgar words which denigrate women would have a contrary effect upon his mind, throwing him into the state of Samadhi. During his Tantric practice, he sat on the lap of a young naked woman reciting Tantric bija mantras and, again, was thrown into the depth of Samadhi. Also, during Tantra, he observed (by the Brahmani's direction) the sexual union of a man and woman with complete and undisturbed equanimity, that is, it did not stir erotic feeling within him. At one time he worshiped his own phallus as the Siva lingam. The Divine Mother appeared in a vision to him as a Mussalman girl six or seven years old with a tilak on her forehead, who walked naked beside him, joking and frisking like a child. Again, he worshiped pure Sakti as the "Beautiful" in a girl fourteen years old, seeing in her the manifestation of the Divine Mother. His perception of the Goddess in all these experiences was clearly there, regardless of any human imperfections. Also, for those of you who would enter your own dark calculations existing within your own minds, you must know lucidly and without doubt that these spiritual perceptions of the Goddess' Presence were in no way involved with the arena of common sexual or psychopathology. Nor were these experiences associated with the misdirected awakening, ascent, or return descent of the form of Sakti known as Kundalini (the Coiled Up Sakti Power), which may occur in some individuals due to a cognitive emphasis on an ego-erotic reshaping of that awakened Energetic Power within.

"Yes, yes! One! One! It is indeed one. Don't you see that it is He alone who dwells here in this way."

He is She and She is He. But that is still the working of the dual mind trying to calculate the nature of the non-dual which is One, but even the thought of one creates the thought of two in its wake. So, thought must become motionless to actually see the Goddess as She dwells here in the way that She does. Yet, most commonly, instead of just coming "here" to this place, we so often spend our entire precious lives waiting in procrastination, putting into tomorrow by believing we must figure everything out first, when Love itself is first. Love alone is the comprehension of Knowledge. Love knows the same Truth that Knowledge knows and yet Love is the easier, quicker, and the more spontaneous and direct course to the goal, as it is the goal itself. But we procrastinate on to the tomorrow instead of immediately embracing the direct feeling of the most precious moment of eternal now as the absolute principle divested of the confusion of time, which in some ways, emotionally robs us of the pure Sakti Experience as that which we are in the spiritual fact of life.

"The farther you advance, the more you will realize that God alone has become everything. He alone does everything. He alone is the Guru and He alone is the Ishta. He alone gives us knowledge and devotion."

As many living beings as there are, there in turn are that many god concepts, guru concepts, and chosen ideal concepts, for cognition within the conscious current is immense. Yet, in deep sleep, none of these three concepts exist whatsoever, for in deep sleep, there is no dual mind to have a concept. The conscious current has become absolutely still for that moment when deep sleep is experienced. The same is ever true in turiya, the fourth state of ever free Consciousness. Of course, when the mind reaches nirvikalpa, if mind advances that far, the final Reality seen and felt is again completely non dual Consciousness. However, one may have that non-dual feeling immediately in pure Sakti Experience where these three thoughts disappear in Her Immense and beautifully overflowing flood of feeling.

"No matter where my mind wandered, it would come back to the Divine Mother."

The spiritually elegant, natural and spontaneous condition of his consciousness ever gravitated toward the Goddess or was in the condition of complete oneness with Her, free of all conditional modifications. You can see anything you want to see or can see, as you are able, in the example of Ramakrishna, and you can become That which you see. Every one of us at some time in life or another experiences some type of Nirvanic plateau, but most of us believe we can't get samadhi, yet it comes to us even unnoticed. Then as we begin to notice that state of mind, it later becomes developed more intensely. Each time this state occurs, the great fright of life stops, for at that moment we see that it is all Mother. The Spanish expression, *"Toda Madre"*, comes to mind, which means "All Mother". This is a response to the inquiry, "How are you?" Its meaning is that one is better than good. The Goddess weaves Her Ways throughout the world we know. Still, the ordinary mind is caught in the trifling dilemma of how long can we experience this All Mother State. Simply: as familiarity increases, the length of time increases. As the mind opens, one is given a genuine and irrefutable blessing from Sakti, that of contemplative joy. Whether the mind wanders into the relativity of embodiment or the divine disembodied, the contemplative joy remains on Sakti, like gravity, without exertion, effort, or struggle; instead of the old habit of chasing the ego or seeking the ego as a reinforcement to one's existence.

157

*"But, Mother, what people call 'man' is only a pillow--case,
nothing but a pillow--case. Consciousness is Thine alone."*

It is by seeing Her, non-dual, in the mind itself, that one will
know that Consciousness is Hers alone. Sometimes the words of
Ramakrishna go completely over my head, and sometimes these
inspired words carry me to a place beyond the words. It is for
these moments that I live and breathe and cherish whatever is
precious within this life.

*"Brahman and Sakti are inseparable. Unless you accept
Sakti, you will find the whole universe unreal --'I', 'you', house,
buildings, and family. The world stands solid because the
Primordial Energy stands behind it."*

Sakti is Excessive Joy. One cannot deny Her. To do so
creates dysconjunctive states of mind or feeling. If you deny the
great Primordial Energy, then you deny life itself. She is the
substance and the stuff of which we are made, shaped, and
composed, as we are within and as we experience the waking,
dreaming, and deep sleep states which are nothing but Her. I do
not want a spirituality which is based on unreality, illusion,
impermanence, or the premise that creation is merely here to
serve the human purpose. The negative contradiction of
eliminating the world as unreal also eliminates one's own being
and participation in Sakti; that thinking creates stress by the
denial of an existence of "you" or of "I" and that this in turn
deposits one into a state of spiritual impediment for one has
denied Sakti and then cannot proceed further than a realization
of egotistical self- importance. That is what keeps us wrapped
up in the fixation on "I" consciousness, which never moves
forward at great speed toward the Experience of Immense Sakti.
Once again, we may here see the unique spirituality of
Ramakrishna.

*"Yes! That's it. Let me tell you that the realization of Self is
possible for all, without any exception."*

The non-dual pure Sakti Experience of the Goddess and the

god person is our inevitable potential, ever waiting and ever present within. Ramakrishna, out of preexisting systems and in conjunctive response to the Goddess Kali, created his own Spirituality, novel, unique, and unified. If Ramakrishna can do it, you can do it, or at least some of it. He demonstrated an example of principles and experiences that need only be assimilated, taken in. We are all simply human and yet Spirituality is everywhere. It is the alertness to Conscious Oneness with the Spiritual Current deep inside, right Here, right Now, without exception, possible for all. Yet, as soon as you identify with a tradition, system, or process, even this one, it immediately identifies you or qualifies your pure Sakti Experience by the touch of, contact with, or dependency on that system, thought, or process in the current of consciousness. Pure Sakti Experience is Direct Consciousness as Immediate Power in the Direct State. Even these words will confine you or identify you some way. In the direct state of immediate Sakti Experience, even the Ideal of the Goddess, the wondrous current of pure Kali, Her name, Her concept, Her identity, is gone from the motionless immediate Current of Experience.

*"As the Master said these words he went into an ecstatic mood.
His body became motionless and his mind stopped functioning;
tears streamed down his cheeks. After a while he said, "O
Mother, make me like Sita, completely forgetful of everything--
body and limbs --, totally unconscious of hands, feet, and sense--
organs--only the one thought in her mind, 'Where is Rama?'"*

It is said that the non-dual state is non-relational, a spiritual position higher than that of the gods, the goddesses, deities or deitesses, or any Chosen Ideal whatsoever. Ramakrishna, completely forgetting his own existence merged in that great non-duality; the pure principle as it is nothing less than pure Sakti Experience. He also practiced a tradition known as Madhura Bhava, the mood of the sweetheart, which is the fifth and last culminating mood state of the five traditional moods that are in relation to the Great Principle. The other four are: the mood of parent to child or child to parent; the mood of friendship; the mood toward the Great Principle as mistress or master as the case may be; and finally the most simple and common mood of serenity with the Principle however it appears. These five mood relations have five stages or layers of emotional content within them. They are: intense affection which causes the heart to soften; the reaction of repulsion toward the one endeared due to an abundance of emotion; the emotion of friendly confidence; the transformation of tragic emotion into the emotion of ecstasy; and the ever-renewing emotion of Love never being old or repetitive. These five stages move through each mood relation and they are determined by the mood of the "I" impulse in relation to the Great Principle. When Ramakrishna practiced Madhura Bhava, he dressed, adorned, and behaved as a woman. He himself tells us that he spent two years as the companion and handmaid of the Divine Mother. It was the worship of Sakti, where he strongly identified himself with Sita, with Radha and as Kali's own. In conjunction with these spiritual practices, there is the very rare state of Maha (Great) Bhava (Mood), when all the stages within all the mood relations happen all at once. In this condition, the emotions become so powerful that they can destroy the human body system if that spiritual, emotional, and physical system is not prepared for the power of those feelings.

You see, it is thought that there are two dominant concepts ingrained in the human psyche, subconsciously and unconsciously, which hold back consciousness from the experience of pure, unfettered non-dualism. These two concepts are that one feels one owns a physical body and that that body is male or female. So, this non-dual freedom is a matter of the depth of identity or the emotional state passing deep beyond these dualistic ideas. Even beyond the limitation of an "I" impulse in relation to the Great Principle or pure Sakti Experience. Ramakrishna is way ahead of his time when he speaks of one named Baburam who he saw in a vision as a goddess adorned with a necklace. Baburam's gender identity was feminine, not masculine, even though the sex of the body was male and not female. To get to the superconscious Sakti

Experience, one must get out of the influence of previous past life impressions and present life identification that one is strictly this or that. Who knows what kind of body one may even seemingly own in a life to come? Nevertheless, these two ideas as independent identities do not exist in the non-dual state. The external existence of a universe as a concrete unchangeable reality only exists that way because consciousness accepts this convergent picture as real. The truth is that the expressions of consciousness in the phenomena of life are massively divergent in their nature. The keynote to all this is Love, into which the impulse of "I" completely melts away in the one thought, the current of consciousness which becomes nirvikalpa samadhi.

"All women are the embodiments of Sakti. It is the Primal Power that has become women and appears to us in the form of women."

This again shows that Ramakrishna was so far ahead of his time. The world in general has yet to catch up. But of course the pragmatic mind will need to remember that women just like men are influenced by the qualities of being either in a state of spiritual harmony with oneself, the state of intense activity in the heroic seeking of a goal, or the state of being brought down by the gravity of heavy emotions. But this in no way denies the truth of his insight. One would almost think that women may appear as chosen ideals of the Primal Power, of Sakti, and as such, in the ultimate sense, are manifestations of the Goddess, therefore exist as parts of pure Sakti Experience in totality. Also, there are reasons why women are innately superior to men. Their intuition functions at a greater level. They do not kill or go off to war for the reasons that men do. They are more connected to life, to the natural world, with the Earth, with birth, with bringing forth life and nourishing, cherishing and adoring the life they create. There are many more reasons as well.

"Please pray to the Divine Mother, who is the Bestower of all bliss. She will take away your troubles."

One may believe that Ramakrishna generated out of the state

of ordinary individuality the highest human potential of living Bliss, ascending the scale of conditions like one rising up the seven musical notes to the final note. Or, one might think he was a genius or a madman or, finally, a conduit in perfect tune with the Goddess. Or, one might consider him to be an eternally perfect being who descended from the state of pure Consciousness as an Incarnation of that Consciousness itself. But do any of these descriptions describe who Ramakrishna was? Do they tell us of the true intimacy he had with the Goddess and She with him? Regardless, whatever he was, in fact, the beauty of this statement is that he holds no power to his own self, his ego. She is the One who removes our troubles. She is the Bestower, the Sovereign, the Empress of Bliss, which is the highest potential.

"The Mother is the Giver of the bliss of divine inebriation.
Realizing Her, one feels a natural bliss."

And She is the Giver of every other gift such as wisdom, surrender, release, and peace, like gratitude, the capacity to forgive, acceptance, and real humility. The ego does not acquire these things on its own, they are gifts from Her, as are true empathy and genuine compassion. For ego to assume that it can show compassion to others is an absurd superior attitude. Love, Kindness, and Generosity are all the Power of Sakti. As is the sense of Spiritual Well Being or Blissful Divine Inebriation, that is to be drunk with Goddess Knowledge rather than drunk on the cognition of the complex of world consciousness. The Natural Bliss that one feels is that simple state, Sahajananda, which is to realize by the cognition of this realization, that it is She (sa) who is thus born (ja) as one's very life, being, and self (ha), as nothing else but pure Sakti Experience.

"What can I do? God alone blesses all. 'Thou workest Thine
own work; men only call it theirs.'"

What would it be like to live and communicate in a world without ego, where our self-value, our self-worth was emphasized in regard to the spiritual content within each person?

Ego is a funny and stubborn thing, like a mirror that refuses not to reflect. The delusive idea of self- importance extends like an ever expanding orbit no matter how far one's psychological evolution has gone. The paradox of identity is ego-based, between "Thine" and "theirs". It becomes astoundingly funny how one can even have a fantastical sense of self-importance over saying how delusive self-importance is! It becomes resolved, and the solution to the problem is gotten only when one looks at one's very most precious possession, that of life itself, like a cast off leaf in the wind, guided only by Sakti, ever sacrificed, even to death, for the sake of Her. But even that capacity to sacrifice or surrender comes only from Her as Sakti within. Does the ego experience Sakti, or does She alone know Herself as She is? The dual idea of "part myself and part She", will never understand the nature of complete Love which is ever gratified by pure identity with itself.

"I cannot say such a thing as 'May you be healed.' I never ask the Divine Mother to give me the power of healing. I pray to Her only for pure love."

It is the nature of the ego to want, crave, seek, and desire power as a vigorous affirmation of what the ego wishes to be in the end. But the ego only gets the power that it wants when once the ego is completely surrendered to the Power which is Sakti. A strange paradox, I would say. The ego wants to create a power form by which it can exist. Those power forms of the ego direct themselves into religious, occult, political, military, economic, and social energy outlets. Yet, Love alone survives all these things. Love alone commands all, directs, defeats, abolishes the misery and suffering made out of these six outlets of the ego's energy. However, its *creative* fulfillment is found only in that Love which is spoken of here. The ego's self-importance stops the potential of the spiritual power of Love. Only then does prodigious fulfillment come. Procrastination in the Precious Now is the hesitation and fear in the ego and so is perfectionism on what was. This Love is not a begging prayer but a Way of Being, a Demand within the self surrendered.

163

Then comes the tender, elegant, sweet power in the communion of Love, which is better than other forms of connection because of its unique and immediate result. It is the Ever New Emotion, creating the ever new mind. Love is the smiling form of a nod from the Goddess which affirms the real context of what ego becomes when it loses the form of the ego that appears to continually rotate within the thought of its identity potentials.

"He said to the Divine Mother: "Mother, what is all this? Stop! What are these things Thou art showing to me? What is it that Thou dost reveal to me through Rakhal and others? The form is disappearing."

As Ramakrishna's mind so often dwelled in the threshold of Mother absolute and Mother relative, that mind would approach and plunge into the eternal absolute and then return through the causal, subtle, and gross fields of normal consciousness as we know it in the form of the time/space matrix. When this would happen, that mind would become filled with massive, infinite ideas, perceptions and insights about where people came from even in past lives, about the nature of their present spiritual condition, and where that spiritual condition would be in the future unfolding of the matrix. These perceptions would be triggered in his mind when he saw someone such as Rakhal or others. Apparently, he would sometimes have to beg Mother Sakti to stop, for it appears that at those times it may have been too much to see at once. Then, She would kindly make those forms of perception disappear from his consciousness.

"'Mother,' I said, 'Who will look after me? I haven't the power to take care of myself.'"

Ramakrishna most honestly admits the helplessness of the human condition, as, ultimately, we are without power unless the Goddess is with us. As it is in Reality, She is always with us, no matter what. Ramakrishna has no egoism about this fact. His sentiment is Absolute Abandon or Total Surrender to the Goddess.

"What power is there in a man?"

Not calling for an answer, Ramakrishna asks this question rhetorically. It is the Goddess who liberates. She is the Power behind all power, even that power which appears as the human being. Yet, humans cannot create a universe, nor can they destroy it. It is She who gives life and spirituality to one and all. Teachers may teach you until they are blue in the face. You may read books till your eyes fall out. You may meditate until your brain melts or repeat mantras until your throat dries up. But unless the Goddess awakens spirituality within you, that spiritual sentiment will remain asleep. Her Great Power is so much more than our simple thought of Deity or Deitess, which is our human idea, concept, or conception of what indeed the Great Power is, in fact. Joy, Love, indescribable by words. Para Sakti, the Great Power, has packed us as individuals, Undivided from Her, where all Spirituality is Already within us.

"The body is really impermanent. When my arm was broken I said to the Mother, 'Mother, it hurts me very much.' At once She revealed to me a carriage and its driver. Here and there a few screws were loose. The carriage moved as the driver directed it. It had no power of its own."

All bodies are momentary, even Ramakrishna's blessed body was momentary. Yet, the Goddess, is Ever Existent. Her Real Joy, Bliss, Power and Ultimate Being never ceases. This is the gist and the essence of the intimate relationship of the Goddess and the God man. Ramakrishna did burst all traditional barriers and conceptual obstructions to spiritual experience. Admittedly, he states that, as the carriage, he has no power. It is all the Goddess. She is the Driver. Can we ever know the Goddess unless She lets us know Her? She does whatever She likes! This deepest, highest of complete spiritual insight is understood in the state of illumination which is absolute abandonment to the Goddess. Not fifty percent, not seventy-five percent, not ninety-nine and nine-tenths percent, but one-hundred percent, total and complete surrender to Her.

"I said to Her: 'Mother, I saw a skeleton in the Asiatic Society Museum. It was pieced together with wires into a human form. O Mother, please keep my body together a little, like that, so that I may sing Thy name and glories."

Realizing the delicate temporal nature of the human body, Ramakrishna wastes no time in seeking and applying himself to the most precious moment of Now, where pure Sakti Experience is felt, known, and exalted with every effort that is left within the fragile delicate frame of the body.

"Mother, I want to be normal. Please don't make me unconscious. I should like to talk to the sadhu about Satchidananda. Mother, I want to be merry talking about Satchidananda."

"Normal" would be the common shared awareness of the waking state, where the diverse minds of other people are dwelling. Ramakrishna wants to be merry and enjoy talking about Existence, Consciousness, and Bliss. He wants to be merry about this Divine Topic and talk with the sadhu (seeker of truth). So he pleads to the pleasure of the Goddess to not make him unconscious in the ecstasy of samadhi. The curious thing is that Ramakrishna would now prefer not to be in samadhi. He would rather be merry, happy with others, rather than having his consciousness swim in the deep currents of the Infinite. How many of us can make such a request to the Goddess?

"I said further: 'I should like to enjoy the society of Thy jnanis (knowers) and bhaktas (lovers). So give me a little strength that I may walk hither and thither and visit those people.' But She did not give me the strength to walk."

How beautiful. For most of us move through life so often feeling that we are victims, that life is unfair and we lose sight of the privilege of existence and the living potential of discovering Love. Sometimes what appears as not so good is, in the long run, that which is best. It is She alone who fully knows what is within the sea of karma. She knows the turnout. So rare it is to see one accept the life that is given by Sakti and without blame

166

toward the Giver.

"A lover of God prays to the Divine Mother: 'O Mother, I am
very much afraid of selfish actions. May I not entangle myself in
new work so long as I do not realize Thee. But shall perform it
if I receive Thy command. Otherwise not."

Since the Love that is felt in pure Sakti Experience is so
Simple and Sweet, it would seem that a natural repulsion to
complexity arises. This is also to create and live in those ideas,
feelings, and movements that come up, out, and forth without
effort; spontaneous non-calculating living. Those entanglements
are not only external activity in the waking state, but these
would also pertain to the stirring of old patterns in the psychic
content, as well as the creation and cognition of new patterns
which are not the natural, intuitive and spontaneous sense of the
Goddess. Only the vigorous embrace of the fresh flow of Her
Current is enjoyed. Put yourself into that one embrace and then
discover everything. It is like wild and free abandon in the
energy of musical notes that carry one into seventh heaven,
where higher emotions are stimulated and are no longer bound
by the usual thought conditions as forms of general or common
conception. Charge up oneself and observe the unfolding of
Sakti Within. She is that seventh note of heaven and She is the
other six notes leading there. But the question still in your
consciousness is: how long can you stay in the seventh note?

"By realizing the Divine Mother of the Universe, you will get
Knowledge as well as Devotion. You will get both. In bhava
samadhi you will see the forms of God, and in nirvikalpa
samadhi you will realize Brahman, the Absolute Existence--
Knowledge--Bliss. In nirvikalpa samadhi ego, name, and form
do not exist."

If you can see what this means, you will instantly understand
that She has already given you these, both knowledge and
devotion, as nirvikalpa and bhava. My thought is that, as bhava,
saguna, and lila, She is the Current of conscious conception or
conscious mood. This is the continuous flow of what is within

the psyche. Yet the curious question then becomes: with what is the psyche identified? The Current of conscious conception is the same function in both the waking and dream conditions. In the dream state, it has the quality of a more free- flowing, imaginative aspect. In the waking state, it becomes more acquainted with the frame of what appears to be logic and reason. This is the strange sensation or adjustment we all experience when we wake from a dream and try to capture what is not usually logical with the logic of the waking mind. But you must admit that it is the same Current of conscious conception and its related moods, emotions, and feelings that experiences the waking and dream state. So you see, that nirvikalpa, nirguna, or nitya aspect is again only She, as the Current without conscious conception. Nirvikalpa is not a conception. Savikalpa is the current of conscious conception as the play of mind. In nirvikalpa, that Current has come to an absolute standstill with no motion, utterly at peace and oneness with itself. This Current which potentially appears as both nirvikalpa and bhava is only Mother. She is the Sakti Experience. When the conscious current is moving, She is the Witness of that conscious current, but when the psyche's identity melts into the Great Unity, so, too, does the Witness of that current and the motion of that current melt away into non dual Consciousness. There, name, form, and ego do not exist as a maintenance of the conscious conception which has some identity, quality, or separative modification of the "I" principle attached to the experience. But you see, in deep sleep, name, form, and ego also do not exist. A moron goes into deep sleep and comes back to the waking state still a moron, but if that moron goes into Turiya, pure consciousness as nirvikalpa, even for a moment getting past the identity involved in the current of conscious conception, then a great change takes place in that person. The Sakti Experience actually moves forward into the psyche and the whole current of conscious conception is transformed into a new mind. There, life in the Goddess begins, as the awareness has now begun, but She was always already abiding as the innate eternal within that very same person.

"But what remains when God completely effaces the ego cannot be described in words."

This is the greatest problem and challenge for human intelligence. No one has yet been able to describe this pure Sakti Experience. So, we put words on Her, like Non Dualism, Great Reality, God, or Goddess. None of those words convey what She is! This remark of Ramakrishna's entices us to get rid of or efface the ego!

"Becoming one with the non-dual consciousness even for a short time is what is called Nirvikalpa Samadhi."

S.

This nirvikalpa samadhi is indeed the Great State of absolute consciousness in pure oneness where all distinction is completely gone. It is truly what the Goddess is, as it must be admitted at the termination of all phenomena in the individual and the universal sense as final conclusion. It is the Goddess who bestowed this Great State upon Ramakrishna. Therefore, She is something more than nirvikalpa, since it is the natural response of the heart to think that the Bestower of a thing is greater than the thing itself. As observed in Ramakrishna, when true nirvikalpa occurs, the signs of the body are lifeless. The breath slows down to an imperceptible degree, the heart rate cannot be detected, the eyes do not respond to light or to being touched, and the body is completely motionless. It would appear that the mind and vital functions have slowed down to such a profound and absolute degree that the consciousness of the mind and vital life have become one with the Great Stillness of Eternity. The connection of that living vitality and mind consciousness has not broken, disintegrated, or left the location of the body, since people do come down from that state. That in itself may be the problem of nirvikalpa samadhi; that is, the coming down from there. What took great effort to reach now takes great effort to come down from. The current of consciousness has now become one with the Great Current of Eternity and, as such, does not exist any more as it is overwhelmed by that Greater Current, the Absolute into which all its personal distinction has become lost. But there is something that stirs in this current of consciousness that does desire to come down from the Great State. There is some factor, function, or principle that desires to make dual that which is now One and after tremendous difficulty to get there to the Great State. What is that function which desires to make distinction in that which has lost all distinction? Or who is She who pulls the mind current down from Nirvikalpa? The effort to go up now becomes an effort to go down. For if this coming down does not take place, then one leaves the human frame behind, as it is said, within twenty-one days, due to not eating or breathing, or the heart doesn't turn back on, or neural activity does not recirculate back to conscious brain activity. Yet, even during the shut down of these life functions, Sakti is there in such a body, somehow supporting the finest imperceptible layer of life within.

Parallels with modern research into near-death experiences may be drawn to a degree. Those who have died technically and are approaching the Great Light are often gripped with a hesitation to completely enter that Light and become one with its Full Luminosity. An impulse to return overtakes them and they find themselves back in the state of conscious waking conditions. Nirvikalpa is "without, free of mind play", as it is nirguna, "without the quality of modifications". Savikalpa is "with mind play", or saguna, "with the quality of modifications". Those who have experienced nirvikalpa have fully died into Reality, for that Great State is the death of the personal ego. In almost all near-death experiences they have only nearly died and so most of these reported experiences are still at the level of the saguna collective complex. Each is described differently according to the traditional training of the mind and the available knowledge in the internal psychic complex, which may or may not be able to interpret the experience. Nirvikalpa has no after-death state phenomena attached to it, whereas near death reports are filled with that phenomena. It is the nature or quality of modifications within the saguna collective that gives us so many various descriptions about those experiences.

"Six months passed that way. Then the Mother's command was heard, 'Remain in Bhavamukha! For the spiritual enlightenment of man, remain in Bhavamukha!'"

S.

No one within recorded spiritual history has ever stayed six months in nirvikalpa samadhi. The body dies after twenty one days. So, the Goddess has demonstrated Her most unique gift to the world in the personal spiritual experiences of Ramakrishna, the God man. In other words, remain in the Mood (bhava) Facing (mukha) Her for the sake of others, for the Sake of Love. Or, do not become totally extinguished of body and mind consciousness in the nirvikalpa state, but remain identified with the Universal "I", the origin of all thoughts and beings, this same Universal 'I' which seeks the good of the many. This is to identify with the Immense "I" of the Goddess, where the lesser sense of the "I" impulse as ego is completely destroyed for all time. In its place there is now only the full disposition, the total quantity, absolute existence, and complete unsurpassed actuality of Her Immense Consciousness. Ordinary minds are perplexed by this and most often worship those beings as Incarnations, when all the while it is the Power of Her, Sakti, which has done these things, even as the manifesting of this identity with and as the Universal "I". This is pure Sakti Experience in the Highest.

"As he was all along dwelling in Bhavamukha, the whole of the universe always, nay, every moment, appeared to him to be composed of nothing but ideas."

S.

Do you think that it might be possible for a human being to be born in this world by a woman, as one who has come out of the immense universal consciousness? One definition of this Bhavamukha is an infinite mass of ideas. This perhaps is the universal collective consciousness, the totality of ideas, which continuously verge at the melting point of absolute non-dualism. All experiences and potentials may be seen in this universal consciousness, the immense collective itself. As the personal is

171

a part of the collective, all that will be experienced by the personal is already there within the collective. By knowing the collective one will know all that is possible for the personal. These two are not separate, as in the thought that the personal will experience this and the collective will experience that. It is all nothing but ideas and these ideas are accessible to one and to all, the personal and the collective, to Ramakrishna and to you. From the Height of the Immense "I" in Bhavamukha, all people, everything there is, are but waves of ideas in that Immense "I". The ego's spiritual blindness is to believe that it moves under the impulse of its own power. Bhavamukha is simultaneously divine indifference filled with Love and Loving Empathy for all beings, for in that state one knows the ultimate destiny of everything, as in what people are, what they are doing, and where they are going. Everyone is moving forward to become one with the Great Cause, which is pure Sakti, none other than that non-dual Consciousness itself.

"In complete obedience to Her command, he forcibly covered his mind, which had got fully merged in the indescribable state devoid of duality and non duality, with the veil of Vidya Maya, the force tending Godward, and engaged himself in carrying out Her behests."
S.

Life itself is made of the Great Infinite Substance which is Sakti. Ego, like a momentary dream on the surface of deep sleep, is the one point keeping us from Perpetual Sakti Experience, whether we see this Great Infinite Substance as non-duality in nirguna or as duality in saguna. It is all nothing but Sakti. After entering the Current of the Goddess without conscious conception, he then reentered Her Current of conscious conception, yet now, this Current of conscious conception was filled or completely covered with the Sakti of Knowledge (Vidya Maya), in full identity with Her, the Immense Goddess, the Great Mother, the Divine Mother, and no ego idea existed in the Current of conscious conception at all. The limited "I", dependent upon the thought of ego impulse, is

172

now gone from the Current of conscious conception, and in that same Current, the Immense Universal "I" of the Goddess takes over. Her Universal Current floods out the current of conscious conception, with the flood of pure Sakti Experience or the Knowledge of Knowing nothing but Her in that same Current. This is Bhavamukha, Her unique, novel, and liberal spiritual gift to the human experience. In the end, the Current, which I am calling the Goddess, cannot be described or comprehended with or without conscious conception, for it is She who has made both and yet the paradox of Her nirguna and saguna aspects does eventually resolve itself in the pure Sakti Experience of Her Immense Love. Love is the one word idea that gets us there! However, even the extraordinary word "Love" is but a cognition in concept of what the Sakti of this feeling is.

"She always kept his mind keyed to a lofty pitch, a high state of Oneness, from which all ideas rising in the infinite Universal Mind were always felt to be his own."
S.

This is the Mood of Her within him, where what was ego consciousness has now become nothing but the Consciousness of Her as pure Sakti Experience. It is the lofty pitch of full identity with the Goddess, where every idea that rises in Consciousness is felt completely as Hers. All confusion as to what is the ego and what is the Goddess is now extinguished. Even the concept of "Oneness" does not fully convey what this is, as ego cannot describe what it is when ego is gone. This most certainly explains how Mother and the person of Ramakrishna became "One". For in this state, everything that is seen or felt is nothing but Mother, even himself, without the idea of himself as an ego conception within the conscious current. It is all Her, this whole universe and the Absolute upon which this universe floats. Some may recall the cosmic form of Krishna, or that demonstration of Inconceivable Difference in Non-Difference that he showed to Arjuna. The essential difference is that Arjuna was terrified by the cosmic form and begged Krishna to take it away, for he still had the dual ego view of that cosmic

173

form as something greater than himself. But Ramakrishna is absolutely comfortable with the Immensity of Mother, for he has felt the non-dual identity, there where the ego has gone and so there is nothing in him to contain the feeling of fear. This was demonstrated in the unique spirituality of the Goddess for the simple sake that this potential may be realized by you. When the many, the great diversity, is seen in the One, then the Universal "I" of Sakti takes over. It is only when this inconceivable great difference appears to feel separate from one's most intimate genuine experience that any emotional distortion might superficially exist. Non-dual identity feels Love alone if one has authentically realized this potential ever waiting within. Dual identity feels many emotions. There is also the explanation that this Bhavamukha is when the wondrous and wonderfully energetic Power of Kundalini Sakti remains at the level of the ajna chakra, the wisdom command center in the middle or midpoint of the brain nucleus, instead of leaving the world in the high exit, through the transcendent axis of the sahasrara, the seventh state of absolute non-dualsim. If this is so, it cannot be an individual condition, for Bhavamukha is the Immense Universal Consciousness. It is not a condition of identity for just a single mind, as in the raising of the Kundalini aspect of Sakti, for and within just one person. She is then clearly known to be the Wisdom Command of the entire universe and Bhavamukha would be Absolute Empathic Identity with Her as She Is!

"Kali and Brahman are identical. Is that not so?"
Yes. It is so. And that oneness, sameness, that empathic identity is known through the movement of Her Divine Current within the sushumna, the very gracious central nerve running from the tip of the spine up out of the top of the skull. This is the vein of Kali's grace filled with the non-dual current of Sakti. It is ever present, noticed by some people with intense spiritual appreciation and yet unobserved by most others. Yet that non-dual current is always moving within this central axial vein of the very gracious Sakti. The current of "I" Consciousness

174

identified with Kali and the current of "I" Consciousness identified with Brahman is the Same Current, and may be realized at any point or center along the sushumna, the sacred artery that descends right out of Sakti's own loving heart into the human experience. Therefore, we are never disconnected from Her at any time, even though we might feel we are not within Her due to the subconscious cognitive projection of other connections or conscious identity relations in time and space with all those circles and cycles, symbols and metaphors of explanation, which are in the turnaround or revolution of consciousness, swallowed into the sushumna or the non-dual current of Sakti. She is ever with us throughout the cadence of Eternity no matter what the mind content projects at any given moment, whether it is dualism or non-dualism or some condition between. So you see, Consciousness and Energy are not different, nor is pure time (Kali) and pure space (Kala), as realized in the Turiya State, when this precious extension of absolute now is completely felt as the knowing of Self. Also, it is an intriguing thought to know that Sakti is always functioning within the sushumna. What do you think carries consciousness from waking to dream, into deep sleep, and then into Turiya and back again? The ego?

"Nitya and Lila are the two aspects of one and the same Reality."

Nitya means inward, innate, one's own, constant, perpetual, eternal, always abiding, essential, and invariable. Lila means play, sport, pastime, diversion, amusement, imitation, appearance, semblance, disguise, charm, grace. The import of these two words has tremendous spiritual value if you do not dualistically separate the two aspects of the same Reality within your mind. Lila is the saguna form of nitya and nitya is the nirguna formless of the lila. One may also say that lila is the amusement or the disguise or the charming pastime of that which is none other than perpetual, essential and innately eternal and constant as your own. Do you see how the two words blend together and create the non-dual feeling of your own Sakti

175

Experience as invariably graceful and charming to the abiding unchanging Self? This Sakti Experience is More than both and these two principles are brought together by Her.

"I prayed to the Divine Mother, 'O Mother, turn my mind at once from the world to God.'"

How could the mind, which is swallowed by the gigantic concept of 'world', ever be turned from there, to a point of Light named God that appears to barely even shine inside anyone's mind? Love is the Power that can do this. Make that Love your own! What good is it for you if it is someone else's understanding? It must be your own to feel complete and undisturbed. A person's time to pass away had then come. In the after-death condition that person had the realization, "Oh, I see now--It is an All Consuming Love!" When this soul came back they tried very intensely to Live that Kind of Love. Is this what we all are doing over and over and over again?

"Therefore I pray, 'O Divine Mother, please don't make me a worldly man if I am to be born again in a human body.'"

I, too, pray to the Wondrous Woman, that if I must return to a human body, I will not forget Her. Or, if this "I" for a time must retain a subtle body, like a dream, that even there I will not forget Her. Or, if this "I" remains, also for some time, as a causal body, which is but a pure cause without a dualistic effect, may "I" there remain with Her. She who is the Great Cause. She who is the Pure Wonder of Love! She who is not limited by the idea of the "I"!

"I have to return your salutes because Mother has placed me in a state in which I see God in everything."

What a wonderful spiritual condition. To see God not just in everything, but in every person. And so sad it is that so few of us ever even see God within ourselves. And if human beings do not see God in human beings, then what will become of human beings through that disregard? Very, very rare is a realized being like Ramakrishna whose humility is overwhelming. He does not sit upon a high pedestal claiming his singular condition. He salutes God, the Mother within everyone!

"Nothing exists but God."

As this is the final conclusion of non-dual thought, what remains is not God, nor Self, nor even the Goddess as a concept of any kind for it is nothing but actual Reality that exists! We have Pure Sakti Experience, no matter what. Whatever is, is Her, and whatever it is that keeps you from seeing this is so, is nothing, for that thing of identity which appears not to be Her is in uttermost Reality, nothing but Her. This is an amazing statement of Ramakrishna's discovery of Reality.

"I become intoxicated at the mere thought of God."

A better word is inebriated, really, for intoxicated has some negative connotation, but, nevertheless, the point is well taken. As nothing exists but God, then everything indeed is nothing but an inebriating reminder of God as being all that is. His mind was so highly tuned to the pitch of the Goddess that just the thought of Her would bring about a change in the mood of that mind; a mood that was so powerful that it is compared to intoxication. But we all change our moods by the thoughts we hold in the conscious current of our minds. So, if that thought is spiritual, we become that thing which we hold in the current of our conception. Seen from this height, everything, without exclusion, becomes an inebriating force of the Sakti Experience.

"If a man really has that knowledge, then he is indeed liberated though living in a body."

We think that What We Are will die, but What We Are, in Absolute Reality, has never completely taken the form of the body and the mind; nor has What We Are ever fully entered, as a limitation, that causal source point of our existence as it is known in deep sleep; a state of being where no waking body nor dream mind exists. There, one is just conscious of joy, happiness, being, and unrealized self-existence. It is here at this causal point of deep sleep that the minute sense of separation begins, as well as ends. From that smallest sense of dualistic separation in the mid- point between multiplicity and Oneness, all other dualistic difficulties are generated. The body is not the problem. The mind is not the problem. It is really only this sense of separation from the Great Cause that is the problem. And so the lifting away of this dual feeling is "knowledge". In the truth of Reality, there is "living" in a body and there is "living" without a body. The existence or non-existence of the body is not the question, from the height of an illustrious, luminous, spiritual standpoint, from the luminous liberated mind. One must simply refine all feelings down to the Essence of Love. If you feel you are free, then you are free. Love has always known this Truth. It is nothing less than to touch and become one with the Continuous Beauty of Life. Then, no dual death reflex is thought of anywhere! One simply leaves the body when living is done. Without hesitation! The heart is open wide to the Sakti Experience! For death is but a name, and wrongly so, that common unawakened minds have placed on what is in Reality non-dual, the Perpetual Beauty of pure Sakti Experience, and by doing so have caused much misery.

(In that case, thinking of God is superfluous.)
N.

Thinking, deep thinking, even the deepest thinking is still caught in the sphere of dualistic cognitive processes. If one holds the thought of God, one may also hold the thought of what is possibly not God. But there is nothing that is not God, so this dualistic thought process leads one out of that innate experience of complete peace, absolute serenity, total tranquility and beautiful bliss. When thought ceases or comes to a standstill, Consciousness becomes evident, and in that Consciousness one finds the Self standing true. Pure Love undisturbed by the cycle of thought then shines through. As long as one is engaged in the dualistic circle of "this is so and that is not so" and so forth, the non-dual consciousness eludes us. What an infinitely beautiful state, when even thinking over the question, the answer, or the even the nature of the Goddess as pure Sakti Experience becomes superfluous. The meaning of this word illuminates this spiritual condition; to flow above, superabundance, beyond what is enough, and, of course, something unnecessary. Sakti Experience is Super-Abundance. Infinite is Always, and so never was not! This universe is an Immense Spiritual Idea and as this is Infinite, it has no absolute beginning or absolute end. That phasing into a single point within the Infinite as a beginning of creation or that phasing out on a single point as the end of creation is dualism, and so cannot comprehend Sakti Experience. It is the same problem when trying to grasp the dual and non-dual as different experiences. That type of thinking which is insistent upon an entering into or an exiting from Sakti Experience actually holds one back from the fullest Experience, the Always Infinite Current of Sakti.

"Let Mother do whatever She likes. I shall know Her if it is Her will; but I shall be happy to remain ignorant if She wills otherwise."

Total Acceptance of Sakti carries one far past the enigma of ignorance or the advantage of enlightenment. One is then free and happy no matter what comes or does not come, for She is the Greater Experience regardless of what is flowing in the Current. Though I, as a poet, do strive for the Beauty of Her Experience, in the end I must beg Her for the modesty to remain happy in ignorance. Peace.

Goddess Work
Sakti Karma

Blessed Be
the Divine Lady of Ecstasy and Rapture
who protects those householders
on the Heroic Path of Blessed Tantra!
As She does for those who
hold no house
in the Divine Path of Tantra!
Blessed Be
the Blessed Lady.
May She appear in my body
as Bliss, Indifferent to Duality!
Blessed Be
Her Wonderful Power
that Carries thought on Her Sweet Current
where Sun and Moon meet
at the Rapturous Crescent
of Her Ecstasy.
Blessed Be
this simple life
the purpose of which
is Goddess Work.
Blessed Be
the Head, the Hip, the Heart
put one by one into
this Goddess Work.
Blessed Be
the Pure Image of Dream
Filled with Her...
holding no weave with the play of meanings
and Blessed Be
the Pure Image of Waking
not entangled in the lower foundation
of extracting interests in things

that are other than Her.
Blessed Be
the Pure Absolute Joy
in the Precious Eternal Moment
of the Dreamless Condition
filled with Her Gift of Rapturous Happiness.
Blessed Be
the New Mind that sees
what the Old Mind was
and the doors that are now
open to the potential of Fresh Bliss.
Blessed Be
this New Mind, this Goddess Mind,
left but to be the Sweet Current
of Her Love......
Ceased, yet Still Awake.
Still, yet moving in the Motion of Her.
Blessed Be
this poet heart
that bleeds for womankind.
And that this wound would be
the perpetual cause of Love.
Blessed Be
that She has caused in me
to be One with the Cause in Her.

Blessed Be
that the life of Art and the Immortal Life
are never separated...
so creativity and fresh discovery
of the ever unfolding Power of Love
never ceases to be but pure excitement,
an exhilaration which is life itself!
Blessed Be
She who crosses the barriers
we have made in ourselves,
to reach us with Her Love.

Blessed Be
those sweet triggers of the Goddess
that release us into irrational bliss...
What may mind do?
To hold to any form, type, tone or identity
is simply still the ego.
Blessed Be
She, who as Sleep is just Consciousness as Joy,
and as Dream, is that skillful power
to assimilate numerous thoughts
symbolically, and all at once,
and as Waking, plays the play
at being bound by what is in appearance, rational,
except at the Moment of Great Joy
when everything is Known as One.
Blessed Be
the Loving Goddess
who has carried the poor me
even beyond the idea of Atma (Self)
which stills holds with a thought
of the ego, both inward and outward.
Blessed Be
each Sacred Moment
as the destiny of death,
the leaving of body,
in each and every lifetime
has already been written by Her,
upon the face of time.....
as is the passionate creation
in the making of each new body.
Blessed Be
that She does not perplex me with
the reflex conflict
of Release and Return,
but has ever freed me from the problem
of nirvana or salvation...
and hell is but the illusion of anger...

and heaven the expectation of distant love.
For me, Her Love is Here,
Now, Immediate.
I am not waiting!
Blessed Be
that there were beliefs before my belief...
and there will be beliefs after my belief...
none knows the one right time in eternity,
only Love knows
the Truth Most Excellent.
Blessed Be
that this mind is
the Mother of Happiness.
Mother teach me
again and again
over and over
what this mind Is!
Blessed Be
that She alone
is the Joy within Joy...
that it is the Current
of Her Spiritual Genius alone
that is ever moving
through the minds of all.
It is She who captures the mind
with Her Living Creative Bliss,
and broadens, challenges and surrounds
that very same mind.
Blessed Be
Her Skillful Power alone
that has taught me to release the contents of mind
in total surrender, in absolute abandon
to Her alone who finds this Peace within us.
It is She who uncovers Peace...
one hundred percent Her alone,
even as we imagine that
part of it is our doing.

Then and then alone
comes gratitude for the gift of life
in this eternal moment,
where one may easily forgive,
for the higher the gratitude,
the more is forgiveness.
As is the greater the humility,
the easier it is to let go of oneself and of others,
and accept oneself as is
and others as they are.
Now, the foundation of self-importance
is loosened by releasing surrender
into Peace, Serene and True,
as genuine humility sets in,
aware and knowing that it is
the Power of the Goddess
that has done all these things.
Blessed Be
the Divine Lady, the Goddess,
the Power of Life, the Energy of Love...
know without a trace
of doubt and free of logic
that She is Real...
not a concept, idea, or conception!
She is Real. Her Power is Real.
Blessed Be
the Pure Joy of this Empathic Identity with Her...
There can be no true fear
where there is Real Ecstasy!
Only one place in the Self
can be occupied by the Self!
Blessed Be
the Sacred Union
where what is got,
has crossed the barrier
and the ego world complex
is left a million miles below

as the pure 'I' rises up
to touch, taste, feel and be,
in Oneness with She,
the Divine Lady of such Loving Ecstasy.
Blessed Be
that the momentum
of what is left here
within the condition of time
is now foreseen
by the Goddess Mind.
Blessed Be
the Deeper Seeing,
free of personality traits,
liberated from ego confinement,
which is a different function
from the 'I' sense, which is so easily lost
in the strange mechanism
of the narrowest perception of this life.
Blessed Be
Sacred Laughter
a thousand times a day
which sweeps the mind clear
into the high sweet moment
of Ecstatic Oneness.
Blessed Be
the Empowering of Her,
the uplifting descent
of Sacred Sakti
ever touching, yet untouched
by the world complex.
Blessed Be
spiritual relaxation
when knowledge and ignorance both
lose all importance,
and Love alone
in Her as Love
alone has meaning!

Blessed Be
Her Gift
the lovingly charged
psychically potent
spiritual Sakti
by which continual images
and visions, as living
moving picture forms permeate
this mind, as Her, my Chosen Ideal,
embodiment of Love,
disembodied Bliss...
Her Ecstatic Rapture
never shaped by condition nor quality.
Blessed Be
that Her Love is the Great Cause
never dual, never separate
from us, and that our Love for Her
is the little cause,
pure with no effect,
yet ever not dual in Her...
this is the high Reality Realized
past all conditioning
like sun waves storming the mind
into the Deep Infinite.
Blessed Be
that the psyche is the center
of all emotions, thoughts, behavior,
and that this exists for awhile
in the face of time, as dream, imagination,
subtle cognition, but comes and goes,
like effulgent waves.
Blessed Be
the body and the voice of the body,
that when listened to is heard
and where the cause and effect
of physical karma is felt...
just as the psychic karma

is felt in the mind...
the psyche betwixt
the little cause
and the body foundation
we know so well with intimacy.
Blessed Be
the apparent fact
with no fixed position,
that Sakti's mysteries
made as creation are
so abundant without a visible end,
that no single perceptual stance
gets it all at once
and we are left reluctantly
identified as human,
with the one resort to Love
this World as the Goddess.
Blessed Be
consciousness, breath, focus,
memory, cognition, and the Point
where effort is left behind...
Sakti, the Goddess, the Lady
takes over, effulgent waves
powerfully caress the immense shores
of the fully conscious ocean
of Her Loving Luminosity,
the Proto Experience,
of Her Blessed Reality.
Blessed Be
that this poet now sees Her
as much within the smallest
thread of the fabric
as in the immense great weave!
She is so hot now,
that everything else is cool
due to the reflex of opposition
in the psyche, caused by

the anguish of Love.
Blessed Be
this sweet inborn tendency,
the best part left with me
to worship and adore
my Loving Kalee
absolutely and non dualistically.
Blessed Be
this Sakti Body of Bliss.
Blessed Be the Mind
and Blessed Be Consciousness.
Blessed Be the Current Focused
between these brain halves,
within the Core Mid Point
naturally without effort
that tends upward,
where You Are There,
conscious, and ever so
not hidden by any secrets...
for Pure Sakti
is the Blessing of pure,
free Independent Spirituality.
Blessed Be
that She may be Reached
by self sacrifice
the complete death of ego
in one single expulsion of breath
total abasement of all self-importance
unique and novel position of bliss
accessible to the bold.
Blessed Be
that She has Become
sacred joy
the beautifully sweet
the deep emotions
the wide open mind
the expansive psyche

the inner forces of
true thought and real feeling
and the Current of Consciousness
running through all.
Blessed Be
that I need not figure out
anything, for She has already
figured out me,
who I am, where I came from,
where I am going,
where I've been,
where I am now.
It is She alone
who knows me as I am.
My Destiny is Her,
when all that was
unravels itself into what Is!
Blessed Be
total contact in this
Sacred Feminine Power...
in one pure breath,
absolute abandon
in what She has made
and in what She is making...
now, poet, without manipulation
you can experience anything
without a belief in
what is the idea
of personal limitation.
Blessed Be
that it has taken only
six years to know Her
as She is, for three seconds,
the full flood feeling of Love...
completely given to Her,
after working through
sleep, dream and waking,

after distilling Her Essence
out of the mixed alloy
of self, mind and body.
Blessed Be
this Flood Feeling of Her Love
which comes when reasoning leaves,
and which again leaves
when reasoning returns.
It is the mystery of obscuration
over what is the face
of pure evidence!
Blessed Be
to the listening
when the Flood Feeling occurs,
where knowledge is learned
that cannot be known...
but forever after
effects one's being.
Blessed Be
the loving luscious conjunction
of woman or man with Goddess...
not a particle of separation
in supersensuous union
turned to non-union
due to the overriding
awareness of previous
Spiritual Oneness,
the Lofty Pitch
of innately realized Love,
stateless and indescribable.
Blessed Be
the Empathic Identity
with Her who is Love.
Love, past and beyond
the circulation of all
emotional or thought configurations,
in the Exquisite Abundance

of Her Sacred Pose
in the many occasions that show
as divine strokes of luck
within the pauses of blessed durations
between and betwixt those moments
when thinking and feeling cease
and before either starts up again,
at One, in the Sweet
and Simple,
Sacred Feeling
of Her Divine Current
having no rational beginning,
nor comprehensible ceasing.
Blessed Be
that death is never death
and that no one ever dies,
Her Divine Breeze
simply blows the dry leaf free,
a Gust of Her Current and the twig snaps,
then Gentleness Endures on.

THE LAMP OF THE TURIYA
The Light of Self Evident Consciousness

"God used to dance then, taking the form of Kali,"....
"We can go into the inner chamber only when She lets us pass through the door." Sri Ramakrishna Paramahamsa.

Creative Impulse

God must Love Dualism. Just look what came from Stardust. You and me. Astrophysicists have detected that the Primordial Ball of Creative Energy (the Big Bang) was full of Hot and Cold spots with just micro measurements of difference. But as the Vaisvanara Jagrat (Cosmic Waking State) spread out from that distant and simultaneously ubiquitous center, these very fine and extremely subtle differentiations later became all this massive expression of dualism (great magnificent galaxies, vast spaces and so on). The physicists have called this heat cold paradigm, "the Signature of God." Or God's original primary cognitive creative thought current.   All this is interesting because material physics and spiritual physics parallel one another and with new insights, it would be quite nice to bring back together, as we might harmonize the natural and spiritual parts of ourselves. Nevertheless, these new insights charge our minds with amazement which opens the door of possibility and the potential of wondrous beauty.

The Lamp Of The Never Dual

The Lamp is the Bliss that leads us out of differentiation. The Never Dual Pure Consciousness assumes two aspects, the Witness Consciousness and Reflected Consciousness.   Even while the appearance of these two principles manifest, it is so in the Never Dual Pure Consciousness. Deep sleep is when the Reflected Consciousness remains in that vibrationless slow wave non dual condition of dreamless cognition. It is unique, but ever occurring when a dream slows down to a stop. Then unbroken consciousness remains there in itself full of bliss without any differentiation superimposed by the conscious individual (reflected consciousness). It sounds almost like the Lamp of Self Consciousness, but not entirely, for this condition is covered with vagueness, even though the mind whose function is doubt, along with all impressions in the psyche have ceased. All identity with the gross and subtle bodies have ceased and one is left with Blissful Non Duality yet to be Awakened.

The Door Of Dreamless Consciousness

Just as waves on an ocean slow down, all notions of names and forms slow down and one is left with Peace innate within the non dualism of dreamless cognition. The obscuration of the gross and subtle identity is gone for a moment. But the potential for that causality of identity with the gross waking or subtle dreaming bodies is still there. There is an imposition in dreamlessness called vagueness and doubt. It is removed by the doubtless conviction that the conscious individual divested of dualistic identity is the Lamp of Self Evident Consciousness. This is the Unrestricted Bliss of Realization, free of grief, free of dualism, experienced through Direct Knowledge of the Great Reality deep within.

Knowledge (Consciousness) is always here, direct or indirect, even though colored by differentiation, that Consciousness is continuously the Lamp of Bliss, ever without stress, grief or anxiety. Ignorance, obscuration, superimposition, indirect knowledge, direct knowledge, destruction of sorrow caused by dualism and unrestricted Bliss are the seven steps to the Roof of the Eternal, the Unchanging, the Ever and Always Remaining.

Waveless consciousness as dreamless deep sleep, curiously enough seems to be the 'door'. Interestingly, if examined deeply, those seven stages all seem to be within this 'door'. Once that doubtful vagueness in never dual dreamless consciousness is clarified, then this deep sleep state (prajna) reveals the

Awakened Never Dual Consciousness (Turiya). Between Relative Thinking and Absolute Thought (Pure Consciousness) there is the Threshold. This is the 'door' of unrestricted dream free cognition. Deep sleep is non dual cognition. There is not even the Witness (Kutastha) here, otherwise referred to as Pratyagatman (the Notion of the Inner Principle of Atma) for if you have an inner you must have an outer (dualism) and in deep sleep this phenomenal appearance does not exist. Also, competent persons of old equated Prajna (profoundly commanding non dual insight) with Isvara (God Consciousness, the God Ideal itself). This clearly shows the wonderful potential for realization and conscious contact with the Atma Principle which we are investigating.

Deep sleep has the characteristic stage of ignorance, being non recognition, it is ignorance of the very presence of the Self. For this never dual Self is obscured by the doubtful vagueness in deep sleep. This deep sleep is the actual superimposition of the forgetfulness of True Identity. The quality of indirect knowledge (cognition) is here too, for in the experience of deep sleep one feels the Peaceful Bliss and the Being Existence aspects of Reality (Existence Consciousness Bliss; Satchidananda). It is felt to be there. It is felt to exist. That is indirect knowledge ordinarily gained through study, dialogue, etc. But this deep sleep has the profoundly real potential for direct knowledge characterized by such blessed awakened thought currents as, I am That Reality, You are That Reality (Tat) and so forth. Indirect cognition says, yes, God, Kali, Atma exists. Direct cognition is conscious awakening to, I Am That. It becomes naturally self evident. Of course, since all thought currents cease in dreamlessness, so do sorrows, joys, depression, fear, everything, so, within the conscious content it is truly the destruction of misery. The seventh stage of Unrestricted Bliss (Ananda = Love, Joy, Happiness, etc.)) is awakened when Turiya Consciousness no longer sleeps the vague sleep of doubt about itself in the midst of dreamless cognition (and of course in waking and dreaming cognition as well, there being no longer any divisional misinterpretation over the nature of the Never

Dual).

The Relative And The Eternal

All that is Relative slows down, leaving the Eternal Self Evidence alone. What is the Relative? Dualism. Differentiation. All the Great Thoughts. The field of the five elements. The five sheaths of the Self, which appears to identify with the sheaths. The picture and the theater of Self is relative. The notion that one may not become satisfied is a relative, false and temporary factor. The idea that there is a permanent real duality between Reflected Consciousness and Witness Consciousness also is relative.

The idea that there is an actual union to take place in this or the next life, that kind of love which is like dropping the sweets to lick the hand, the concept that the clay is different from the cup out of which it is made, all this is relative. The objective psychosomatic disposition is relative, as is sorrow, fulfillment, achievement or the idea that things must be doing and done. Actually, the conceptual cognitive notion that there are Four States of Consciousness is a relative belief system identified with the three states as they are experienced within the Substratum. And all those meditational bouts where we try to rebut the psychosomatic posture we have assumed are also quite relative. On the other hand, no one can express what is Eternal. It is simply beyond words, a feeling (bhava) at best. No verbal mantric cognitive power can invoke It fully, being also relative. Yet, since this is so, we are forced somehow to speak of the Atma, as the Fourth (Turiya) State of Consciousness Supremely Free and this Self Evident Consciousness in relation to the three states.

Kali Is God Dancing

How is it that God is dancing as Kali? She is dancing as the Self Bliss (Atmananda). It is this Self Love (Bliss) which is the Lamp of Reality. How is it so? Because it is said that Infinite

Love is always felt for the Self as the Primary Feeling in any relative particular context. This emotion, mood (bhava) extends partially to whatever is related to Self and not at all to things in no way related. That is why we grieve when a loved one dies, but when a stranger dies we a barely feel anything. The Self is more precious than one's own life or one's own mind. It is the dearest of all objects, being the cause of all Happiness (Atmananda : Self Happiness). Where there is an Expanse of Love, there is an Expanse of Joy, the Self being the Source of Joy, the Sovereign of all Happiness. How can one who has this Love for the Self, in the absence of all dualism, have any love, fondness, enjoyment of or attachment to objects in particular? How can such a one with this Love, ever see anyone or any object as being inimical, unfriendly, with aversion or animosity or enmity?

Kali is God dancing as this Love, ever unchanging in the presence or absence of waking, dreaming or deep sleep. She is Turiya dancing as the Three States. The Cup which is made from Clay is not different from Clay. It is this Immediate Love, not mediate. One cannot even correctly say Love of the Self. There is no connection (of) to be made in Direct Non Dualism. It is Never Dual (Advaita). So it must be termed Atmananda (Self Love).

Now, if Cup is Chidabhasa (Reflected Consciousness) and Clay is Kutastha (Witness Consciousness), the cognition of dualism is sheer imagination on the part of Chidabhasa. It does not exist for Kutastha. In a sense, Chidabhasa is infatuated with its reflected identity with the waking, dreaming and deep sleep states. It is an affection Chidabhasa has for the three bodies (states). But this affection for the three states is in fact in the three states and is not innately natural to Chidabhasa. Reflected Consciousness and Witness Consciousness are non differentiated as Self Luminous Consciousness. This is the natural spontaneous joyfully evident nature of the Self Lamp illuminating its own light.

Remembering there is only One Reality, there can be only One Witness Consciousness and ultimately speaking, there can then only be One Reflected Consciousness. This is the Mirror (Witness) and its Reflection in the purest sense. Diversity (the complex multiplicity of dualism) comes later with the infatuation that waking, dreaming and deep sleep are our real nature. "It is common experience that the states of waking, dreaming and deep sleep are distinct from one another, but that the experiencing consciousness is the same." Pancadasi VII - 211. This consciousness illumines the three states, each with its own light.

FIRST LAMP

Consciousness illuminates the Waking State. The Five Elements shine bright with Consciousness. Waking is the active gross physical body composed of these five elements. Called the sheath of food, made from the five elements. The light of the Sun is the Lamp of Waking (optical light and the Day). This is symbolical and actual, as Light or Illumination is present from the waking state all the way up to ultimate enlightenment. 'A' is the letter for Waking.

SECOND LAMP

Consciousness illuminates the Dreaming State. The dream body is the passive subtle body made of thought currents manifesting as the pranic body or emotional sheath, the mind sheath functioning as doubt and belief, etc., the intellectual sheath (vijnana maya kosha which is the same as Chidabhasa), which is the reflection of clear sightedness due to Pure Consciousness in the mirror of the intellect. The light of the Moon is the Lamp of the Dream State. Lunar light symbolizes the dreamland, the night (as distinct from day: Sun, Waking). Also lunar light is a reflection, which is the luminous light (taijasa) of the dream state. Just like a lamp reflected in a mirror, so is Dream Consciousness. Thought currents, mind imprints and emotional shapes in the Subtle body are what carries from lifetime to lifetime. 'U' is the letter for Dreaming.

197

THIRD LAMP

Consciousness illuminates Deep Sleep. This is the Causal body of Deep Sleep, if it may be called a body, for this is the Ananda maya kosha, the sheath covering of Pure Bliss. The very joyful quality of this mass of non dual consciousness shows its innate God nature. The light of fire is the Lamp of Deep Sleep. Why fire? Because fire as such has the potential of manifesting light, here, Turiya Consciousness as being Fully Awake. Fire also burns everything in its path, here it is like the nature of deep sleep in that all and every dualism is burned away in the dreamless consciousness of non dual awareness. The lamp of fire has the potential of illuminating the waking and dreaming consciousness coming out of deep sleep. And if deep sleep is transformed by conscious awakening (from the Ultimate right through to the waking state itself) the potential for conscious contact with the Never Dual Luminosity of Turiya is there.

This is tending in the direction of the Eternal, where the potential coming out of deep sleep toward waking and dreaming is illuminating the Relative. One is direct contact, the other is the path of return. Now, it is said that if Brahman Vasana (the Deep Impression or Potential for God Consciousness; or Kali Vasana; the Potential for the Consciousness in the Goddess Kali; or Atma Vasana, the deep impression of the Genuine Self) goes deep into the Causal body of dreamless sleep, then the force of the three qualities (gunas : harmony, passion, and weightedness) can no longer affect or effect consciousness. In some ways Dreamlessness may be compared to Nirodha, that position in consciousness where activities, thought currents or feeling moods (waking or dreaming) come to a standstill, and before these begin again, subjective-objective dualism disappears, ceases and simply drops off. Here, consciousness is bright with non dualism. 'M' is the letter for Deep Sleep.

198

FOURTH LAMP

Never Dual Illumination is the Nature of Turiya. It is the Lamp behind and yet within the lamps of the three states. It is the Self Evident Light of Consciousness. At once Singularly Itself (Eternal), yet simultaneously illuminating the three states (the Relative). Since the Luminosity of Turiya is the Light of Knowledge and Consciousness, the Light of Being and Existence, the Light of Love, Bliss, Joy and Happiness, it cannot be compared or described in reference to optical light as in the waking consciousness, reflected light of internal consciousness as in the dream state or the potential light as depth cause and profound effect, which one might think of as the dreamless seat of consciousness. The Fourth (Turiya) Lamp cannot be described by the relative lights of the three states. Nor may the letter symbol, AUM (OM) fully indicate This Reality Directly, at best, all symbols and talk are only indirect indications.

A Thought On Kutastha

Interestingly enough, the word Witness comes from Wit, meaning Wisdom, Knowledge, Understanding, later the meaning became observer, watcher, seer, perceiver and knower. The Witness principle is only the 'Witness' when something is before it, to wit, waking or dreaming objects. In Deep sleep no objective projection is there, so this principle cannot really be called the 'Witness' at that point. In the state of non dualism no otherness as objective projection is being watched or observed, as it were. It is Absolute Thought as Pure Consciousness, without thought currents moving before it, a Mirror without an image upon its surface.

The Picture

A beautiful illustration is given in the Pancadasi. It is very simple. There is the Canvas (Turiya). Then the canvas is Whitewashed (Dreamless Sleep). Next, the Sketch is done (the

Dream State). Finally, Color (the Waking State) is filled in to make the Picture Complete.

The Theater

One may find the example of the Theater also given in the Pancadasi. The Light that lights the Theater is Kutastha. The Patron in the theater is the ego-mind (the principle of consciousness identified to the body mind complex and the sense of being latched to the doer and enjoyer idea). The Dancer on the stage is the Intellect (Vijnana maya kosha: Chidabhasa, to which one might add the Reservoir of the Memory which holds in the psyche, imprints, impressions and potentials). The Sense Organs (the ten functions of sensing and agentship are manifestations expressing consciousness objectively in the waking or dreaming states) are the Musicians playing their instruments. The Sense Objects (the five gross and five subtle elements which may possibly be compared to atomic materials and finer quantum energy phenomena) are the Audience.

These, in sum total, are what is meant when Sri Ramakrishna says, "the twenty four cosmic principles." Now, the Kutastha Light is what Illuminates the entire Theater. This Illumination is There, whether or not the patron, dancer, musicians or audience are there or not. If they all disappear as Chidabhasa disappears into Kutastha or if they all remain, Kutastha stays Unchanged.

The Results (The Four Signs of Self Illuminated Joy)

Cessation (due to the dissipation or finishing of dualism) or Release from sorrow, suffering, grief, distress and sadness. The Fulfillment of all desires, qualified by the remark, "Desiring What?", any longer, for all that is to be enjoyed has been enjoyed by the spiritual feeling that comes as a result. The Feeling has been engendered that everything to be achieved has been achieved. And all that needs to be done is already done and nothing remains to be done. These are the four signs which may be summarized by Ramakrishna's address, "The Mother reveals to me that She Herself has become everything." As Mother Kali is everything, then all dualism has ceased, all is fulfilled in Her, all is done, all is achieved. Seeing that She alone is Real and that every dualism only somehow expresses Her glories, is, as Ramakrishna states, "... very deep thoughts." And, "It is God who does all these things. I do not know anything."

Further Signs of Happiness as Atman, Kutastha, and Within Chidabhasa

Chidabhasa loses the sense of ego centered self seeking. Becomes embarrassed by this. Becomes humble. Submits or surrenders to and then begins to imitate Kutastha, renounces and no longer identifies with the limited vision of the chidabhasa complex. Chidabhasa, like a courtesan who has become ashamed of herself, becomes ashamed of having identified with the doer enjoyer agentship. Chidabhasa takes up a fresh course in imitation of Kutastha. One must cross over the bridge of reason to the Other Shore in order to understand the feeling content of these results.

Reflected consciousness, even after Illumination, may once in a while go back to momentary identification with the chidabhasa complex (body mind). The psychosomatic complex does not abruptly end but gradually dies down. Realization is not a vow or promise, it is establishment. Karma continues, as it were, wearing out eventually. Worldly and heavenly joys are no longer a concern for chidabhasa and never were for Kutastha. Even the teacher ideal is left to those who are entitled, because for Kutastha all activities have ceased, even that of thinking one is a teacher. As Ramakrishna said, "One can get human gurus by the million. All want to be teachers."

As it is, what others see (on Chidabhasa or Kutastha) is but imagination, onlookers imagine attributes. The thought is that anything short of seeing Satchidananda in another person is imagination. The statement that only a sage may recognize another realized person might be grasped by this idea, When we look at Ramakrishna, for example, what we most often see is what we think him to be through our imagination. Does one see Ramakrishna as Satchidananda, which is fact what he is, or does one see him endowed with the attributes within our imagination? It is like this with everyone, from the Viewpoint of Never Dual Reality. What does imagination have to do with who one really is? The chidabhasa reflection imagines a serpent over the Rope, a ghost on Tree Stump or fire on a Bush with Red Berries.

If one has this Self Evidence (the Spiritual Dignity of Atman, the Authentic Self), then why is it ever necessary to listen again to Vedanta, Tantra, Samkhya, Yoga, etc. That listening is for the sake of clearing the wavering doubt out of Chidabhasa. Even meditation is just for that sake of Chidabhasa who might confuse Kutastha for the body. Karma goes on and thousands of meditational bouts will not change what is so. Even the imprints and impressions which form the behaviors of the chidabhasa complex continue in some form or another. But these dealings, these plays in the theater cause no harm to Kutastha, nor change this Principle in any way.

Even so, distraction (Chidabhasa's imagination) and samadhi (God Consciousness) are dualisms of the mutable mind. The polarity of the Witness and the Reflection is still very much a dualism. Where Ramakrishna shows the balance, "Nevertheless, this is the state of my mind: unceasing samadhi and bhava." Most beautiful, either God Consciousness or the Mood (Bhava) of God Consciousness. Chidabhasa's distraction does not play into it. If it so happens that Chidabhasa does come up, then the mood within the reflection of Consciousness is that of Consciousness (Kali, Atman, God).

Chidabhasa's unshakable conviction is that there are no separate experiences in the entire universe. Identity has moved from self centered individuality to the expansive identity of the universal and even more, just to the Oneness of Kutastha itself, who as Infinite Consciousness in the background of all experiences, experiences everything. A kind of universal polyphasic cosmic mind. This is how all desires are fulfilled, how everything is always done and how everything is ever achieved, as well as the cessation of dualism. If there is only Self, then where is the other?

This Associationless Consciousness is not concerned with past karmic phenomena nor even with social or scriptural codes. One who know this feels no harm in doing good for the sake of others, already having the <u>feeling</u> of obtaining all that is to be obtained. Let the body perform worship. Let the mind think of the AUM symbol. Let the reflection of Consciousness meditate on the Personal or merge in the Impersonal, what change can any of that cause in Kutastha?

Chidabhasa, now being bright by the Luminosity of Kutastha, sees the True Self and the Actor (the aspect of consciousness engaged with the idea that it is the waking, dreaming and deep sleep states) as different as the eastern and western oceans. There is no more confusion, nor concerns over the body mind complex that Chidabhasa once long ago thought it was. The only concern at this point is within illumination, concern with the brightness of Kutastha and the Happiness of just being the Atman.

Laughter and humor comes for Chidabhasa who sees those who hold to and dispute over the doctrine of the Relative or the Eternal, like two deaf people engaged in a quarrel. Let one have ideas about the Eternal, let the other engage in the dramatics of the Relative, it changes nothing really. If Illumination has let go of these two ideas, then what can be effected if others so desire to engage therein? Atman Consciousness is unobstructed and needs nothing to revive its own Self Illumination, the dawn of which has melted the realm of dualism, which in Never Dual Reality was already and ever ceased. Even if the realm of dualism is perceived, as is the natural case, the perception cannot in any way affect or effect Illumination in Itself. Can an edgeless weapon harm an Invulnerable Warrior?

The power of dualism in fact was an invaluable assistant in realizing the non dual. Now, these corpses of dualism just lie there on the battlefield, Chidabhasa having no fear of them, these as such declaring the magnificence of the Emperor. Does this not remind one of Mother Kali ever victorious standing upon the corpse of Siva, ever revealing the Never Dual Truth? Action or actionlessness are related to the phenomenal body to which Chidabhasa no longer identifies. But among people of the world, Chidabhasa's actions will be more or less in accord, harmony and abiding with them. Though inwardly Chidabhasa has given all this up.

Chidabhasa now acts and feels as a parent would toward their children. Great Empathy. Tremendous Love. If they get angry, disrespect or even beat the body of this Chidabhasa, this never broken bright loving consciousness does not feel sorry for them nor angry at them, but only feels affection for them, unaffected by their praises or blaming. Chidabhasa's primary feeling behind all phenomenal behavior is only the one empathic loving intention to awaken a knowledge within them of the actual presence and reality of Kutastha, of Atman and of the Happiness that may be realized by Chidabhasa.

In the Waking State, Chidabhasa sees that Kutastha is There, continually thinking on That until the Waking State is finished and done with. In the Dream State, Chidabhasa's thought currents continually dwell on that Kutastha. In Deep Sleep, Chidabhasa actually disappears, or melts like a salt doll in the sea, into the non dualism of Kutastha. The Truth is really quite simple. It is everything else that is so complex. A Story to illustrate. Ten people were crossing a river in a boat. A Storm came up. The boat was tossed. They swam to the other shore. Arriving there they became frightened that one of them was lost, each person only counting nine survivors. But when they remembered to Count The Self, they found all ten to be just fine. Regret was gone and each rejoiced in their own spiritual Self Esteem. Wonderful and Blessed is Illumination. Wonderful and Blessed is Kali. Wonderful and Blessed am I. "Prema (Love) is the rope by which one can reach Satchidananda." Sri Ramakrishna.

The ideas presented in this article have been mostly gleaned from *The Gospel of Sri Ramakrishna* and the *Pancadasi* of Sri Vidyaranya Swami translated by Swami Swahananda, published by Sri Ramakrishna Math.

References

The Lotus and The Flame:
Monastic Teachings of Swami Aseshananda
from the notes of
Swami Yogeshananda
The Eternal Quest, Inc.
The expression, "felt awareness" comes
from the Swami's published notebook.
Minor Upanishads
by Advaita Ashrama
Numerous quotations are borrowed
from these beautiful Upanishads.
Vedantasara of Sadananda
translated by Swam Nikhilananda
Advaita Ashrama
A few ideas were inspired by this text.
Mandukyo Upanishad with Gaudapada's Karika
translated by Swami Nikhilananda
Bonanza Books, New York
Some ideas about the four states
of Consciousness are are borrowed
from Gaudapada.
Pancadasi of Vidyaranya
translated by Hari Prasad Shastri
Shanti Sadan, London
A most profound inspiration
into the pure clarity of Advaita Vedanta.
The Gospel of Sri Ramakrishna
recorded by M.
Ramakrishna Vivekananda Center, New York
Many quotations are borrowed
from M.'s record of Ramakrishna's words.

Sri Ramakrishna: The Great Master

by Swami Saradananda
Sri Ramakrishna Math, Mylapore, Madras, India
I cannot speak my unending gratitude
to this most wondrous work.
The Siva Samhita
translation by Rai Bahadur Srisa Chandra Vasu
Munshiram Manoharlal, Allahabad
Some concepts are borrowed
from this Tantra.
A Brief History of Tantra Literature
by S. C. Banerjee
Naya Prokash, Calcutta
All quotes from the Tantra Texts
are from this excellent work.
History of the Tantric Religion
by N. N. Bhattacharyya
Manohar Publishers, New Delhi
"To become as a woman."
quoted from here.
Jung: His Life and Work
by Barbara Hannah
G.P. Putnam's Sons, New York
Jungian ideas came from here.
The Serpent Power
by Sir John Woodroffe
Ganesh & Co., Madras

About the Author

Richard Chambers Prescott is a writer and publisher of twenty books of poetry. He has had five plays published by Aran Press in Kentucky and over seventy essays and articles published from the U. S. A. to India. His essay, *The Lamp of the Turiya*, has been translated into Dutch and published in the Amsterdam journal, *Vedanta*. Over the last several years, some articles and essays have been printed in *Prabuddha Bharata* and *The New Times*. The intent of his writing is to join the spiritual and psychological aspects of human nature. He has donated to the publication of a text on the woman saint, Gauri Ma. Grascott Publishing has published two books of humor by Swami Bhaskarananda, *The Danger of Walking on Water* and *One Eyed Vision*. Some of his collected essays have been published in the texts, such as, *Because of Atma: Essays on Self and Empathy* and the work entitled *Measuring Sky Without Ground: On the Goddess Kali, Sri Ramakrishna and Human Potential*. His manuscript, *The Goddess and The God Man: An Explorative Study of the Intimate Relationship of the Goddess Kali with Sri Ramakrishna of Dakshineswar* came later and is perhaps the crown of those creations. Then, *The Mirage and the Mirror* was born out of continuous pondering on the Goddess. His most recent text is *Inherent Solutions To Spiritual Obscurations* which is a comparison of Tibetan Dzogchen and Indian Advaita in three parts, *The Wonder of The Dakini Mind, Letting Go and Soaring On* and *Resolution in Pure Mind*.

His early seven books of poetry, *The Sage, Moonstar, Neuf Songes, The Carouse of Soma, Lions and Kings, Allah Wake Up*, and *Night Reaper*, are on the passionate emergence, the coming forth of spiritual desire, *Neuf Songes (Nine Dreams)*, being the crest wave of that time. *Kings and Sages* is a poetic sojourn through discoveries in East Indian doctrines. *Three Waves* is a poetic text on the transformation of tragedy into the love of life, that then becomes spirituality. *The Imperishable* is a collection of Tantric and Vedantic essays. *The Dark Deitess* is a sensitive text on the enigmatic stages of Goddess worship. *Years of Wonder* is a recounting of time spent in searching for the spiritual. *Dream Appearances* is a one-fourth of a century study and examination of the spiritual connection within the dream state. *Remembrance Recognition and Return* is a record of personal spiritual return to the Goddess. The seven *Dragon books: Tales, Dreams, Prayers, Songs, Maker, Thoughts, and Dragon Sight: A Cremation Poem* are an evolution of the creative mind culminating with the poetic affection for non-dualism and the composition of his own cremation poem. *Kalee Bhava :The Goddess and Her Moods, The Skills of Kalee, Kalee: The Allayer of Sorrows* and *Living Sakti: Attempting Quick Knowing in Perpetual Perception and Continuous Becoming* are purely expressions for the Goddess, conveying states, emotions, methods, techniques, direct insights, fresh discoveries, and a few personal spiritual ideas. *Disturbing Delights: Waves of the Great Goddess* are twenty-one journal volumes which are written, illustrated, and published by Mr. Prescott. *Tales of Recognition* is seven stories of spiritual journeys through the past and the future, death consciousness and return. *Spare Advice* is a short novel on the tragic comedy of two souls searching for truth. *Racopa and the Rooms of Light* is a play taking place in the after death condition. *Hanging Baskets* is a comedy about psychiatry. *Writer's Block and Other Gray Matters,* written with his marriage companion, S. Elisabeth Grace, is a collection of comedy drama one acts. *The Resurrection of Quantum Joe* is a comedy on physics. *The Horse and The Carriage* is a comedy on disparagement. Mr. Prescott has been published side by side with other journalists, some professors, and renunciate women and men in the text *Eternal Platform* by the Ramakrishna Mission Ashrama in Ramharipur, India. He has also been published in the journal text *Matriarch's Way* and *Vitals Signs: The International Association for Near Death Studies.* He has just recently had an essay entitled *Sri Ramakrishna As Personal Companion* published in *Global Vedanta.* His works are in some libraries, universities and spiritual sanctuaries in the U.S.A., Europe,

Russia, South America, and India. Writing has been his spiritual practice for thirty years.   Including all volumes, he has over eighty published manuscripts, most of which are privately distributed. His works, of over twenty years, are now mentioned in the *International Poet's Encyclopaedia,* Cambridge, England. As of 1998, he is forty-six years old and has been married for seventeen years.

Printed in the United States
86894LV00002B/115-132/A